Nicholas Royle is the author of four short story collections – *Mortality, Ornithology, The Dummy and Other Uncanny Stories* and *London Gothic* – and seven novels, including *Counterparts, Antwerp* and *First Novel*. He has edited more than twenty anthologies and is series editor of *Best British Short Stories*. Reader in Creative Writing at Manchester Metropolitan University, he also runs Nightjar Press, which publishes original short stories as signed, numbered chapbooks, and is head judge of the Manchester Fiction Prize. His English translation of Vincent de Swarte's 1998 novel *Pharricide* is published by Confingo Publishing.

WHITE SPINES
Confessions of a Book Collector

NICHOLAS ROYLE

SALT

CROMER

PUBLISHED BY SALT PUBLISHING 2021

2 4 6 8 10 9 7 5 3

Some of this material appeared first in a different form in Nicholas Royle's blog *White Spines*. Some material from the chapter 'Last Orders at the White Hotel' appeared first in a different form in the *Independent on Sunday*.

First published in Great Britain in 2021 by
Salt Publishing Ltd
12 Norwich Road, Cromer, Norfolk NR27 0AX United Kingdom

www.saltpublishing.com

Salt Publishing Limited Reg. No. 5293401

A CIP catalogue record for this book is available from the British Library

ISBN 978 1 78463 213 7 (Paperback edition)
ISBN 978 1 78463 214 4 (Electronic edition)

Typeset in Granjon by Salt Publishing

Printed and bound in Great Britain by Clays Ltd, Elcograf S.p.A

For my mum

'You want something physically in your hands, don't you? It's the whole point of collecting.' Customer in Church Street Bookshop, Stoke Newington, London

Picadors are involved here and there (8).
Rufus, *Guardian*

'That's the point of second-hand bookshops. Being closed.'
Rob Gill, Gosford Books, Coventry

Contents

Introduction

On a weekday in the middle of March 2020, I get in the car in Manchester at 6.15am and drive in the direction of the Peak District. Up on the moors somewhere after Woodhead I see what look like three dark woollen jumpers flapping madly in the wind. Lapwings, it would seem, are like buses: you don't see one for years and then three come along at once. The wild, joyful unpredictability of their aerobatic display is exhilarating. Lapwings, that is, not buses.

The roads are quiet and I enter the outskirts of Norwich at 10.30am. In the boot are two boxes of chapbooks. A chapbook is like a pamphlet. I'm getting one box-load signed in Norwich, the other in Ipswich, then back home for tea. Maybe around midnight. But not before, I hope, seeing my mum in Ipswich as well.

I find my way to Andrew Humphrey's place close to the centre of Norwich; he and Ipswich-based Robert Stone are the latest two additions to my Nightjar Press roster of authors. Andy Humphrey signs his 200 chapbooks in good time (under an hour is good), which means I have time to make another call before heading down to Ipswich. I park the car on a meter and walk around the city centre. Most places are closed, but I did phone ahead to check that where I want to go is open. What I didn't do, though, was save a picture of its location on a map and now I have no phone signal. Is Norwich one of those old city centres, like Canterbury and Chichester, full of cathedrals and other old buildings, but no phone masts? Eventually, almost by luck, I find myself on the right street and there it is, Oxfam Books & Music. This is where I go to commune, to rejoice, to give thanks and receive blessings. Part of me always wants to stop and take a moment before entering. But another part of me is too impatient and I feel myself being drawn in.

It's a good branch. I can tell that as soon as I enter. The careful way things are laid out, the well-stocked 'literature' shelves, the general sense of order. I start looking in a few books. The prices are not cheap. I remember when that used to bother me about Oxfam Bookshop Chorlton in Manchester, them tending to charge £3 for a paperback instead of the more typical £2.50 at my local Didsbury branch, or 99 pence at Dalston Oxfam in Hackney, which is also local to me, some of the time. I rationalised it. Chorlton is well managed. This branch in Norwich is obviously well managed. I get the feeling they know what they're doing. If they charge £4 for a paperback, they must know someone will happily pay it and that's more money for Oxfam and its good causes.

I find, to my delight, a Picador I don't think I have, *Nomad* by Mary Anne Fitzgerald, a 1994 edition of a 1992 non-fiction work subtitled *One Woman's Journey into the Heart of Africa*. There's no direct link between the content of this book and the emotion I feel in finding it – I rarely read non-fiction books and, if I'm honest, I'm unlikely to read this one – but the pleasure I feel as I take it from the shelf and look at the cover, which I am pretty sure I have never seen before, is real. The cover illustrations (front and back), which are credited to Mack Manning, employ mixed media – old photographs, handwriting, a photograph of the author, and postage stamps. I find there's something irresistible about postage stamps on book covers.

Later, at home, I'll look for other postage stamps on other Picador book covers and will not find as many as I thought I might. The signs are initially good as I start from the beginning of the alphabet – they are shelved alphabetically, by author – and soon come across a 1995 edition of Julian Barnes's *Letters From London 1990–1995* sporting not one, not two, not three, four, five or six postage stamps, but a lucky seven, all photographed, by Andrew Heaps, stuck to various appropriate artefacts: a Stan Laurel stamp on a bowler hat; a second-class stamp on a Labour rosette; a Charles and Diana stamp, torn in half, attached to a picture of the Queen. There's a postage stamp from the Russian Soviet Federative Socialist Republic on the cover of Lesley Chamberlain's *Volga, Volga* and a couple of pretend postage stamps on the covers of Tama Janowitz's *A Cannibal in Manhattan* and Jill Tweedie's *Letters From a Fainthearted Feminist*. I also find another cover by Mack Manning, although this one is credited to Mac Manning, on Gavin Bell's *In Search of Tusitala: Travels in the Pacific After Robert Louis Stevenson*. Non-fiction books often seem to have rather long-winded titles, or rather they may have a short title designed to intrigue and a longer subtitle that has the job of describing, more prosaically, what the book is about. For instance, *White Spines: Confessions of a Book Collector*.

Also to my great pleasure – we're back in Oxfam now, in Norwich, in the middle of March 2020 – on the 'literature' shelves, I find a 1973 Penguin edition of *Quartet* by Jean Rhys. Nine out of ten copies of Jean Rhys's *Quartet* that you will find will be of a particular Penguin edition with a film tie-in cover and non-standard lettering on the spine. I owned a copy of this edition years ago and never read it and somehow the book and I parted company. Although I would like to have the novel, and the possibility of reading it, back in my life, I can't have that non-standard spine messing up my Penguin shelves. I could shelve it elsewhere, with other non-standard A-format paperbacks, but with that spine, frankly, it wouldn't look good anywhere. The 1973 edition, however, which I'm looking at now, is perfect. Author's name in black, title in white, both out of orange. When Penguin still went for a uniform look on the spine, and cycled through a series of different designs, this was the one that I liked best – and still do – probably because when I bought or was given my first Penguins – Graham Greene's *A Sense of Reality* and *The Power and the Glory* – in the mid 1970s, that was the spine, that was the template. Author name in black, title in white. (Cover illustrations, on the Greene titles, by Paul Hogarth.)

I am still browsing when I hear the shop manager – or volunteer – answer a phone call.

'We're only open for the next two days,' he says, 'because after Saturday we're shut for four weeks – temporarily.'

I get home around midnight after a successful visit to Ipswich, where Robert Stone signed his box of chapbooks and I met my mum for a coffee, and then a long drive back along the A14, up the A1 and over the Peaks, where I stopped, briefly, to listen to the weirdly metallic cries of lapwings in the darkness. To writer and musician Virginia Astley, creator of the 1983 album *From Gardens Where We Feel Secure*, the cry of the lapwing sounds like an oscillator on an early analogue synthesizer, the VCS3.

On my Picador shelves at home I find I've already got *Nomad* by Mary Anne Fitzgerald, so I was wrong about not having seen Mack Manning's cover before, but it doesn't matter. The duplicate copy can join what I have started calling my 'shadow collection', the purpose of which is so far unclear to me. The Penguin edition of *Quartet* can join my other Jean Rhys titles on the Penguin shelves. Months later I will post a picture of my modest Jean Rhys collection on Instagram and someone will comment that she is their favourite writer. Someone else will say, 'These are brilliant.' Another commenter will post a black heart emoji and another will say she has an edition of *After Leaving Mr Mackenzie* with a photographic cover, which I will immediately think I need to look out for, to go with my Faith Jaques-illustrated edition. An old friend will post, 'Get some bloody writing done. #displacementactivity'.

I am, by then, getting some bloody writing done, because I have a deadline, and deadlines help, especially the sound of them whooshing by, as Douglas Adams once said. But, really, I've been writing this book since I was nineteen or twenty, using 'writing' in the very loosest sense. Researching, perhaps.

Christmas, 1980. My parents gave me a single. I've no doubt they gave me some other presents as well, but 'Dark Entries' by Bauhaus is the one thing I know they must have given me that Christmas, because it was released in 1980 and I definitely remember being given it one Christmas and I wouldn't have wanted to wait more than a year before owning it. I had heard it on John Peel; he played it several times during 1980, as well as a session from the band that I still have on home-recorded audio cassette. The 'Dark Entries' picture sleeve featured a detail from a painting credited on the back as *Venus Asleep* by Paul Delvaux. Having never previously heard of Delvaux, I became at that moment an instant, lifelong fan. A pale-complexioned, wide-eyed woman occupies the centre of the image. She wears an elaborate hat of scarlet feathers, her upper body covered by a tight black garment that gives her torso the appearance of a dressmaker's dummy – with arms. Her right arm is down, extended a short way from her body, her left arm bent at the elbow, so that her left hand is raised, palm open in an ambiguous gesture as she approaches an upright skeleton, which, like the backdrop of classical structures, is bathed in moonlight. In the background, a tiny female nude embraces a thick white column. There was about this image a mood, an atmosphere of sinister melancholy that appealed to me immediately and profoundly. It was a *coup de foudre*, although I may not have known the term at the time and probably would have said, if you had asked me, that it was love at first sight.

My second date with Delvaux took place within months. Having written a fan letter to Peter Murphy, singer and lyricist with Bauhaus, at the Northampton address on the back of the 'Dark Entries' sleeve, I was thrilled to receive a reply, on stiff yellow card that he had folded and squeezed into my stamped addressed envelope. He told me that *Venus Asleep* was owned by the Tate Gallery, as it was then called, in London. I duly made the trip to the capital, unaware that only a fraction of a major gallery's holdings will be hanging at any time, but I was lucky. I was excited to see that the detail reproduced on the sleeve of the single accounted for less than a third of the painting, which featured the sleeping Venus of the title in the foreground and four other female nudes in addition to the small figure in the background. The moonlight washing across the bones of the skeleton, the columns and steps of the classical buildings and the bodies of the female figures was provided by a mere crescent, which could not possibly, on an actual night in the real world, have cast so much light.

In September 1982, aged 19, I moved to London to study French and German at Queen Mary College, University of London. The college was in the East End, but I moved into an intercollegiate hall of residence on Cartwright Gardens, between Euston and St Pancras, just south of Euston Road. If you came out of Hughes Parry Hall and walked south, away from Euston Road, within less than a minute you were on Marchmont Street, passing Gay's the Word bookshop on the left and, on the right, if it was there then, which it wouldn't have been, because he was still alive, a blue plaque recording the fact that Kenneth Williams had lived in a flat above his father's barber shop at No. 57. I know Kenneth Williams was still alive because some time that year or the year after or, in any case, certainly before 1988, I walked past him on Tottenham Court Road, just a few minutes' walk west of Marchmont Street. Russell T Davies has said that Williams rarely strayed far from the area around King's Cross and that he never ventured further west than the Edgware Road.

I was walking north, on the right-hand side of Tottenham Court Road, having just crossed Great Russell Street, and there was Kenneth Williams walking towards me, a slight figure in a dark raincoat, of similar height to me. I recognised him at once and smiled, and he smiled back. I had never been a fan of the Carry On films, but I had loved Williams's contributions to *Round the Horne*, which we would listen to at home, whether repeats on the radio or on my dad's reel-to-reel tape recorder, alternating with *The Goon Show*.

But, to return to Marchmont Street, go back ten paces to Great Russell Street, turn left, walk past the site of the old

Cinema Bookshop at Nos. 13–14 on the right, and, on the left, offices upstairs at No. 102 where I worked at the International Visual Communications Association (IVCA) between October 1987 and November 1988. Some readers might remember the Cinema Bookshop, a tiny space crammed from floor to ceiling with books on the movies; given my lifelong love of film and the fact that I worked just across the road for a year, it doesn't make a lot of sense that I only went in there a handful of times, unless it was simply that I was more often drawn, as I had been when I was a student, to Skoob Books.

The first time I went looking for Skoob Books, which in the autumn of 1982 was located on Sicilian Avenue, a pedestrian cut-through from Vernon Place to Southampton Row, it took some finding. It wasn't until the mid-1990s that Sicilian Avenue made it into the *A–Z*. In Skoob, they shelved all their Penguins together; I had seen that done elsewhere, all those orange spines. In addition, beyond the Penguins, in the next room, there was a wall of white spines. These, I saw on closer inspection, were Picadors, and I had never seen Picadors shelved together like this. (Why, I vaguely remember thinking, would you do that?) I'm not even sure I had seen any Picadors at all before. Maybe I had, in Paramount Books on Shude Hill in Manchester, or on Dick's market stall, Ipswich, where my family had moved in the summer of 1982, but if I had, they had not made much impression. It was when I found, among these tall, white-spined paperbacks in Skoob Books, a novel called *Ice* by Anna Kavan, that I knew there was something special about Picador.

The cover of the Picador edition of *Ice* features a painting of a female nude. The time of day is night, the setting a puzzling combination of interior and exterior. The female figure stands face on to the viewer, eyes closed, a lacy white gown draped over her right arm while in her right hand she holds a burning candle. To one side of her is a cobbled street, to the other a red carpet leading to a set of stairs and a closed door. If it weren't signed in the bottom-right corner – P. DELVAUX – you would still know the identity of the artist, if you had seen his *Venus Asleep*. This painting, *Chrysis*, dates from 1967, the same year *Ice* was first published by Peter Owen – a nice touch and, I would guess, not a coincidence.

I have bought numerous copies of the Picador edition of *Ice*. I have given several to friends as presents, most of those, once it became a sort of joke, to my good friend Adele Fielding, and I have had to replace copies loaned and never recovered. (I drop a quick line to Dell to ask her if I should include the grave accent on the middle 'e' in Adele. She responds: 'I don't mind what you call me, but my actual name as given by my parents is Adele Fielding – my parents were only aware of an accent as being something that you needed to get rid of to get on in life.' Anyone who knows Dell knows how fabulously she has got on in life, and her Rochdale accent is as broad now as it was the day she left Syke, for London, in 1982.) The edition has become scarce, for which perhaps I should take some blame. At the time of writing, there are only three copies available on AbeBooks. There are newer editions with forewords and afterwords by notable writers, but for me the Picador edition (complete with Delvaux cover and introduction by Brian Aldiss) is unbeatable. It was one of sixteen titles published by Picador in 1973.

The list was launched the previous year, in October 1972, by Sonny Mehta, as an imprint of Pan Books, with the aim of publishing outstanding international writing in paperback. They launched with eight titles: *A Personal Anthology* by Jorge Luis

Borges, *Trout Fishing in America* by Richard Brautigan, *Heroes and Villains* by Angela Carter, *Rosshalde* by Hermann Hesse, *The Naked i* edited by Frederick R Karl and Leo Hamalian, *The Bodyguard* by Adrian Mitchell, *The Lorry* by Peter Wahloo and *The Guérillères* by Monique Wittig.

I have copies of all of these. I have copies of the sixteen titles published the following year. I also have— Actually, I don't have copies of the nineteen titles published in 1974. I only have eighteen of them. But I'm getting ahead of myself. This is supposed to be an introduction.

One of the striking things about the eight books, looking at them today, is how slim they are, how unbloated they appear. No literary agent or commercially driven editor told these authors that a novel has to be 90,000 words. Six of these books are around 150 pages; *The Lorry* is 250 pages and *The Naked i* just over 300. When an Instagrammer posts a picture of the seventeen books she has read in January, or February, they all look like new releases and they all have great big fat spines, with the odd exception by Max Porter. It's great that people are reading new books; I just wish they weren't all so long. Before I was commissioned to write this book for Salt, I worked for them as a commissioning editor, acquiring approximately twenty-five books over nine years with an average length of just under 50,000 words.

Also striking are the covers of the eight Picador launch titles. Three utilised existing paintings, by Dalí, Grünewald and Hundertwasser. The Brautigan cover was based on the first US edition. Mitchell's *The Bodyguard* used an original photograph by Roger Phillips and *The Naked i* employs graphic design, credited to Paul May, inspired by, but an improvement on, the first US edition. *Rosshalde* was the first in a series of six books by

Hesse to appear in Picador with cover illustrations by Guernsey artist Peter Le Vasseur, who was to do at least one other cover for the imprint in a similar style, for John Livingston Lowes' *The Road to Xanadu: A Study in the Ways of the Imagination*.

The cover for Wittig's *The Guérillères* was by the English surrealist painter and prolific book and album cover artist John Holmes, who, discovered and nurtured by art director David Larkin at Granada Publishing (who would go on to be part of the team that set up Picador at Pan), had already done notable covers for Germaine Greer's *The Female Eunuch* and Nabokov's *Despair* for Paladin and Panther, respectively, and would go on to do covers for Picador editions of Beckett and Pynchon as well as Jung's *Man and His Symbols* and dozens if not hundreds of covers for other publishers.

If my relationship with Picador started with *Ice*, it underwent a change at Christmas 1983, when my parents gave me a copy of *Black Water: The Anthology of Fantastic Literature* – that title/subtitle formula again, but, unusually, on a book of fiction – edited by Alberto Manguel. At a little under a thousand pages, this landmark Picador anthology, published that same year, contained a small number of stories I had already read several times, such as Franz Kafka's 'In the Penal Colony', EM Forster's 'The Story of a Panic' and Horacio Quiroga's 'The Feather Pillow'; numerous stories I hadn't read before by authors I liked very much, including Saki, Daphne Du Maurier, Graham Greene, Jorge Luis Borges and Marcel Aymé; and dozens of stories by writers I had never read, but who I would read, in this book and in other books, over the years to come.

I don't know if I asked for *Black Water* for Christmas or if my parents just knew.

I now own two copies of *Black Water*. On a Sunday in April

2017, I visited a branch of Oxfam, where I found, in the short stories section (I like it when a second-hand bookshop has a short stories section), two books side by side. One was *Black Water*, the same Picador edition I already had, and the other was *Stepping Out, Short Stories on Friendship Between Women* (Pandora), edited by Ann Oostuizen. I noticed a dedication in *Black Water*: 'Dear _____, fondest love, _____, 25.12.83'. I thought, I know someone called _____, and I happened to know that she knew or had known a woman called _____. And then, in the copy of *Stepping Out*, I saw, on the flyleaf, in blue ballpoint, '_____ _____'. The copy of *Black Water* had obviously been _____'s as well, inscribed to her by _____ _____. How wonderfully ironic that this gift from _____'s friend _____ had now been given away along with a book of stories about friendship between women. I decided not to buy the books and left, realising about half an hour later that I had to buy them, after all, and went back and did so.

If I ever decide I don't need two copies of *Black Water*, I know someone who would happily accept the inscribed copy. WB Gooderham is the author of *Dedicated to . . . The Forgotten Friendships, Hidden Stories and Lost Loves Found in Second-hand Books* (Bantam Press), which grew out of Wayne Gooderham's website of the same name, which grew out of his collection of second-hand books containing dedications, the more personal the better. On top of Wayne's wardrobe in the north London flat he calls the Bunker are boxes and boxes full of books that he has 'absolutely no interest in reading' but that he has been collecting for many years for the dedications written within them. I think of Wayne as a fellow traveller, although as I write these words in February 2021 no one is doing a lot of travelling; maybe virtual cell mate would be more appropriate. The point is that I probably have as many books as Wayne does that I have absolutely no interest in reading.

I also have, as I'm sure Wayne does, hundreds of books that I have read, and hundreds of books that I want to read, and hundreds, well dozens, of books that I have read and want to reread, as well as a certain number of books that I do regularly reread. Another friend (I say, 'another', which presumes I can call Wayne a friend), a very old friend, the writer Conrad Williams, has a dislike, if not a deep, pathological loathing, for that word – 'reread'. I know what he means. At least, I think I do. You know the sort of thing. 'I'm rereading Proust.' 'I was rereading *Hamlet* the other day.' 'This summer, when we go to Tuscany, I am looking forward to rereading Nabokov's stories.' That sort of thing. They want you to know they've read Proust or *Hamlet* or Nabokov's stories before. In fact, they're terrified lest you think they're so ignorant and poorly read that they're only just getting around to reading Proust or *Hamlet* or Nabokov's stories.

When I say 'the writer Conrad Williams', I mean the author of *London Revenant*, *The Unblemished* and *One Who Was With Me*, among many other novels and short story collections, rather than the literary agent with Blake Friedmann who is also a novelist (*Sex and Genius*, *The Concert Pianist*). The subject of writers sharing a name with another writer is a subject I will return to.

For now, as my deadline approaches faster than the speed at which I can write, I'm engaged in reading, or in some cases rereading, those first eight Picador launch titles. A couple of days ago I finished Angela Carter's *Heroes and Villains*, but I won't comment on that yet as I don't want to start off on a negative note, especially not in relation to such a well-loved figure. Even

I, a poor strategist, can see that that would be rather foolish. I'm currently reading Richard Brautigan's *Trout Fishing in America*, which I thought I might have read before, but it's not at all familiar and you'd think it would be, what with all the fun he has with different interpretations of who or what is meant by Trout Fishing in America. I've barely finished reading *Trout Fishing* and moved on to Monique Wittig's *The Guérillères* when, in my current lockdown Scandi noir, 2017 Norwegian crime drama series *Monster*, police chief Ed Arvola, played by Bjorn Sundquist, is sitting at home reading *Trout Fishing in America*. His wife asks him what it's about and he says, 'Definitely not about trout fishing. Just lots of weird stories.' This is not an unfair assessment, although there's more about trout fishing than I expected. The best story, or chapter, comes towards the end. The Cleveland Wrecking Yard is selling a trout stream, but selling it in foot-long lengths that are stacked up outside the back of the shop. '"We're selling the waterfalls separately of course,"' says the man, '"and the trees and birds, flowers, grass and ferns we're also selling extra. The insects we're giving away free with a minimum purchase of ten feet of stream."'

Having owned a copy of *The Naked i* since the mid 1980s and dipped into it many times, it's only recently that I've read it from start to finish. It's quite a thing to read Kafka, Borges, Cortázar and Ellison one after another. I hadn't read Richard Wright's 'The Man Who Went to Chicago' or Carlos Fuentes' 'Aura' before and both are among the highlights. Rereading Ted Hughes's 'Snow' reminded me that I once applied to Manchester's Cornerhouse for a little pot of funding to edit a mini-anthology called *Snow* of stories called 'Snow', which would have included reprints of stories by James Lasdun, Jayne Anne Phillips and Miles Tripp alongside the Hughes and an original story by one of my students. The application was un-successful. My favourite story in *The Naked i* is Sylvia Plath's 'Johnny Panic and the Bible of Dreams', which begins, 'Every day from nine to five I sit at my desk facing the door of the office and type up other people's dreams.' An administrator in a hospital, Plath's narrator also takes her work home, where it consumes her. I once put together a book called *The Tiger Garden: A Book of Writers' Dreams*. Every day I sat at my desk typing up other people's dreams. Because it was a charity project intended to benefit Amnesty International, I was unable to offer payment to contributors. 'I don't dream,' wrote actor and writer Dirk Bogarde in response to my request, 'and not for "free" anyway.' The book was dismissed by critic Harry Ritchie as 'uniquely pointless and stupid', so he's not going to enjoy the current book, which will feature some of my dreams about books, writers, bookshops and critics, including at least one in which Harry Ritchie appears. Since it's widely believed that there's nothing more boring than other people's dreams, I'll try not to include too many and will use them as section breaks, which could be easily skipped, or studied, or simply enjoyed, according to your preference. They'll look like this, with a date.

Saturday 29 October 2016
I found two white-spined Picadors in a second-hand bookshop. I can only remember – or perhaps I only properly saw – one of them, a non-fiction book about the Tarot.

Not to be confused with snatches of overheard conversations, which will also be dated and will include a location and brief note on who is speaking, and be laid out like this.

Friday 31 January 2020
Thai Café, Stoke Newington, London.
Couple, late 50s, eating dinner.
Her: It's interesting.
Him: That's not much to say about a novel. All novels are interesting.

As far as I know, there haven't been any Picador non-fiction books about the Tarot. There was Calvino's *The Castle of Crossed Destinies*, but that's fiction.

Having recently read Virginia Woolf's *To the Lighthouse*, I'm not sure I'd agree that all novels are interesting.

Susanna Moore's *In the Cut*, a brilliant erotic thriller that would be one of my top ten Picadors, endears itself to me on only the second page: 'Some of them admitted that before completing the Virginia Woolf assignment they'd smoked a little dope and it had helped.' I don't, but I can imagine it might.

There will be chapters in which the main focus will be on various things, like: covers; inclusions – my preferred term, possibly even my coinage, for ephemera found in second-hand books; other people's books; names and inscriptions; Picador Classics; second-hand bookshops; French books and bookshops; writers with the same name as other writers; memories of Picador authors. Throughout, I will be hoping to throw some light on to what makes Picador so special that I decided to collect every single B-format Picador paperback published between 1972 and 2000, when the publisher abandoned its commitment to the white spine with black lettering in a more or less uniform style (which has started to sound to me like a fairly long-winded yet niche specialist subject on *Mastermind*). What it will not be is a history or biography of Picador; nor will it be a systematic guide to second-hand bookshops like a *Skoob Directory* or *Drif's Guide*. I'll try to stick to the point while at the same time allowing digressions. Adelle Stripe, responding to my series of lookalike photographs on social media, called me the 'Cindy Sherman of Northern Literature', which I liked, but I hear myself going on a bit in this introduction, which has topped 5,000 words, and I wonder if I might not be the Ronnie Corbett of Contemporary Letters, and I mean principally for his armchair monologues rather than the fact his feet didn't quite reach the floor. And, if that's the case, who is my Ronnie Barker?

I might be indiscreet, but I'll try not to offend. I may occasionally go into slightly bewildering detail, but I'll try not to be boring. Someone suggested to me that this book might be like 'that Nick Hornby book, but about books instead of records'. If it is, it will be by accident, because I haven't read it, although I have read Giles Smith's excellent Picador memoir *Lost in Music*, which came out in the same year as *High Fidelity*, which, it now occurs to me, was a novel anyway. In November 2020 I read Chris Paling's *Reading Allowed: True Stories & Curious Incidents From a Provincial Library* (Constable), which I found in the excellent Bopcap Books in Levenshulme Antiques Market, which was briefly open between one lockdown and the next. Novelist Paling's highly readable and likeable memoir of his career-switch from BBC radio producer to public librarian does a number of the things I had been hoping to do in *White Spines*, which was mildly concerning but also perhaps reassuring. If Chris Paling can do this, so can I, sort of thing.

Cover versions

Thursday 5 March 2009
I'm with Graham Joyce and another, unidentified member of the England Writers team, and David Beckham. I shake hands with Beckham. His hand is curiously light and bony. Graham and the other writer, both in football kit, stand either side of me, dwarfing me, and we have a bit of a laugh about it. I ask if it is a good idea to draw attention to the short stature of the goalkeeper, since it seems I am to be the goalkeeper for this match, not Graham.

Everyone I meet in Leicester – on Monday 8 May 2017 – says, 'It's not as warm as yesterday.' I can believe it; it only warms up when I am walking briskly between bookshops. The meeting I'm in town for, at De Montfort University, is on the Tuesday morning, early enough that they're putting me up in a hotel on the Monday night. A little online research suggests I will be able to fill an afternoon easily enough before paying a visit to the family of my late friend, the writer Graham Joyce.

I start at Maynard & Bradley on Silver Street in the city centre. It's a charming shop with an affable owner, but I come away empty handed. I survey a smattering of charity shops with the same result. Tin Drum Books on Narborough Road looks more promising. It's the classic second-hand bookshop: tall bookcases, full shelves; pleasing level of order despite tattiness and frayed edges; older gentleman sitting behind the counter quietly getting on with whatever the proprietors of second-hand bookshops get on with. I inspect the shelves, checking non-fiction first, saving up fiction like the icing on a cake. I don't find anything in non-fiction, so I move on to fiction. I start at the end of the alphabet and pick out *Man Descending* by Guy Vanderhaeghe. He sounds Belgian but is Canadian; the fact his book is a short story collection published in the 1980s by Sceptre is good enough for me. It's not all about the Picadors. My heart beats a little bit faster when I spot the tattered spine of William Trevor's *The Children of Dynmouth*. I have a copy in Penguin, but this is a King Penguin, so the chances are it could have a James Marsh cover. I tease it out and see the eyes floating in the sky, the lighthouse nose and the bird for a mouth. The book is in poor condition, but I love these covers. I love them like I love those by Grizelda Holderness for Emma Tennant in Picador and Tom Adams' covers for Fontana's Agatha Christie series. I assemble a smallish pile of books (Charles Nicholl's *The Fruit Palace* and Justin Cartwright's *Look at it This Way* in Picador, Louis Aragon's *Paris Peasant*, which I already have in Picador but this is a Picador Classics, so, since I also collect the black spines of Picador Classics, I have to have it, and Anita Desai's *Games at Twilight* in King Penguin) that come to £11.50. I head to the counter, wishing I felt able to say to the man that £2 seems a bit steep for the William Trevor, given that it is literally falling apart. He counts them up and says, 'Let's call it £10, a nice round number.'

The next shop on my list is Treasure Trove on Mayfield Road. As I walk I look at the books I have just bought. The Anita Desai short story collection has a cover by Poul Webb, who illustrated a whole series of Anita Desai covers for King Penguin in the 1980s: vividly coloured landscapes and gardens, some with figures, some without, but most featuring a bird in flight. The bird may not be the first thing you see, but once you've seen it, you can't unsee it. The James Marsh cover on the Trevor novel also features a bird, which is typical of Marsh, across his many book and album covers, but not of this particular series of books for Penguin, which are all representations of human faces made out of unusual features, including a letter box for a mouth and irises made out of jet engines. The *Dynmouth* cover reminds me of Marsh's cover for a Picador book, Randolph Stow's 1979 novel *Visitants*, with its suggestion of a face using two flying saucers and an arum lily. (In February 2021, as I write this chapter, I'm charging through Monique Wittig's *The Guérillères*, translated from the French by David Le Vay, and, on page 52, I read, 'It is during this movement that they exhale a perfume of arum lily verbena which spreads instantly through the surrounding space.') As an enthusiast, rather than an art historian, I'm not very good at categorising art, but artist and designer John Coulthart describes Marsh's style as 'hard-edged, post-Surrealist'.

Most notable about the Picador Classics edition of Aragon's *Paris Peasant* is not the cover, if illustrator Max Ellis will forgive me, but the biographical note about the author, which begins and proceeds in the conventional manner – it's factual, neutral and dry, precisely how a biographical note should be – covering his being a founder of the Surrealist movement before converting to communism, then distinguishing himself as a soldier in WWII and in the Resistance. Then, we read, 'His post-war fiction was crudely propagandist and he became little more than a poseur with dyed red hair in the years before his death in 1982.'

I find out later I could have reached Mayfield Road by going up New Walk, the most beautiful street in Leicester. On London Road, I pass the Church of St James the Greater, where in 2014 I attended Graham Joyce's memorial service. It's a cliché, of course, but Graham was one of those larger-than-life, passionate, funny and generous characters you simply can't quite accept are no longer around once they've gone. Dying far too young at 59, he was as committed to defending the goal-mouth for the England Writers football team as he was to defending disadvantaged groups generally.

The Mayfield Road address for Treasure Trove turns out to be a private residence. What can you do except take a step back and stare up at a building resentfully? Maybe you assess how recently the change of use took place? Can you still smell books in the air? In this case, 21 Mayfield Road doesn't look as if it has ever been a second-hand bookshop. You start to doubt the reliability of Google. You wonder if Donald Trump is to blame. Or the Russians. Better for the blood pressure just to walk on, in this case south into increasingly leafy neighbourhoods, eventually stumbling upon the charming villagey centre of Clarendon Park, with its twin bookshops either side of Queen's Road run by Age UK and LOROS (a local hospice charity). In the former, where ladies of a certain age gather for lattes at the tables in the window, I find an Edmund White collection in Picador that I have never seen before, *Skinned Alive*. You see some White titles a lot – *A Boy's Own Story*, *The Beautiful Room is Empty*, even *Nocturnes For the King of Naples* and *Caracole* – but *Skinned Alive* is a new one on me. Also: a King Penguin edition of JM

Coetzee's *Waiting For the Barbarians*, with, tucked in between pages 98 and 99, a newspaper clipping of a letter from Coetzee to the *Times Higher Education Supplement* dated 7 October 1988 in which he, as a professor at the University of Cape Town, writes in support of the cultural and academic boycott of South Africa.

I remember the clip on YouTube in which Coetzee introduces British writer Geoff Dyer to a festival crowd at Adelaide Writers' Week in March 2010. Dyer gets up and goes to the microphone. 'Thank you, John, and thank you, everyone,' says Dyer. 'What an honour. If someone had told me twenty years ago that I'd be here in Australia and I'd be introduced by a Booker Prize-winning, South African, Nobel Prize-winning novelist, I don't know what I'd have said. I mean, yeah, what would I have said? I would probably have said, "Well, that's incredible, because Nadine Gordimer is my favourite writer."' Dyer's face breaks into a smile, the audience fall about laughing and Geoff glances across at the Booker Prize-winning, South African, Nobel-Prize-winning novelist to see if he appreciates the joke. On Coetzee's granite face there is not a flicker.

Over the road in LOROS I buy a copy of Graham Joyce's thirteenth and penultimate novel *Some Kind of Fairy Tale*. I ask the shopkeeper if he knew Graham. He didn't, but when in conversation I mention that Graham had been a fan of Coventry City, the man opens up. He's a Derby fan himself. He doesn't watch *Match of the Day*, he says, because he can't bear it when men talk about football. Neither of us comments on the irony as we proceed to have a friendly and apparently mutually enjoyable chat – about football.

I have a sense that Clarendon Books, around the corner on Clarendon Park Road, could be the highlight of my afternoon and, indeed, when I get there the signs are good. In one of the boxes outside is a copy, albeit in poor condition, of Christopher Kenworthy's short story collection *Will You Hold Me?* I've known Chris as long as I knew Graham, since the late 1980s. He has lived in Australia for many years now. His collection contains some of my favourite short stories. They are as affecting as they are odd. 'Odd', in my opinion, or in this context anyway, is an entirely positive descriptor.

As I push open the door of Clarendon Books, the carpet beneath it rucks up. I poke my head around a pile of books and apologise to the proprietor. 'It's been happening all day,' he tells me. Clarendon Books is similar to Tin Drum Books, although with more books crammed into less space. I find a Picador by John Cowper Powys that I don't have – *Weymouth Sands*. When I get it home it will join five others of his books and the six of them will account for an impressive nine inches of shelf space. Cowper Powys, a writer of unusually long books, died the year I was born, our lives overlapping for only three months. It says on the back of *Weymouth Sands*, '. . . the stones of Chesil Beach are as much characters as the human beings.' Some might have said something similar of a more recent novel by another author.

I reach, breathlessly, for what looks like an early Picador. It's Peter Wahloo's *The Lorry*, one of the first eight, which I don't have and have never even seen. I look at the cover, which, when I get it home, will be one of only two Picador covers in my collection to feature the work of Salvador Dalí, the other being the artist's own and only novel, *Hidden Faces*. Gingerly I open *The Lorry* to the flyleaf, expecting its scarcity to be reflected in the price, but it's actually cheaper than the other books I've selected. I take four books to the till and remove a £10 note from my wallet that I hope will cover the cost (I should really be able to add four prices together in the time it takes to reach the till from any position in Clarendon Books). 'Let's call it £8,' says the man. 'Thank you very much,' I say as a feeling of warmth similar to the one I had in Tin Drum Books starts to suffuse my entire being. I leave the shop and, as I walk back to Queen's Road, I tot up what the books should have come to – £8.05.

Sunday 6 October 2019
Coffee Circus, Crouch Hill, Crouch End, London.
Couple, 30s.
Him: I've got two Philip Pullman books signed by Philip Pullman. I still haven't read them.
Her: Is there a reason you haven't read them?
Him: Fantasy versus reality.
Her: Robin really liked them.
Him: Robin *would* like them.
[Pause.]
Him: There's a place there that does pizza and Chinese food.
Her: That's not trustworthy.
Him: Jack of all trades. Master of none.
Her: Exactly.

Probably the next Picador I owned – after *Ice* and *Black Water* – was Emma Tennant's fourth novel, *Hotel de Dream*, originally published in 1976 by Victor Gollancz and issued in paperback by Picador in 1983. The cover is by Grizelda Holderness and depicts a house on the side of a hill and two human figures, one female and one male, caught up in a huge blue wave, along with a dining table and cloth, a teapot and four fish. A crescent moon hangs in the sky.

'I loved doing the Emma Tennant pictures,' writes Grizelda Holderness after I contact her via her website. 'I was young.

It was a time of innocence. I was lucky to be there.' She did four more covers for novels by Tennant for Picador, among them Tennant's seventh novel, *Alice Fell*. 'Gary Day-Ellison gave me the book, *Alice Fell*, and said, "Draw me a picture." He "employed" so many of us, just young and starting artists, mostly from Fine Art, whose work he liked, and he gave us all a life-line. Freedom and money! Also respect and self-respect, and courage – no, actually, it was something *much* more than that. It was "I trust you to do your best for me, and if it fails it doesn't matter." I think this is the best thing you can say to anyone in the world. Any child.'

Grizelda Holderness did at least one other Picador cover – for Norman Mailer's *Ancient Evenings* – as well as a number of covers for other publishers. For Serpent's Tail she did, rather pleasingly, a cover for *Mer de Glace*, a 1992 novel by Alison Fell that won the Boardman Tasker Award For Mountain Literature. A few years later, when I was editing *The Tiger Garden*, I included a dream from the novelist Nicholas Shakespeare. He dreamt that he was at a colloquium on VS Naipaul, who is present and answering a question about his sentiments regarding the Japanese sense of humour, when the door bursts open and 'an unshaven man staggers in, his long hair gathered back in a pony-tail. Ignoring Naipaul, he walks up to the serious young questioner and says: "I'm sorry, Matthew. Alice Fell has been assassinated. She was doing an interview and her cameraman and sound recordist were the assassins. You have to come." I have no idea who Alice Fell is, but it is evident from the collective gasps that everyone else does (a figure, I start to imagine, rather in the mould of the East German novelist Christa Wolf). My eyes water for a woman I've never heard of and the dream ends with Naipaul giving his blessing for Matthew and the pony-tailed man to depart.'

Shakespeare confirms to me by email that, as far as he can recall, he was aware of neither *Alice Fell* nor Alison Fell when he had this dream, on a visit to Benin in the mid-1990s. I have three books by Shakespeare in my Picador collection. I bought *The Vision of Elena Silves* from Oxfam Bookshop Leeds in Headingley in August 2017 and *The High Flyer* (to replace an existing copy in poor condition) the following month for a pound in Halcyon Books, Greenwich, on the second of my three visits, spaced out over three years, to their 'closing down sale'. I bought another copy of *The Vision of Elena Silves* from Oxfam Books & Music Crouch End at the end of August 2020. Drunk with happiness at finding the Crouch End Oxfam open for the first time since March of that year, I bought nine books that day, one of which I *knew* I already had (Shakespeare – as was the case with *The High Flyer*, it was in better nick), one of which I *thought* I already had (Mario Vargas Llosa's *The Time of the Hero* – I did), and one of which I thought I *didn't* have but later found I *did* (Uwe Timm's *The Snake Tree*).

'Picador, for a short, magnesium-flare span,' Shakespeare says, 'was a little like *Granta* under Buford, or *Horizon* under Connolly. I know how proud I felt to be on the list.'

If *Hotel de Dream* was my third Picador, Knut Hamsun's *Hunger* would have been my fourth, but it could be the other way around. I was attracted to both of them by their covers. Picador published seven Hamsun novels, six of them in a series with covers illustrated by Paul Leith depicting figures in various landscapes in a sort of Nordic naïve style, like a cross between Edvard Munch and Henri Rousseau.

If you're not supposed to judge a book by its cover, why do publishers employ designers and art directors and why do they commission artists and illustrators and photographers? Why has the cover reveal become such a thing – an event – on social media? Why do virtually all publishers periodically reissue a successful author's backlist with new covers?

Gary Day-Ellison joined Pan/Picador in May 1977 as the most junior of four graphic designers. 'I had been art-directing the Association of Illustrators magazine in an attempt to make a better portfolio,' he tells me in March 2021. 'David Larkin called me and seemed intrigued when I said I wasn't ready for such a major publisher yet. He told me to meet him at the nearest pub to King's Reach Tower that evening at six. He quizzed me about my decisions and choices on my first issue and a half of the magazine, then offered me the job. I was made joint art director by Christmas, then I was groomed as David Larkin's successor as he migrated to New York. I was art director from then on. Latterly I adopted the publicity art department too. I was offered title of creative director. I was very idealistic and (pompously?) said every department should be creative if they were on their game. I settled for design & art director. Dumb on reflection!'

In March 2021, I have 959 Picadors in my main collection, excluding 35 in the anomalies section, and of those 959 a certain number will be accounted for by doubling up on titles where series have been rejacketed. This means people like Barnes, Calvino, Chatwin, Doctorow, McEwan, Ondaatje, Raban and others. Of Ian McEwan's outstandingly good first collection of short stories, *First Love, Last Rites*, for instance, I have three Picador editions: photography by Barnaby Hall (which forms a pair with *In Between the Sheets*); design by Kyle Burris, photography by Robin Cracknell (in series with several other titles); and the one that represents my favourite early McEwan editions, illustrations by Russell Mills, photography by David Buckland

and typography by Vaughan Oliver. It's Mills' multimedia assemblages, like his other multi-layered covers for Picador including Don DeLillo's *White Noise* and Josef Skvorecky's *The Engineer of Human Souls*, that really catch the eye. Mills is also a recording artist: I'm listening to one of his albums, *Strange Familiar*, as I write these words.

And as I write *these* words I'm listening to *Tiny Colour Movies* by John Foxx, because Foxx, like Mills, is another artist as comfortable in the recording studio as he is in the design studio. Under the name Dennis Leigh, the original Ultravox vocalist turned solo artist has produced numerous book covers for various publishers including, for Picador, the one that adorns Evan Eisenberg's *The Recording Angel*.

The point is I would often buy books just for their covers. In the summer of 1982, having finished school and moved from Manchester with my mum and younger sister to join my dad outside Ipswich, I mostly cycled into town to mooch around between Andy's Records and Dick's book stall. I bought a paperback off Dick. The combination of the publisher (New English Library) and the cover (a green-tinged photograph of a seashore with yellow, white and red type) reminded me of James Herbert's *The Fog*. I still hadn't quite got over – or understood – an episode at school, when a teacher I particularly liked had spotted a book sticking out of my briefcase. 'What's this, Royle?' he asked, plucking it free and holding it up for all to see. '*The Fog*, sir,' I said. 'I'm rereading it.' Mr S smiled and gave a little laugh and – and this is what I never understood and still don't to this day – the whole class laughed with him. OK, so it wasn't *Middlemarch*, but nor was it a copy of *Mayfair*. I was unlucky. On another day it could have been Robbe-Grillet's *ciné-roman* version of *L'année dernière à Marienbad* sticking out of my bag.

Precociously, perhaps, I loved the *nouveau roman*, even at that age, as much as I enjoyed horror stories.

But they all laughed. Even _____ _____, who I knew for sure would have had a copy of *Mayfair* in his bag, or at least in his locker.

I read the novel I bought from Dick's book stall and found it kind of interesting. At the end of the summer I went to London to go to university, as mentioned above, and forgot about the book with the green cover. Some years later I thought of it again and wanted to reread it, but couldn't find it, neither in my room in Hughes Parry Hall nor in my bedroom back at my parents'. More years – many years – passed and something reminded me of it and I decided I really had to reread it. What had it been called? The haunted something? Who had it been by? Somebody Hillman? I could remember the cover, the green light, the wet sand, the distant sea. The haunted shore? That was it. *The Haunted Shore* by MN Hillman. Or was it NM Hillman? One or the other. I tried second-hand bookshops, library catalogues, book searches. The British Library catalogue. As a last resort I contacted the publisher, New English Library. It felt like cheating, because I knew they would have the answer, although the British Library should also have had the answer. But, still, nothing.

Then, in 2007, the *Independent* ran a double-page feature on well-known writers' unsuccessful first novels. It was only a tiny thumbnail image of the cover, but I recognised it immediately and realised my mistake. *The Haunted Shore* was *The Haunted Storm* and MN Hillman turned out to be Philip N Pullman, who, in the intervening years, had become phenomenally successful, but would not permit any reissue of his first-published novel. Not only that, but he wouldn't permit any discussion of it. He wouldn't sign copies of it. But he couldn't stop me going online and paying a ridiculous amount for a copy and reading it. Was it terrible? The French have a phrase – *pas terrible* – which of course literally means 'not terrible', but also carries with it the clear message that something is definitely 'not very good either'. For years I would hear the expression being used without really understanding it, and now that I think I do, I like to use it every so often. *The Haunted Storm* is *pas terrible*.

Finally, to draw this chapter to a close, poetry. I don't understand poetry. I don't know what it is. I don't know what it's for. I don't know when it's any good. At school, for A-level, we did something by Gerard Manley Hopkins and Gray's 'Elegy Written in a Country Churchyard'. I didn't understand either. I didn't know what they were. I didn't know what they were for. I was being told both were good. We also did Ted Hughes, who I decided I did like. I learnt his 'Cadenza' off by heart and came up with my own rather subjective interpretation, which Mr Craze rejected. 'But, sir,' I began, 'surely literature is a matter of opinion.' A pair of lips could be seen curling into a smile in the depths of Mr Craze's beard. 'Yes, Nick, literature is a matter of opinion,' he said, 'but you're wrong and I'm right.'

On Wednesday 16 November 2016, I was walking from Stoke Newington, north London, to Euston station and called in at one of my favourite branches of Oxfam Books & Music, the Islington branch at the Angel end of Upper Street. That day I found a Picador I didn't already have, Stephen Brook's *LA Lore*, and a Picador Classics title I also didn't have, *The Collected Stories of Tennessee Williams*, and then I spotted a Paladin. I had started collecting Paladin paperbacks, not with quite the same single-mindedness that I collected Picadors, perhaps, but whenever I saw a white spine with the Paladin logo at the bottom I would at least get it out and have a look. Looking more closely I saw the familiar logo had an unfamiliar addition, the word 'poetry'. But I had already laid my fingers on the top edge. Oxfam Books & Music Islington used to shelve poetry and short stories together, by the way. The front cover made me catch my breath. The design was very simple, clear and elegant. Classy. At the top was the poet's name – Lee Harwood – in caps, then the title – *Crossing the Frozen River* – lower case, italics. Underneath this an asterisk, then 'Selected Poems', in caps again. Then a large image and underneath that 'A Paladin Original' and the logo again.

Penguin may not have invented the 'paperback original' in 1989, but since the launch of the Penguin Originals list in that year, I have been susceptible to the use of the word 'original' on a book cover. It sends a clear signal to readers, critics, reviewers and literary editors. This book may not be a hardback, but we wish to draw your attention to the fact that it is being published for the first time. It is worthy of your attention. It is special.

The image is special, too. I don't recognise it and have to turn the book over to see that it is a pastel, *Study For the World's Body*, by RB Kitaj. It's somehow a simple and a complex composition at the same time, wonderfully compelling, and while it has an immediate impact on the viewer, it doesn't dominate the cover, which still has plenty of white space around the image and those two blocks of type. Anyway, I bought it and from that moment on made sure not to leave any second-hand bookshop without first checking the poetry section for further volumes in the Paladin Poetry series.

The dream I had in which Graham Joyce and I met Beckham was one of several I had about Graham while he was still alive.

So far, I've only had – or remembered – one dream about him since he died. On Saturday 19 March 2016 I dreamt I was on a coach, or series of coaches, travelling somewhere, into somewhere, into some great, more primitive interior, only when we get there it's much more built up. Our vehicle, which has become a fire engine, has been parked on a zigzag line close to a pelican crossing. I want to get our driver back so he can park it properly. Although I think maybe we'll get away with it because it's a fire engine. Later, the vehicle is a train. I'm talking to Joe Stretch. We are talking about a series of books that are copies of or references to other books. There's one that's meant to be Margaret Atwood's *Oryx and Crake*, which I say I haven't read. We talk about Graham Joyce. Graham's wife Sue has asked a series of questions that we are somehow answering and I say it's just like we are talking to Graham, because Sue knew him so well for so long.

That doesn't quite make sense, but it was a dream.

Back in Leicester, May 2017, I spend a lovely evening with Graham's family. Graham's daughter Ella has written a poem about her dad and she lets me read it. I understand it. I know what it is. I know what it's for and I know that it's good.

Later I head back to my hotel along New Walk, which must be the most beautiful street not only in Leicester but in the whole of the East Midlands. And the West Midlands, come to that. It feels enchanted, like a street in some kind of fairy tale.

I Find You, Dad

There is a hole you left
and now
the stories flow less easily

and the magic is harder to see
but long ago you showed it to me

and if I saw it once I will see it again
because you are in everything I do

and I find you

in
the reflection of light on a sea in Spain
a tea light in a tiny ceramic house
the moon above the Sierra Nevada
a book I read before I can remember reading
books
a vinyl played on an old record player

the smell of old leather
and wine at a new year's eve party

an old book of poetry half chewed by a much
loved pet

and a smile from my brother
and a story from my mother

and then the edges of the hole are softened and I can

f
a
l
l

into it

like

     falling

        asleep.

ELLA JOYCE

2

Last Orders at the White Hotel

Tuesday 7 September 2004

I was walking, with my wife, past the distinctive white house in Altrincham where I lived between the ages of eight and 19 and I noticed demolition/rebuilding work going on. I could see into the back garden from the front. We went in and encountered a man with bushy fair hair in his 30s or 40s. I told him I'd lived there, getting the dates wrong by a decade. He explained that he spent little time there, just weekends. I asked if I could look around. The kitchen had a high surface with no way of climbing up, or putting your feet under. Upstairs it was impossible to make any sense of the rooms. Nothing, including the staircase, was how it had been. The man gave me a card relating to the home and to himself. My wife pointed out DM Thomas's name under a credit for 'Film'. Maybe this meant Thomas was responsible for films made about the house. Or maybe it meant the white house was to be turned into a *White Hotel*. The man was not Thomas but he was clearly linked to him. Presumably when he wasn't at the home, he was down in Cornwall with Thomas in some capacity.

৵৬

In Hughes Parry Hall, a number of staff lived on site, including the warden, the vice-warden and a number of hall tutors. The vice-warden was a jolly man with a permanently amused expression called David Brown, who lived in a flat on the thirteenth floor. From memory, which can be unreliable, David Brown played a lot of squash, unless I just associate him with the sport because of the location of his flat, under the squash courts. What I remember clearly is being invited there, to his flat, along with a group of other freshers for a welcome drink, enjoying the view from his windows and feeling strangely excited by the idea that while around 200 students would come and go every year, David Brown lived here permanently. The warden lived in another wing, the low-rise section, above the refectory, in accommodation that might have been more spacious and luxurious – I have only the vaguest memory of being inside it on a single occasion – but the vice-warden's flat had a height advantage. If you're going to live in a tall building, you need to be high up. My own room, 7.14, was only half way up, but with a great view of St Paul's Cathedral.

Sitting in one of David Brown's armchairs, I noticed a magazine on his coffee table called *London Magazine*. I imagined it might contain photographs of landmark buildings, articles about the history of Harrod's or the Great Fire of London. Picking it up, I found it packed with short stories, poems, reviews. The vice-warden – a subscriber, he told me – pointed to a whole row of copies on a shelf.

I don't remember what issue it was, but it would make sense if it was the August/September 1982 double summer short story issue, featuring a story by Charles Wilkinson, whom I would meet three decades later at the funeral of our mutual friend Joel Lane.

I started writing short stories the following summer and would submit them to, among other places, *London Magazine*, but I committed a sin typical of young writers starting out. I didn't read the magazines I was submitting to. I didn't read *London Magazine*, I didn't read *Ambit*, I didn't read *Stand*. Or not at first. Alan Ross would send very kind rejection slips from *London Magazine* saying, 'Not quite right for us' or 'Not quite there yet' while Martin Bax would send slightly tetchy ones from *Ambit* recommending a subscription. Running a small press, four decades later, I get it. I have met Martin Bax many times since and he is charming and generous, the perfect gentleman, and his first novel, *The Hospital Ship*, was probably the fifth addition to my Picador collection.

I'm still awaiting a reply from *Stand*.

The first *London Magazine* I bought, second hand, was the October 1968 issue, for a story and cartoons by Roland Topor. I saw Polanski's adaptation of Topor's novel *The Tenant* at the National Film Theatre not long after arriving in London and thereafter would buy anything with the Frenchman's name on it. I didn't properly start collecting *London Magazine* until the 90s when I came across a good number of them, reasonably priced, in Goldmark Books in Uppingham, Rutland. Goldmark Books – indeed, Uppingham itself – was somewhere you were only likely to come across if you were driving from, say, Kettering to Oakham, or in either direction along the A47 between Leicester and Peterborough and you happened to take the turn-off for the small market town that was home to a well-known independent boarding school, the best homemade Battenberg cake in the world (from Baines Bakery on High Street) and Goldmark.

Or you may have driven there deliberately, the yellow cover of the *Skoob Directory of Secondhand Bookshops in the British Isles* splayed on the passenger seat.

Within a minute of starting browsing, you would be offered a coffee. Time it right and that could turn into lunch. You would never leave without a book you had been hunting down for ten years.

Once you found Goldmark Books, it was inconceivable that it wouldn't be your favourite second-hand bookshop until the day it closed its doors.

Mike Goldmark was born in 1944 in Welwyn Garden City, his parents having fled Austria five years earlier. He moved to Uppingham in 1972 and soon became a partner in a second-hand bookseller's by offering the owner the £500 he needed to remain afloat. In 1974 he bought the premises on Orange Street and moved the business, of which he was now the sole owner, across. The bookshop thrived and eleven years later a wing was added to house the Goldmark Gallery. In 1986 he branched out into publishing.

In 2004, Goldmark told me he was going to close down the bookshop and concentrate on the gallery. Much as I loved the gallery, having also become a customer there, buying dark, intense, sometimes grotesque paintings by Barry Burman, I instantly felt a deep sense of loss, then immediately went into denial. He would never do it.

A month into 2005, Goldmark did indeed close down the bookshop, giving away the entire stock. With an unusually heavy heart, having pitched an article to the *Independent on Sunday*, I paid Goldmark my first visit of the new year.

'To begin with, the bookselling side was much more important,' Goldmark said. 'I loved it, and the truth is that I still do. For a number of years I did both and then I think the bookshop suffered, firstly because it wasn't getting enough attention and secondly because the internet started to change everything. Years and years ago we'd take fabulous amounts of money on a Saturday. A couple would come in and they'd find six books each and they'd spend thirty or forty quid. They'd have spent an hour and a half with us. They'd have had a coffee and a chat and I used to get real enjoyment out of it. The books were relatively small amounts of money, but we sold so many that the business was tremendous. I've just watched it change over the years. Now, very, very seldom does anyone come in and buy six books. You're more likely to get a couple coming in and they find "one each, darling", and one's a fiver and the other's seven pounds fifty, and then they have a discussion about which one of the two they're going to buy. And if you went round to the Falcon Hotel an hour later you'd find them in there buying a round of gin and tonic that's going to cost twice that.'

Every time I visited the shop, I would find something I wanted, I told Goldmark for the hundredth time, whether it was a first edition by William Sansom or a Derek Marlowe paperback to replace one I had lent to someone and not got back. Maybe it was a short story anthology missing from an otherwise complete set, or back copies of *London Magazine* containing stories by Edward Fox or Alan Beard.

'I think that happened with a huge number of people,' said Goldmark. 'It used to feel to us and to other people as if the whole thing were magical. We never went anywhere to buy. We just stood here and the stuff came in. Quite early on I went to a bookshop in a little town just down the road and a guy came in with a box of books and the bookseller in there looked at the box and he said to this chap, "All crap. I'll give you a fiver." And the guy picked up the box, didn't say anything and walked out. I was just leaving at the time. We got outside and I said to this chap, "I've got a bookshop down the road. Do you mind if I have a look, because actually there are a few things on the top that look fine to me?" And he said, "They're yours." I said, "We haven't worked out a price yet," and he said, "I wasn't going to ask the man for any money. I was going to give him the books, but after that . . ." And he gave me this box of books. I found out very early on that the truth was that people selling books were not necessarily looking for the most money they could possibly get. We just tried to be as nice to people when we were buying as we were when we were selling. And the result was that car-loads would arrive from all over the country. If we needed something in particular – I don't know whether I dare say this – we used to *think* them in. It is actually true. It used to happen quite often.'

Signs informing customers of the closing-down sale had gone up towards the end of 2004. I still didn't believe then that Goldmark was serious, even when I tried to buy a few *London Magazine*s and he told me to help myself to the whole shelf.

'We had a sale, sold a few books, and then I wasn't sure whether the rest were worth much,' Goldmark told me. 'Somebody said, "How much? I'll take the lot." And we let him have them. As it happens he complained bitterly because I think he thought he was going to make a fortune just passing them on to someone else without doing anything.'

That must have left a sour taste?

'No . . .'

Although, after a pause, Goldmark added a four-letter word that was startling in those surroundings, the walls hung with original engravings by Eric Gill and William Blake. Through the open doorway, I was taunted by the sight of the empty, skeletal shelves.

Visiting the shop in 1994 and chatting with Goldmark, I had raved about Iain Sinclair's new novel, *Radon Daughters*, which I had just reviewed for *Time Out*. I was a slightly more ignorant fool then than I am now and did not know I was talking to the man who had published Sinclair's first novel, *White Chappell Scarlet Tracings*, in 1987. He had handed me a copy, which he allowed me to pay for, but insisted I also have a free copy of Sinclair's *Suicide Bridge* in the original Albion Village Press edition.

'Sinclair had been a customer almost since the beginning. I trusted him so much that if I got a first edition I would put it in a pile. He would come once a month and I would show him the pile, unpriced, and I would accept whatever he gave me. It was a lovely way to deal. He gave me one or two scraps of stuff that he'd published. None of which I understood at all. *Suicide Bridge*. Things like that. He told me that he was going to write a novel. I told him that if he couldn't find a publisher I would publish it. And months later he came back. He had wanted three months' space. I remember him telling me he'd been thinking it for fourteen years and it was a question of actually getting it down on paper. I think I offered to give him the money and he wouldn't take it. Then he found a parcel of books on Jersey – or Guernsey, one of those two – and I flew out there, bought them. He took some of the best of them. I think that gave him the three months that he required, when he had sold those. Then I didn't see him for another six months and he came and said that the book had gone out and been turned down by everybody. He wasn't going to hold me to what I had said, but I said no, I'd publish it. He said, "Do you want to read it?" and I said, "No, I don't think that would be a good idea." We had no sales force. We had no marketing. Nothing. And it turned out we didn't need it. All we had to do was make a really nice book and the publicity just came out of the woodwork at us. And that happened the second time a few years later when we published Aidan Andrew Dun's *Vale Royal*. Again we had no idea how we were going to sell the book. And the right person walked in through the door, the right journalist, and away we went. That's the way we do most things.'

While the second-hand books had gone by 2005, new books would continue to be produced, the publishing operation expanding alongside the gallery.

'I've always wanted to be in a situation where I could do three or four really good books a year, of the sort that other people don't want to publish, and to produce them beautifully, and hopefully illustrate them as well. And maybe, one day, I'll get to read again.'

It was a strange and rather sad fact that for years this passionate lover of books, who in 1995 hired the Royal Albert Hall at a cost of £20,000 to put on a poetry reading featuring Allen Ginsberg and Paul McCartney among fourteen other poets and performers, had been unable to read. 'I just get extremely tired when I start doing it. I'll read an article and I read reference books every day for work, but that's all. It's bloody embarrassing.'

Maybe it was just hard to find the time. Never content to stand still – unless as part of his daily tai chi practice – Goldmark was already thinking ahead to some point in the future when the gallery would have gone the same way as the books and he'd be using the space on Orange Street to teach chi gong.

'I'm more excited about life and business than I've ever been,' he announced. 'Do you want another coffee?'

Goldmark Art has since expanded into the space previously

occupied by the bookshop and new books have continued to be published, beautifully.

Saturday 18 May 1996

I want to talk to Iain Sinclair, so I find the section of the refectory/department store where he should be sitting, according to alphabetical ordering, but he's not there. Bob Geldof is there. I ask Bob if Sinclair is around. He says he'd brought along all his Sinclair books (to get them signed? He says not, but why else?). I ask him what his favourite is and he ums and aahs, finally stumbling over his pronunciation of *Downriver*. I say mine is *Radon Daughters*.

Also in the 1990s, I started collecting *Ambit* with the same level of enthusiasm as I was now collecting *London Magazine*, my collection more than doubling in size in 2012 after I was kindly offered – by his family, via writer and curator Gareth Evans – the pick of the late Dai Vaughan's collection of literary magazines.

I have never properly collected *Stand*, but will pick up the odd copy if it contains a story by Ron Butlin, which it usually does.

That same edition of *London Magazine* that might have been lying on David Brown's coffee table carried an ad from Penguin for their paperback edition of Graham Swift's latest novel, *Shuttlecock*. The previous issue, July 1982, had advertised a forthcoming publication from London Magazine Editions, the magazine's book publishing arm, namely *Learning to Swim*, the same author's debut short story collection. Both *Learning to Swim* and later *Shuttlecock* would become Picador titles once Swift moved to the publisher (for paperback only, at first) with *Waterland*.

By the time of *Last Orders* in 1996 Swift was fully a Picador author and his new novel about a group of old guys who travel from London to Margate to carry out the last wishes of their late friend was that year's Booker Prize winner. Around about the same time, married to my first wife, Kate, and with our children not yet born, I had the space (and time) to put my small Picador collection in a white bookcase which I kept on the first-floor landing in our house in Shepherd's Bush. It didn't quite fill the bookcase – a small or medium-sized and medium-height Billy from Ikea – and so I filled the rest of the bottom shelf with other B-format paperbacks, using whatever Sceptre, Abacus or King Penguin paperbacks I had, which happened also to have white spines, plus maybe there were some orange and black spines in there just to fill up those last few inches.

I was working full time at *Time Out*, but when I wasn't working, or sitting at my desk in the attic pretending to write, surrounded by hundreds of books from dozens of publishers, an anarchy of formats, bindings, sizes and colours, I would sit on the soft oatmeal carpet on the first-floor landing staring at these shelves of white-spined books, studying the differences between each one and the next. The authors' names and the titles, obviously, but also the order in which those appeared on the spines. When Picador launched in 1972, the title came first, all in caps, followed by the author's name in lower case with initial caps. In the late 1980s, these elements switched positions and styles, the author's name being rendered in small caps with initial caps. I have been asked a number of times if this switch bothered me. I can understand that. There seems no particularly good reason, for example, why the spine on the first Picador edition of Bruce Chatwin's *The Songlines*, dated 1988 (my copy kindly donated by Richard Clegg, an excellent reader and enthusiast from Oldham), with a cover showing *Red Landscape* by Fred Williams, should read THE SONGLINES Bruce Chatwin, while a reprint dated the same year with a cover by über-fashionable design house The Senate goes with BRUCE CHATWIN The Songlines. But still, in any list of things worth getting worked up about, that would come quite near the bottom.

If I could just acquire a few more Picadors to edge out those Sceptres and Paladins and King Penguins on the bottom shelf I'd have a bookcase, a white bookcase no less, full of white-spined Picadors. It would be a thing of beauty. It would be a small masterpiece and it would be easier to achieve than the masterpieces I was trying to create at my desk in the attic.

It wasn't the only collection of mine in the house. In another bookcase was a complete set of *The Pan Book of Horror Stories*, from volume one to volume 30, including my own first professional sale, 'Time to Get Up', which was the eighteenth story I had written, in volume 26; a complete set of 17 volumes of *The Fontana Book of Great Horror Stories*; and a tantalisingly incomplete collection of *The Fontana Book of Great Ghost Stories*, for some reason lacking – and still lacking today – volume 14. But it wasn't only books. I don't mind admitting I had collected train numbers. And bus numbers. These were more intangible, but you could buy little books in which the numbers were listed and you underlined a train number – or a bus number – when you 'copped' it.

On the inside of a cupboard door in the kitchen was my collection of bread labels. You know those little plastic adhesive ties you get around the end of the plastic bag your supermarket loaf comes in? With the Best Before date on? If you remove it carefully, it will stick to the inside of a cupboard door, and if you stick it right at the top of one edge of the cupboard door, you can fit a good 50 or so underneath it on an average-sized kitchen cupboard door, and then start the next column back at the top and so on until you fill the cupboard door and can move on to the next one.

I started doing this in my first London flat, in 1985 in Archway, above Usher Brothers electricians. The charming Mr Usher was my landlord. Maybe that was why I started collecting bread labels, sticking them to the inside of the kitchen cupboard, like a prisoner ticking off the days. When I left the House of Usher five or six years later, for a shared-ownership studio flat in South Tottenham, I started afresh, and when I moved from there to Shepherd's Bush, the same. In the 2010s, when I started buying posh bread, I stopped collecting. During lockdown, however, far from baking my own sourdough, I found myself opening up the kitchen cupboard door with increasing regularity, reaching up, lining up, watching the angles, pressing down with the pad of the index finger, perhaps only partly because I was buying more supermarket bread again, and partly because now it really did feel like counting the days. This was what I had been in rehearsal for.

There was a dash of controversy around Graham Swift's *Last Orders* when someone said it was too similar to William Faulkner's *As I Lay Dying*, but this was a bit of a non-story as Swift had pre-empted such talk by acknowledging it himself. Indeed, the resemblance had been deliberate, a tribute. Haunting second-hand bookshops and charity shops, branches of Oxfam Bookshop and Oxfam Books & Music in particular, with increasing frequency and regularity over the last ten years or so, I couldn't help but notice that the Picador book one saw in such places most often was *Last Orders*. Only one other Picador title has come close to challenging *Last Orders* for this honour and that is Andrea Ashworth's *Once in a House on Fire*. A long way behind, but still more frequently spotted than other Picadors, will be John Lanchester's *The Debt to Pleasure*, Kate Grenville's *The Idea of Perfection*, Michael Ondaatje's *The English Patient* and any of the many Picador titles by Bruce Chatwin, Clive James, Kathy Lette, Norman Lewis and Eric Newby.

In the Oxfam Bookshop on Kensington Gardens in Brighton, on Friday 26 May 2017, both *Last Orders* and *Once in a House on Fire* were in evidence and it occurred to me that I could mark the singular achievement of *Last Orders* by buying up copies whenever I saw them and allowing them to form the basis of an art project similar to, but not as good as, Rutherford Chang's collection of copies of the Beatles' *White Album*. In 2014 I had seen the New York-based artist's collection of over 1000 copies of the first pressing of the Fab Four's ninth studio album at Fact in Liverpool. It had made quite an impression on me. More than a thousand copies of the same – white, essentially blank – artefact would mean little if they were brand new, sitting in a warehouse or stacked up in HMV waiting to go on sale, but, being second-hand, they were much more interesting, as they were now the same but different. Far from being minded to reject copies that had been defaced or otherwise spoilt, Chang welcomed disfigured sleeves with enthusiasm. That was the point, or part of the point. I would find the same, perhaps, if I started collecting copies of *Last Orders*.

On Wednesday 5 July 2017, therefore, I bought a copy of *Last Orders* from Dalston Oxfam in east London for 99p. With the exception of a small number of specially priced items in the window, all books at Dalston have been priced at 99p for some years now. My plan to emulate Chang's collection of the *White Album* had developed into an idea for an event at the Whitstable Biennale, after discussion with co-curator Gareth Evans. Over the coming 18 months I picked up 36 copies of *Last Orders* from charity shops in Bath, Bristol, Brighton, Nottingham, Newcastle, Manchester, Shrewsbury and all over London. Inside some of them were boarding cards, in-flight menus, tickets to an aquarium, Tatton Park Mini Explorer tickets. One copy was inscribed, 'I stand listening to your music. I am still. People swirl and speed. Thank you for this gift. Becks x.' Two copies were donated directly by Richard Clegg of Oldham.

Is it a good thing or a bad thing for an author if their book is the one found most often after being given away? I have no idea how Graham Swift would feel about it. Speaking for myself, I am only ever pleased to see one of my books in a charity shop. Although, maybe you're slightly less pleased if you take it down from the shelf and find it contains your own inscription, either to a reader who bought the book at an event and got you to sign it or, as does happen, to a friend. Less pleasing again is when someone else goes to the trouble to tell you they've come across a signed, inscribed copy of one of your books that's been given away. The classy thing to do if you find an inscribed book – and you know the author – is either never to mention it or to write about it in a memoir about collecting books, but leave their name out of it.

Wednesday 3 April 1996
[Night of lunar eclipse.]
All I can remember from a series of irritating, frustrating dreams, in too hot a room, too strange a bed, above a pub in Padfield, Derbyshire, is that I was giving my Penguin editor Hugh Barnes a hard time. He kept showing me books and I kept saying they were rubbish. He showed me things he thought were really cool, including a gimmicky presentation pack that

was a teaser for John Lanchester's *The Debt to Pleasure*. It was a clear plastic envelope containing a proof of the book and a fillet of fish. I told him I'd got the book and had read it. He said he was disgusted with my attitude.

I finally read *Last Orders* in November 2018, having more or less decided and/or accepted that I was not going to do the planned event at Whitstable after all. I bought what I decided would be my last copy of the novel in Oxfam Bookshop Herne Hill and started reading it on the walk back to Denmark Hill, where I would get the London Overground back to Dalston.

I've been a reader-walker since I was a student. I did most of my finals revision walking around north London. Since reading and walking are two of my favourite things, why not combine them? I don't bump into things, or step in things. My eyesight may not be great but my peripheral vision is second to none.

I found *Last Orders* a bit of a struggle for much of the first 150 pages. All the voices sounded the same to me. I couldn't remember who was the butcher and who was the used car salesman and who was the greengrocer, not to mention who'd slept with whose missus and who was actually whose son or daughter. It took some determination and a sense of duty to keep going. But I was glad I did. What brought the book alive for me – spoiler alert – was Jack's request to Ray that he put a big bet on a horse for him, with Ray to choose the horse, but a big bet to win £20,000 so that he could clear a big debt that would otherwise be passed on to Amy. Amy, being, I think, Jack's wife, but maybe she'd been sweet on Ray, and who was June, Amy's daughter? Who was her dad? Why did Jack never go and visit her in the home where she lived, badly disabled? You're wondering, will the horse win or will the bet be lost? What Swift does next is the best thing in the novel. The horse wins, but Ray, instead of going straight to the hospital to tell Jack, goes home to change out of his clothes, which smell of the bookies, and falls asleep. He is woken later by a phone call from Amy to tell him Jack's gone. It breaks your heart, and that's no lie.

The last section, in Margate, is also very well done.

Whoever used to own the copy I bought from Fulham's Hurlingham Books and jotted down notes and remarks on every other page until page 167 should have carried on reading. Once you've put in the hard work demanded by the first 150 pages or so, you might as well stick around for the enjoyment of the second half. After page 167 the Hurlingham Books reader puts down his or her pen. Still, I'm not shedding a tear for the missing interventions, which had ranged from underlinings and question marks to a teacherly 'History – used to be heath!' in response to Ray's line 'Blackheath isn't black and it isn't a heath'.

I watched the film as well (not on the walk back from Herne Hill to Denmark Hill), directed by Fred Schepsi in 2001. The director's adaptation is true to the novel in all but one detail, which just happened to be that same best thing in the book. In the film – further spoiler alert – Ray tells Jack he's bet on Fancy Free (Miracle Worker in the novel) and Jack watches the race on TV from his bed, seeing that Fancy Free romps home, and promptly sparks out in that happy knowledge.

Apart from this somewhat mawkish cop-out, the script is otherwise faithful, even down to lots of lines of dialogue being lifted straight from the book. Some of the flashbacks look far too stagey, such as the visit to a brothel in Cairo, but the contemporary stuff works well, mainly because of the performances. Helen Mirren, in particular, is very good, and Bob Hoskins, too, and I would happily watch David Hemmings and Tom Courtenay do nothing very much at all for 90 minutes.

The Herne Hill Oxfam Bookshop is one of the good ones. What am I saying? It's one of the very good ones, one of those you never leave empty handed. On my previous visit, on Monday 30 October 2017, I had bought a copy of DM Thomas's *The White Hotel* in what I consider to be the 'correct' edition, by which of course I mean the King Penguin edition. I read *The White Hotel*, the King Penguin edition, at some point in the 1980s. All I remember about the experience is being knocked out by it, and not even especially minding the fact it started with several pages of letters (the epistolary novel is not my favourite kind) followed by ten pages of verse. On Monday 10 October 2016 I found, on some bookshelves in Nexus Art Café in Manchester's so-called Northern Quarter a copy of the King Penguin edition of *The White Hotel* previously owned by my Manchester Metropolitan University colleague Helen Darby. The books were not for sale, but I asked permission to bring in my own copy, of a slightly different edition, and exchange one for the other, which was granted. My copy looked the same from certain angles, with the same cover illustration by Peter Till, a Magrittean vision as if drawn by Topor, of a woman on fire standing by a choppy lake with a whitish hotel also in flames on the far shore, but it had an orange spine, not the classic white spine of King Penguin. It also had an inscription, dated September 1992: 'To Nick, Thank you for all your interest, help and support since we met – I really hope we stay friends. Lots of love, Eileen xxx.' I didn't know an Eileen in 1992 – I was sure of it – so I swapped my copy with Nexus Art Café for the one that had been Helen's.

In September 2017 I walked across Clissold Park in north London to Blackstock Road, which runs between Highbury and Finsbury Park. I remembered catching a fleeting glimpse from the top deck of a bus of a second-hand bookshop there. It turned out there were two, across the road from each other. Animal Aid and Advice was chaos, with lots of books in boxes and some on shelves, but I found a Picador I didn't have – Rebecca Brown's *The Haunted House* (her first novel) – and two copies of *Last Orders*. Across the road was the much better kept House of Hodge, a charity bookshop that supports a number of animal charities (among them, funnily enough, Animal Aid and Advice), and further up the road towards Finsbury Park was a Christian charity shop, Second Chance, where I bought a Picador edition of Bruce Chatwin's *The Viceroy of Ouidah* because it had a different cover to the one I already had, and, for another possible future art project, another copy of the King Penguin edition of *The White Hotel*.

Helen Darby's copy of *The White Hotel* isn't the only one in my collection (to date, 35 copies, still growing) that bears the name of a previous owner. In October 2017, I bought a copy of *The White Hotel* in Sharston Books, Manchester, that had previously – in August 1982 – belonged to Charlotte Everest-Phillips, whose PhD thesis *The Patronage of Humphrey, Duke of Gloucester: A Re-evaluation* is listed on Amazon, at the time of writing, as currently unavailable. A *White Hotel* that I found in Oxfam Bookshop Chorlton, also in Manchester, in January 2020, had belonged, in 1988, to Enid R Pinch, whose *Optimal Control and the Calculus of Variations* appears to be in print with Oxford University Press, although it's not cheap. Enid Pinch's Twitter profile describes her as 'Retired Mathematics lecturer, Quaker, amateur cellist, failed cyclist'.

One of several copies I've found in Greenwich's Halcyon Books had been a birthday present for 'Mum' from Barnaby and Sam. A copy found in the Bloomsbury Oxfam Bookshop, in June 2018, had been owned by Jonathan, who had had bookplates printed saying 'Jonathans Ex Libris', sadly without an apostrophe. Other previous owners of copies include Susan Cameron (the wonderful Next Chapter Books, Sheffield), Kate Slade (Dalston Oxfam, east London) and Ann, whose copy was inscribed, in 1983, 'Be well, even if you're far away. Love Justin x.' Ann's copy came from Oxfam Books & Music Islington in June 2020, after the end of the first UK national lockdown.

Writing in the first week of March 2021, with the end of the third UK national lockdown still some way off in the future, I am hoping that my small collection of copies of *The White Hotel* will be involved in an event at Salford's White Hotel venue, in the summer of 2021, to mark the fortieth anniversary of the publication of *The White Hotel*.

Tuesday 30 June 2020

Oxfam Books & Music, Islington, London.

Two female volunteers at new till on first floor, behind Perspex screens, wearing masks and gloves.

Volunteer 1: The first month I went mad emptying my flat. Decluttering. So I didn't feel anything. I went in the garden in the afternoon.

Volunteer 2: [. . .]

3

Amber crud

Saturday 6 December 2008

Behind the precinct in Chorlton is a large fresh fish market. There are different entrances to buy different kinds of fish. I see 'TUNA' and the name of another kind of fish carved into the stone above a doorway. I keep walking right to the end, where I find myself in a section selling old tat like a flea market or car boot sale. I pick up a book about experiences either in the war or in the film business – or possibly both – by a Brice Burroughs. I become aware that the author, an old man in a wheelchair, is behind me with his daughter and grandson. I chat to the daughter. I'm going to buy the book. It's in good nick with glossy photographs and maps like OS maps. But do I keep it for myself or give it either to Ian Cunningham or to Jonathan Coe, as I realise that both would really appreciate it? It matters that I decide quickly, so that I can get it signed and dedicated appropriately.

In *Sleep Has His House* – first published in 1948 and issued in paperback by Picador in 1974 with another Paul Delvaux cover as a companion volume to *Ice* – Anna Kavan writes, 'A big country estate in the finest old-world tradition . . . In sun-speckled shady groves deer daintily roam the preserves they share with the handsome game birds. As if suspended in amber, fish hang in the clear streams.'

Formed from fossilised tree resin, amber may contain bits of bark or insects, perhaps ants or flies, even small invertebrates. A fish would be a tall order, but then Kavan's lovely image is a simile, and, in any case, she is writing in what she calls, in her foreword, her 'night-time language'. I've had a copy of the Picador edition of *Sleep Has His House* almost as long as I've had a copy of *Ice*. It could even have been the sixth addition to my collection. You don't see many copies of the edition around these days – at the time of writing, none is listed on either eBay or AbeBooks – although I did pick up a spare copy in October 2020 in Streatham's excellent British Heart Foundation Books & Music, which had been recommended to me by two south London acquaintances, Chris White, a fruit & veg business journalist and amateur photographer with a good eye, and Michael Caines, founder of the quarterly *Brixton Review of Books*, which can be subscribed to for not much more than the cost of postage, or picked up for free in various bookish places south of the river, including Oxfam Bookshop Herne Hill and the lovely Kirkdale Bookshop in Sydenham, where they sell new books in the front and second-hand books in the back and in the downstairs area (I pretended I hadn't seen the sign asking customers to leave bags at the desk).

Sleep Has His House – of which I no longer have a spare copy, so I must have given it away to somebody – is not as straightforward as a book of dreams, like, say, Jack Kerouac's *Book of Dreams* or *Joseph Cornell's Dreams* (edited by Catherine Corman) or William Burroughs' *My Education: A Book of Dreams*, which Picador published in hard and soft editions. I had bought the hardback of the Burroughs when it came out in 1995 and swopped it in 2017 with Anne Brichto of Hay-on-Wye's Addyman Books for the paperback that had come out in 1996. I'm not much of a businessman – the hardback is worth about three times the value of the paperback – but I know what I want. Peter Reich's *A Book of Dreams*, an early Picador from 1974 and the inspiration behind the Kate Bush song 'Cloudbursting', is not a book of dreams; everyone goes on about unreliable narrators, but has anyone done any decent research into misleading titles? (I mean 'misleading' in a good way; *A Book of Dreams* is a perfectly good title for something that is not a book of dreams.)

A wasp or mosquito or other creature trapped in a lump of amber is called an inclusion and is characterised as a snapshot of the unimaginably distant past, a glimpse of deep time, very much like, for example, the item I found in a copy of Agatha Christie's *Hallowe'en Party* bought from Abacus Books in Altrincham in July 2016. I hardly need point out that it was a Fontana paperback with a cover painting by Tom Adams. I accept that other editions exist, but I don't understand why anyone would want one. With the odd exception (*The Body in the Library*, when for a week in 2010 I was holed up in a tiny office in Manchester's Central Library trying to write a story called 'The Library in the Body' that ended up being called 'The Blue Notebooks') I haven't read Agatha Christie in years; I collect her books mainly for the Tom Adams covers. (I enjoyed *The Body in the Library* a great deal, however, especially the bit where a young boy tells a policeman how much he likes detective stories: "'I read them all and I've got autographs from Dorothy Sayers and Agatha Christie and Dickson Carr and HC Bailey.'")

Inside *Hallowe'en Party*, at page 81, I found an unsealed, unstamped envelope addressed to GH Bedspread Offer No 267, PO Box 6, Kettering, Northants, and inside that were a coupon and a cheque, both bearing the handwriting of Mrs EJA Arthur of Stourport-on-Severn, Worcestershire. The cheque was even signed, but the king size 'parchment' bedspread was never ordered.

There's more in the way of soft furnishings in one of my three copies of the Picador paperback of John Lanchester's Whitbread First Novel Award-winning *The Debt to Pleasure*. A copy I found in Oxfam Bookshop Chorlton on 20 August 2020 contains a hand-written note at page 49 about pencil pleat curtains, 90 inches by 66, £160. There's a phone number that turns out to be for Marks & Spencer customer retail services and a name – Emma. Even a stray L, on its own, but possibly the initial letter of Emma's surname. I have a colleague, Emma L, who I've seen in that branch of Oxfam on two separate occasions. I want it to be her note, inside what had been her copy of *The Debt to Pleasure*, but it could equally be a reference to Emma Barclay curtains. Not that I'd heard of Emma Barclay before I started looking into pencil pleat curtains, nor of pencil pleat curtains, for that matter, but they are, I gather, a thing.

Only ten days earlier, I'd found another copy of the same edition of the novel, with, at page 173, a memo from the Chateau Marmont, Sunset Boulevard, Hollywood. The presence of a fax number, but no email, dates it, roughly. Pencilled: an asterisk, a name that could be Kara or Kare, @ 1.30pm, and, written above that time, 1.25.

By November 2016, although I had acknowledged to myself that I had definitely set out on the path of collecting all the Picador B-format paperbacks published between October 1972 and the new millennium, it was still not quite the case that I would buy whatever I came across, if I didn't already have it. I wasn't quite at the point where I would buy all different editions of the same title, nor was I quite ready to buy certain authors.

On Saturday 12 November 2016 I drove to Oldham to pick up a small white bookcase I'd bought off eBay; the collection numbered around 380 at this point and was growing apace, but in fact this bookcase was for the much smaller but expanding collection of similar paperbacks from Sceptre, Abacus, Paladin, Vintage and King Penguin. From Oldham it was a short drive to Holmfirth, where I knew there was an actual second-hand bookshop as well as charity shops. 'Est 1983. Large. Gen stock,' according to my 1996 edition of the *Skoob Directory*, it sounded promising, but turned out to be disappointing, with a brusque sign on the door – 'No food or drink' – and a bookseller moaning to a customer about a previous incident when he had seen some children pushing books to the back of a shelf. If he'd wanted them like that he'd do it himself, he told the customer he'd said to the children. 'And if the parents had said, "Don't talk to my child like that," I'd've said, "I'll talk to them how I like. It's my shop."' I didn't stick around long enough to see if he also had a sign up saying, 'Leave Bags at Counter'.

Wherever several charity shops are gathered together in a small town centre or village, a number of phenomena will generally occur. Firstly, in at least three of these shops staff will be playing the same terrible radio station, so that you might leave Barnardo's to escape 'Young at Heart' by the Bluebells, only to enter Mind in plenty of time to hear the last three verses of the same wretched song. Secondly, the same middle-aged man in a Fred Perry shirt you spot thumbing through the albums in Shelter will somehow also be flicking through the vinyls in Sue

Ryder by the time you get there. And if you see any Picadors at all, they will be by Kathy Lette.

If there's an Oxfam I'll either go there first or leave it till last, since experience has shown me that Oxfam is usually the best of the bunch. But I have also discovered that some Oxfams are better than others. A lot depends on the source and nature of donations, but I've seen also that good management can make a big difference. In Holmfirth I pop into Oxfam first and find a Picador I don't have – Rachel Cusk's *The Country Life* – although – and obviously I don't know this yet – I will replace this copy early in the new year when I will find one in Manchester for only 20p with an interesting inscription and I will give away this Holmfirth copy, along with a spare copy of Jane Solomon's *Hotel 167*, to Ailsa Cox, in return for Jim Crace's *Arcadia*. This will take place in a Picador Swapshop that I will organise as part of a seminar I will be giving to creative writing students at Edge Hill University towards the end of January 2017. Ailsa Cox, the world's first professor of short fiction, will have invited me to address her students, one of whom, Bill Bulloch, will also take part in the Swapshop, offering me Patrick McCabe's *The Butcher Boy* and Kay Redfield Jamison's *The Unquiet Mind*, both of which will already form part of my collection (but it will be a different edition of *The Butcher Boy*), in return for my duplicate copy of *The New Gothic* edited by Patrick McGrath and Bradford Morrow.

In Debra ('for people whose skin doesn't work') I find another Picador that's new to me, Emily Perkins' *Leave Before You Go*, and in the Forget Me Not Children's Hospice shop I see Kathy Lette's *Altar Ego* and Nicholson Baker's *The Fermata* (Vintage). They're only a quid each and it's a children's hospice and I only ever had the first edition of *The Fermata*, a handsome hardback from Chatto & Windus, because I had reviewed it. I look at the Kathy Lette and wonder if it's time. I open it and my eye alights on a line on the opening page. 'I stared in disbelief at the meringue dress which I had drunk only skimmed water for four weeks to fit into.' I puzzle over 'skimmed water' for a moment before I get it and then I wonder if the joke works if you have to think about it. And then I wonder if the line might have been better with the bit at the end moved to the middle. 'I stared in disbelief at the meringue dress, to fit into which I had drunk only skimmed water for four weeks.' Maybe not.

I get both books and then, in Age UK, I spot another Kathy Lette, *The Llama Party*. Because I bought *Altar Ego*, I'm kind of bound to buy this one, so I take it from the shelf and turn to the first page. Paragraph five begins: 'Tash yanked down his underchunders.' It's not quite what I've come to expect from Picador. Take Knut Hamsun's *Hunger*, for example: 'On the bed, right under the coloured lithograph of Christ, and very close to me, I made out two shapes, the landlady and the new sailor; her legs showed very white against the dark quilt.' If you wouldn't rather read that than 'Tash yanked down his underchunders', then I don't know why you're still reading this.

Still, when I flick through *The Llama Party*, I find it has an inclusion, at page 105: a 'colourings' card from the Body Shop with lipstick shades on one side and eyeshadow shades on the other. It holds the same irresistible appeal for me as a paint chart, or a collection of definitive postage stamps. Things that are the same but different. The previous owner of *The Llama Party* has circled various shades on both sides and ticked certain other colours, while having also written the name 'Beth' beside lipstick shades 21 Oyster Pink and 30 Melon.

Saturday 5 July 1996

[After launch party for *Saxophone Dreams* at which I met the Albanian ambassador and his wife.]

Someone comes to collect, from me, the remaining files for the particular *Time Out* guide I'd been working on. Possibly Brussels. There were files on an IBM-compatible PC which had to be got off on disk. And a couple of files or so on a Mac.

Later, outside – see a lion, a dead lion, partially buried. Its rump and poodle-like tail stick out of the dusty earth.

Later still – Derek Jarman's belongings are being auctioned because his family are moving overseas. I read about this in a newspaper. Possibly the *Observer*'s *Life* magazine. I notice his typewriter and wonder if I could afford it. Then: three Albanian diaries at £10 each, somehow coming to £40. I think I should buy them but don't know if I'll be able to read Jarman's hand-writing. A telephone number is given for further enquiries. 0800 something.

Occasionally, I'll buy a non-Picador second-hand book that I don't really want, if it has a sufficiently interesting inclusion. I try not to buy hardbacks any more – and have lately started getting rid of hardbacks, replacing them with paperback editions where possible – but I made an exception for JZ Young's *The Life of Vertebrates* (Oxford) from the RSPCA shop in Didsbury Village because it contained a newspaper article and a pressed flower. Later I decided these weren't actually that interesting and gave the book away again, with its inclusions.

I made another exception for another hardback, Lady Cynthia Asquith's *The Duchess of York* (Hutchinson). Oddly, the book is undated, but the text concludes with a date – September 1927. I bought it from Halcyon Books in Greenwich solely for its inclusion, at page 97, a letter written in black ink on a page neatly torn from the staff list of an independent school in south London. The sender is female, the recipient male. It is dated '10.30pm, Thursday' and reads as follows:

My darling A_____,
I LOVE YOU with every part of me – you are my life – everything. I don't know what I'd do without you to love me. I need you to love me.

Please look after yourself for me. I know it's selfish of me to ask you to just 'get better' but I know everything will be OK – we will be OK.

I think I've being detaching myself and making things difficult cause I'm scared about what will happen – and if you do leave me, then at least I think I won't miss you because I've mentally walked away. But I <u>hate</u> myself now, for giving up hope. I haven't really. I never will. Stop hoping and having faith. DON'T give up – for me. Please don't give up.

You can do it. It's possible. Because I can't stop loving you. NOT ever. No matter what. However much. To my best friend – I'll miss you this weekend. Be good for me. Love, K_____ always XXXXXOOOOO God Bless you always.

See you on Sunday evening. Keep texting me.'

A different tone is struck in a letter found in a Penguin edition of Robert Graves' *Claudius the God* acquired from Oxfam Bookshop Bloomsbury Street. A man, T____, writes to a woman, K____, from an address near Wootton Bassett:

Dear K____,

    If at all possible I would like to meet you over Christmas, for a drink, or a day out? I will be at Crayford from the 23rd inst. until the 2nd of Jan.

    Yours in hope

    T___

Tucked inside the back cover of Richard Holmes's *Coleridge: Early Visions* (Penguin), which I found in Oxfam Books & Music Islington, was a long, handwritten letter from a male, N___, to a female, K_____, the book having been given to K_____ by another male, H____, who is mentioned in N___'s letter. The letter is mostly about friendship, with references to writing up PhDs and academic positions at various universities. Undated, it was written in the garden of an Oxford college on a Saturday morning.

Some inclusions – like N___'s letter to K_____ – tantalise with partial information, but, given an internet connection, a curious nature and a couple of hours when I should have been writing, can be worked out. (I'm pretty sure I now know the identities of N___ and K_____.) Others give nothing away, but are no less fascinating, such as the small piece of white paper six inches by three and a half inches that I found inside a Penguin Modern Classics edition of Nabokov's *Pale Fire* purchased from Oxfam Bookshop Chorlton in February 2017. Lodged between pages 94 and 95, the paper has a few apparently random letters on it from a typewriter:

        k o   o p

        p

Readers of a certain age may have seen or even produced similar documents. What child of the 1960s or '70s with access to a portable typewriter didn't from time to time feed a blank piece of paper into an Olivetti or a Silver Reed and plonk away at random keys before becoming bored? My *Pale Fire* inclusion could be one such accidental concrete poem. When I hold it up to the light I see an additional number of blank impressions, where a letter has failed to engage with the ribbon. If I use brackets to represent these uninked additions we end up with:

(j)k o(i)(i) (p)o p
(o) p   (m) (k)(l)

Pale Fire is a novel of clues, but there is none on either page 94 or page 95 to suggest that the typed text might be some kind of code.

I had already splashed out £10 for a copy of the 1977 Picador edition of Richard Cavendish's *The Black Arts*, in November 2016 from Manchester's Paramount Books, when I came across a second copy four months later in Finsbury Park's Crisis shop in north London for only £2. I would have happily handed over another tenner just for the inclusion at page 273, a suitably aged and stained page torn from an exercise book with, to begin with, some chemical notations in black ballpoint, and then two names with numerical values attached to each letter and some further workings-out. When I first saw these, I assumed, because this is the way my mind works, that this was black magic and I was looking at a record of an attempt by a sorcerer to place a curse on two named individuals. Now that I've read the chapter in *The Black Arts* on names and numbers, I'm convinced the book's previous owner was simply working out the 'number' of his 'name', as well as the number of someone else's name, perhaps that of his partner. Anyway, I couldn't resist having a go at working out the number of my own name. I used the 'Hebrew' system rather than the 'modern' system, since that's the one Cavendish uses in the book and the previous owner of the book used it too. If I apply the 'Hebrew' system to my name, this is what we get:

$$\text{N I C H O L A S R O Y L E}$$
$$5 \quad 1 \quad 3 \quad 5 \quad 7 \quad 3 \quad 1 \quad 3 \quad 2 \quad 7 \quad 1 \quad 3 \quad 5$$

I add those numbers together to get 46, then add 4 and 6 to each other to get 10, then add 1 and 0 together to get 1. The number of my name is 1.

According to Cavendish, 'People whose names add to *one* have great fixity of purpose and an unswerving drive towards achievement in their own particular line. They are *single*-minded, or *one*-track minded. They are powerful characters – positive, obstinate, self-reliant and self-assertive, ambitious and aggressive. They have excellent powers of concentration and good memories.' Hmm.

Cavendish died in 2016 at the age of 86. *The Black Arts* appears to be in print in the US with an imprint of Penguin Random House. I recommend it.

Monday 12 April 1999
In or near Doncaster to visit the other Nicholas Royle – or his wife. I realise I've left it too late to get back to the station to catch the InterCity back to London. I catch a bus. On the top deck are two Mrs Royles. I talk to one. The other is shy. In a desperate bid still to get my train I jump off the bus and look for a cab. I

end up in a village walking down a road next to a golf course. I'm looking for a way in over a high fence.

Later, I'm with another Nicholas Royle. He's a magician and he's perfected a trick in which he can make two facsimiles of himself appear in the same room as himself. One is hitting a tennis ball with a racquet, keeping it up. Another is sitting watching him. Dressed as a baby, he has a grown man's legs sticking out of the bottom of his baby-style leggings. A third Nicholas Royle adopts a pose a few yards away. I talk to the one with the tennis racquet. He has thick fair hair.

On Saturday 11 February 2017, I set out to find a copy of Ovid's *Metamorphoses*, which I need for a story I'm writing about hoopoes. In my local Oxfam, in Didsbury Village, I donate a pile of books from either Cancer Research in Stockport or Sue Ryder in Chorlton, somewhere that was selling them for four for a pound anyway, which seems a shame if someone has gone to the trouble of donating books, but if they can't shift them for more than 25p each, then at least it's better than giving them away.

They don't have Ovid's *Metamorphoses* in Oxfam, but I have a look at an Abacus edition of Paul Bowles's *Let It Come Down*. I don't know the book, but it looks good and it's a white-spined Abacus, and the cover, by Peter Sherrard, is red hot. Because I'm intending to walk to Sharston Books, which seems like the likeliest place to find Ovid's *Metamorphoses*, I'll pick the Bowles up later.

Sharston Books is a 40-minute walk away, over Simon's Bridge across the Mersey, then following the river round for a bit before diving into the network of hidden paths between the static caravans, which lie in the shadow of the motorway, and Royle Green Road. Like a maze dreamed into existence by installation artist Mike Nelson, Sharston Books sprawls across two floors, connected by a creaking funhouse stair, and two or three shipping containers in the car park. You can lose an afternoon here easily and, depending on who's on the till, the amount you end up paying is likely to be a pound or two less than you thought it would be.

I finally buy a tatty old copy of Tim Winton's *Cloudstreet*, a Picador I've had my eye on here before but not bought in case I found one in better nick elsewhere, plus another Picador, Mario Vargas Llosa's *The Green House*. I thought I might have *The Green House*, but my phone suggests not (I keep vaguely up-to-date photos of my Picador collection on my phone and check them if in doubt) and when I think about it I'm sure I can picture it on Kate's shelves in her new house.

As I write these words, in March 2021, I am reading another of the eight Picador launch titles from 1972, Hermann Hesse's *Rosshalde*, translated from the German by Ralph Manheim. In it, Johann Veraguth, a painter, is effectively separated from his wife. They live on the same country estate, with their youngest son Pierre, but while Frau Veraguth lives in the main house, her husband spends nights and most of his days in his separate studio down by the lake. Pierre, on whom he dotes, visits him and they take walks together. The older son, Albert, is absent, although does return, but is estranged from his father. I'm half way through and am enjoying it, although the pain that Herr Veraguth feels as he contemplates the possibility that divorce will mean he loses Pierre, as well as Albert, reminds me of the day when my wife and I told our children that we would be separating. My son walked out of the room and my daughter looked confused and embarrassed. I am more thankful than

I am able to put into words that we managed to achieve an amicable separation and divorce without any damage being caused to the children or to my relationship with them.

Back in Didsbury Village I return to Oxfam to find they still have the Paul Bowles. I feel I should make some remark to the manageress, Wendy Elliott, née Royle, who sells it to me, some remark about the cover, to the effect that I'm not buying it for the cover, in case she judges me for it, but I don't. I try the RSPCA for the Ovid. They don't have it either but they do have an early-1990s Picador: William Bedford's *All Shook Up* looks familiar, but I don't appear to have it. Then, I realise, I can have a look in Bob's for *Metamorphoses*. Bob's got loads of Penguin Classics at the Didsbury Village Bookshop. Bob's bound to have it.

He doesn't.

Didsbury Village Bookshop is a narrow, labyrinthine, bare-boarded room, behind the delightful Art of Tea café-bar, that appears to be mostly made of books. Those that aren't actually holding up the walls are piled up on the floor or spilling out of boxes that Bob – Robert Gutfreund-Walmsley – hasn't yet unpacked. Sadly, Bob's prices resemble London prices, and Skoob Books prices at that – £4 for a Picador or equivalent. I suggested to him once that he'd sell more than twice as many books if he were to reduce his prices by half. He said he didn't care. I think maybe he loved books so much he couldn't bear to part with them, rather than didn't care. There's a breed of misanthropic, or maybe just depressed, second-hand booksellers who are undemonstrative at best, and downright rude at worst – Shaun Bythell, in his *The Diary of a Bookseller*, refers to 'a stereotype of the impatient, intolerant, antisocial proprietor' – but Bob certainly wasn't one of these. Indeed, he was drawn

to customers. Whether you were in the shop or in the Art of
Tea, or passing through both, to visit Paul Hodson, the picture
framer whose workshop is accessed via the bookshop, there was
no escape: if Bob saw you and recognised you, he'd sing to you,
usually a Sinatra number. Maybe you weren't that keen on being
serenaded, but what you really had to avoid was a conversation
about politics. What was a Hungarian-born Tyneside-raised un-
derdog-supporting book-loving crooner doing standing in local
elections for Ukip, you wondered. 'Good old Bob' was the best
response you could come up with to that.

What Bob does have is Ovid's *Heroides*, not the book I need
for my story, and even if it were, I'd prefer it to be from the
A-format series of Penguin Classics in black covers from the
1970s and '80s. This is a B-format from 1990. But, when I flick
through it, my thumb stops at page 23. There's an inclusion and
it's a good one, a photograph of a middle-aged man sitting at a
boxy desktop computer in a Royal Mail office. There are notices
pinned up and a 1994 calendar on the wall with weeks high-
lighted in blue, pink and yellow highlighter, perhaps indicating
colleagues' annual leave. Among the notices is a document with a
yellow cover sheet that says, in bold black type, BOMB ALERT
PROCEDURES. Our man, meanwhile, is hunched over his
desk, chin in his hand, head turned to look at the camera.

It sounds a bit dull, I realise, but to me, found like this
entirely at random, in the pages of a book you might not immediately associate with a humdrum workplace, it's pure gold.
Still, I would never normally buy this book and, since we're in
Bob's, it's £4.50. Basically, I'd be paying £4.50 for a photograph
of an unknown man sitting at a desk. So I show it to Bob and
explain. He says I can just have the photo, so I suggest I buy a

Picador and put it in that. Bob's happy with this and so am I – I choose Tama Janowitz's *The Male Cross-Dresser Support Group* – and he knocks a quid off and I pay him and head out the door. 'Respect!' says Bob, as he always does. But when I get home I think maybe I should have bought the Ovid. But, then, do I want the photograph for my collection of books with inclusions or for a separate collection I've been assembling, in recent years, of found photographs, alongside other growing collections of found business cards and found playing cards (acknowledging the pre-eminence in this specific field of Merseyside-based artist Cathy Butterworth)?

I decide that in the hierarchy of collections, the collection of inclusions comes above the collection of found photographs, and the photograph of the Royal Mail man at work cannot – or should not, I suppose I should say – simply be transplanted from one book to another, so I have to go back to Bob's at some point and buy the Ovid. I don't get around to this until April, when I'm planning a workshop exercise based on inclusions. I'll have 12 writers in the group and only 11 good examples of inclusions for the particular exercise I want to do. I've still got the photograph, but it needs to be in the book I found it in for the exercise to have integrity, so back I go to Bob's, wondering if he'll still have *Heroides*. Who am I trying to kid? Will he still have a copy of Ovid's *Heroides* in a not-particularly-attractive edition for £4.50? Of course he will, and he does. He also has a Penguin edition of Iris Murdoch's *The Unicorn*, which I already have, in the excellent series with photographic covers by Harri Peccinotti, but this one has an inclusion, at page 87, a business card in the name of Bill Quilla Ingham of Apartment Services Paguera with an address and phone number in Mallorca and, added in green ballpoint, the name Karen. So I buy that as well.

The inclusions collection has grown and continues to grow. It could be subdivided now into categories: money, tickets (for trains, to exhibitions, to various types of performances), photographs, numbers, phone numbers, maps, boarding cards, business cards, loyalty cards, postcards, hotel memos, love letters, begging letters, boring letters. What they have in common, perhaps, is their being accidental. Most of these artefacts will have been left in these books by accident. And if I find them, I find them by accident. (Although, I have started to look for them.) In many cases, the people who left those things in those books when they sold them or gave them away will still be walking around, reading other books, living their lives, while some of them, maybe more of them – one imagines house clearances, sales or donations of entire libraries – will have died. Is the previous owner of a voucher, found in a copy of Michael Ondaatje's *The English Patient* bought from Oxfam Bookshop Marylebone High Street, entitling them to one free adult spa session at Elveden Forest on the back of which they had drawn a family tree going back four generations, still alive? I know that at least one of the friends or acquaintances listed on the Filofax address book page I found inside another copy of *The English Patient*, with a different cover, that I bought from St Vincent's in Dalston, died in 1995, because I just looked her up and read her obituary.

I already had a copy of the Picador edition of Aragon's *Paris Peasant* (translated by Simon Watson Taylor and with, it turns out, another perfect cover illustration by Peter Le Vasseur) when I saw another copy in Paramount Books in Manchester on Friday 18 August 2017. I checked it out and found it contained, at page 63, an informal graduation photograph, most likely the (lost) property of the young woman in the photo, in white blouse and black gown, standing between proud parents. From the haircuts and clothes, I would date it to somewhere between the late 1970s and mid-'80s. The parents, even allowing for the ageing quality of some '70s fashions, look like older parents.

Robert Gutfreund-Walmsley, aka Bob, owner of the Didsbury Village Bookshop, passed away on 27 November 2020, aged 82.
    Respect.

4

Other people's books

Tuesday 16 October 2018
I was walking behind a man carrying a load of paperback books. Among them was an edition of BS Johnson's *Christie Malry's Own Double Entry* I'd not seen before. It had a couple of mustardy colours on the spine and some torn paper. Not in great condition.

I must have been dreaming about the King Penguin edition of *Christie Malry*, which I had actually seen before because I bought a copy from the Bookshop Experience in Westcliff-on-Sea in 2017. It has a front cover image by Dan Fern of a torn page from an accounts ledger. The dream was likely to have been prompted by a visit to Next Chapter Books in Sheffield just the week before, on 11 October 2018, when I found another edition of *Christie Malry*, in Quartet paperback, and, also in Quartet, *All Bull: The National Servicemen* edited by Johnson. Both these Johnson paperbacks have a previous owner's name on the flyleaf, Andrew Hinchliffe. Dave Bartholomew, who runs Next Chapter Books, also stocks new books from Sheffield-based Longbarrow Press and from Atlas Press and CDs from Martin Archer's avant garde Discus Music label.

❧

JG Ballard's *The Atrocity Exhibition* (Panther), M John Harrison's *Climbers* (Gollancz), Rupert Thomson's *The Insult* (Bloomsbury), Ramsey Campbell's *Dark Companions* (Fontana), Robert Irwin's *Exquisite Corpse* (Dedalus), Alain Robbe-Grillet's *La Jalousie* (Les Editions de Minuit): all books of mine that I've lent to people and never got back. While I would maintain that these books are still mine, they've each been in someone else's possession for so long now, longer in most cases than they were ever in mine, that those people might feel they have become theirs. They may genuinely have forgotten how these books came into their possession. Or they might feel a little jolt every time they see them on the shelf. Oh, I must give that back to Nick, sort of thing. Or, I must give that back, but to whom? They might even have given them away, or – some of these missing books are worth quite a bit – sold them.

All readers, unless they refuse to lend books, have – or more accurately don't have – books like this. I've replaced *The Insult* with the same edition – the first edition – but it's not the same. I would never have allowed my copy to become so scuffed and bumped. I don't mind buying a book that's not in great nick, but I mind replacing one that was in excellent condition with one that looks as if it's spent a couple of years in the boot of a stock car. As I glance at or handle my replacement copy of *The Insult*, I know it's not really mine. It's not the one I had. More to the point, it's not the one I read and fell in love with. I'm reminded of my loss and it still hurts. I don't remember lending it to anyone, but I feel that I did; I just don't know who.

I do know what happened to my first edition of *Climbers*. I lent it to an ex-girlfriend. Whether we were still together when

I lent it to her I can't remember, but a confused sense of honour combined with a horror of revisiting the aftermath of that relationship meant I could never ask for it back. So, I've written that one off, but I haven't written off the Paladin paperback edition of the same novel, its cover a painting by John Harris of a man in a red helmet clinging to a fissure in a sheer rock face. There have been later editions of *Climbers* and I probably have at least one of them, no doubt with an introduction by Rob Macfarlane, but, that introduction notwithstanding, later editions feel so different they're almost like another book. The Paladin edition is the perfect conjunction of book, format and edition, and I made the rookie error of lending it to someone, or rather, lending it to someone and not keeping a record. But then doesn't keeping a record of who you've lent a book to seem against the spirit of lending a book in the first place?

I spent years assembling my collection of Ballard novels in A-format Panther editions. I remember the excitement I felt when I found *The Atrocity Exhibition*, with its cover illustration, probably by John Holmes, of a bandaged figure holding a glass of red wine, but this edition is not on my shelves today. It could be anywhere. I could buy a replacement for £35, but (a) £35, and (b) I'd know it was a replacement.

I didn't know I was missing *Dark Companions* until Stephen Jones wrote to me to ask if I wanted to contribute a short piece about my favourite Ramsey Campbell story to a commemorative issue of a magazine being put together to celebrate Campbell's seventy-fifth birthday. I could find all my other Campbell collections, to look through and pick a story, apart from that one. Weirdly, both editions I'd had – the much-loved Fontana one and the not-so-much-loved US edition – were missing.

Another mystery is what has happened to my copy of Alain

Robbe-Grillet's *La Jalousie* in its beautiful Editions de Minuit edition. I know I'll find a replacement sooner or later, perhaps in a second-hand bookshop in Paris, assuming that Covid and Brexit ever allow us to travel there again, but which *connard* has my copy?

If I had written my name in any of these missing books, maybe they would have been returned. But, apart from when I was very young, it's something I never do. At school I was encouraged to write my name in the front of a book. There would even be, in some cases, such as if the book came from the school's Book Department, a red grid stamped on the flyleaf requiring you to write your name, form and year. In the front of a Livre de Poche edition of François Mauriac's *Le mystère Frontenac* I wrote my name, along with 'Msiiip' and '1979'. Two places above my name was that of Michael Crick, who I remembered standing for Labour – and winning – in a mock election the year I had started school. At the end of the 1979–80 school year I should have returned *Le mystère Frontenac* to the school Book Department, but for some reason failed to do so.

Instead I returned it 37 years later while making a half-hour programme for BBC Radio 4 called *Late Returns*, in which I also took back a pile of Albanian literary magazines to the University of London Library (I shouldn't even have had them in the first place) and a copy of Robbe-Grillet's *Les Gommes* to the library of the nineteenth arrondissement in Paris (I'd borrowed it in 1985 when living in Paris and forgotten to return it). My producer, Geoff Bird, and I interviewed Michael Crick and a number of other people including poet Vahni Capildeo and novelist and short story writer AL Kennedy to get their views on the late returning of library books. The day the programme was broadcast, Thursday 9 February 2017, I went to Liverpool on the way to Edge Hill University, where I was due to say a few words at the opening of an exhibition. I like going to Edge Hill, for the nice folk there, both staff and students, and because it means I can visit Liverpool, by which I mean Oxfam and News From Nowhere, both on Bold Street, and Kernaghan Books at the Bluecoat, and Reid of Liverpool on Mount Pleasant, and Henry Bohn Books on London Road, where there is invariably a small gathering of book- or music-lovers putting the world to rights with the proprietor.

Upstairs in Henry Bohn the first thing of interest I see is a slim hardback with a white spine and faded red lettering, *Birds by Character*, by Wallace, Rees, Busy, Partington and Hume. The front cover carries an intriguing subtitle: *The Fieldguide to Jizz Identification*, reminding me momentarily of a book we found in a telephone box across the road from the *Time Out* offices towards the end of the 1990s. A fake alternative version of the *Time Out London Guide*, of which I had been the most recent editor, the *Time Out 'O' and 'A' Level Guide* had a masthead page including my name as editor and that of my managing editor Peter Fiennes, but the 112 pages were filled with reproductions of what are generally known as tart cards, plus some lurid passages of erotic writing and odd bits of anti-British Telecom polemic. In the back, a note advises readers to 'Check out the latest news on London Prostitution' and gives a URL that begins with paranoia.com, which, weirdly, defaults to Disney's website. There was also an email address, but an email sent to it bounces straight back. We never found out who was behind it, whether artists or pranksters, or both, or whether it was to be taken at face value as pro-prostitution anti-BT propaganda.

However, jizz, it turns out, in ornithological circles, is the general *character* of a bird. 'Jizz is instantly appreciated,' say the authors of *Birds by Character* in an introduction, 'but its meaning is understood only through experience. This book aims to be the ultimate tool for gaining exactly that experience.' But it's eight quid and I'm not convinced, so I put it back and move to the shelves opposite where I find Hermann Hesse's *Rosshalde*, one of the first eight Picadors. I know I already have a copy at home, but a later printing and therefore not, like this copy, the first paperback edition from 1972. It has a name in it, Edward Beattie, and a date, '7 Nov 72'. He crosses his 7s, in the European style. Forty pence the book cost him, almost 45 years ago, less than a month after it was published. Did he buy any of the other first eight Picadors, or just this one? I find another book with his name in it. Sartre's *Le mur*, in Livre de Poche, a 1971 edition. Beattie's name appears in a different form – 'EW Beattie, 6 May (Nice', without a closing bracket. On the first page of the text of the novel there's an inclusion, a folded, typed flyer for a screening of a film, *Satguru Has Come*, of the life, to date, of 15-year-old Guru Maharaj Ji, taking place on Wednesday 16 May at 7.30pm in the Percy Gee Quiet Room. The date means it's 1973 and the Percy Gee building locates the screening at the University of Leicester. But on the back of the flyer Beattie has written 'Poste Restante, Siena, Italia'. I also spot, close by, a lovely, smallish-format Minuit edition of Beckett's *En attendant Godot*. 'Edward Beattie, April 1973.' For years I have been buying almost anything I see in Minuit, the principal publisher for exponents of the *nouveau roman* and publishing only authors who write in French. I don't know enough about Beckett's way of working to know if they bent their own rule to work with him. Did he write everything in English and then translate it into French or did he write some of his books in English and some in French and then translate them into French and English respectively? If I carry on wondering about this while also looking for more French books I want to buy or more books with Edward Beattie's name in, suspecting that there might be more books on the shelves in front of me that tick both boxes, I'll miss my connection to Ormskirk, so I take what I've got – plus a pre-selected Picador edition of Bruce Chatwin's *Utz*, his delicately poised short novel about a collector of porcelain figures – and head downstairs to pay.

I decided to read *Utz* for the first time later that year. It was my first Chatwin and I enjoyed it a great deal, not in the sense in which editors, myself possibly among them, sometimes use the verb 'enjoy' when rejecting a submission – 'I enjoyed reading your story, but regret that it is not quite right for our list' – but in the sense that I really, genuinely did enjoy it. I particularly enjoyed an exchange of dialogue on page 42. Utz remarks that Adam was not only the first human but also the first ceramic sculpture. The narrator asks, '"Are you suggesting your porcelains are alive?"' and Utz replies, '"I am and I am not . . . They are alive and they are dead. But if they were alive, they would also have to die . . ."'

I wonder if it has ever occurred to me that my books are alive. It's undeniable that I love them and treat them with the kind of care one might reserve for living things. I am perhaps overly concerned with their appearance, but I also respect and can become deeply involved with their contents. I'm not quite sure how inclusions fit into this increasingly uncomfortable analogy, but I think I can see that what attracts me about the inclusion of a previous owner's name written on the flyleaf is partly the suggestion of another mystery or narrative running alongside the author's – who was this person and why did they give away or sell this book? – and partly the illusion of contact, even the possibility of contact, the sense you might get that the world is small. Some name/date combinations, you sense that with a little bit of detective work you'd track them down, like 'Holger Norgaard, Nov 1976' in a copy of Flann O'Brien's *The Third Policeman* (1974 edition, reprinted 1975), whereas with others you know you'd never get close, such as 'Sylvia, May 74' in Gurney Norman's *Divine Right's Trip* (1973).

It's thrilling to find a book previously owned by someone you know, like the Penguin edition (one of an extensive series of photographic covers by Van Pariser) of Muriel Spark's *The Go-Away Bird* I found in Abacus Books in Altrincham that bears the name LT Bohl (in red ballpoint), formerly a teacher at my school; or the Picador edition of Rudolph Wurlitzer's *Slow Fade* previously owned, in January 1985, by Philip Hamer, with whom I had contact when he wrote for Manchester's *City Life* magazine; or the Penguin Modern Classics edition of Joseph Conrad's *Under Western Eyes* that I found in Sharston Books that contains the name G Hammond and a handwritten note at page 287, dated 27.1.92, reading, 'Dear Dr Hammond, I'm sorry I missed the 10 o'clock tutorial but I was stuck in a traffic jam on the motorway for nearly 2 hours. Helen Thompson.' After a little bit of detective work I realise that Dr Hammond is someone I used to say hello to when we passed each other on the street and then I realise, with a brief falling sensation in my gut, that I haven't seen him for a while.

A couple of weeks later in February 2017, I return to Henry Bohn in Liverpool. I'm still working on the hoopoe story for my forthcoming collection, *Ornithology*, and I think the jizz book might help. Like all the best second-hand bookshops, at

Henry Bohn they have some tat outside that they're as good as giving away, except that at Henry Bohn tat might include, as it does today, Picadors like Clive James' *Unreliable Memoirs* and Jonathan Raban's *Arabia*. I've already got both, but at 10p, it would be crazy not to. They'll go in the shadow collection. Inside the shop and upstairs – I can imagine my former colleague at *Time Out*, Sarah Guy, frowning over this use of 'upstairs', since 'upstairs' is meaningless without context, and Sarah, editor of the *Time Out Eating & Drinking Guide* for many years, would not allow it, because it was not clear whether it meant upstairs relative to the ground floor or upstairs on the ground floor rather than in the basement, assuming 'basement' was even allowed, which I can't remember – once I've checked that they still have *Birds by Character* and have taken it down from the shelf, I go back to the other wall to see if there are any more French books previously owned by Edward Beattie. There are numerous books containing his name and different addresses, several in Leicester, also Leeds, Liverpool and Paris. One of the Paris books contains an inclusion, a payslip, which allows me to conjecture that he might have worked for a year as an assistant d'anglais in Paris, as I did, as part of his degree at Leicester. I am tempted to buy all these books and embark on a project to research his life. I wonder if it's a vain idea. When I pick up any one of Edward Beattie's books, hold it under my nose and flick through the pages and breathe in, as I do with every book I pick up – I haven't mentioned this before, perhaps because it is so habitual, so instinctive, it almost goes without saying – I wonder if among the familiar aromas generated by the decay of volatile compounds in the paper is another faint smell, that of mortality. Assuming he went to university while still in his teenage years, Beattie must be ten years older than me, which doesn't make him old, but it makes him older than my dad when he died. I hope Edward Beattie simply decided to declutter.

All I really know about him is he went to university in Leicester, could read French, moved around a bit and had – hopefully still has – a sense of humour. His old copy of Sartre's *Le mur* contains another inclusion, a postcard of Ventimiglia, with a bird's-eye view of the city, stretched along the Medierranean coast. In the foreground, framing the view, is the bough of an orange tree laden with fruit. The caption on the back reads, 'View from the airplane', to which Beattie has added, in beautifully neat, tiny handwriting, 'flying through an orange tree'.

Saturday 15 February 1997
In a car, pursuing a car with chess-players in it. Reach a junction – sharp left to the motorway or straight on for Mobberley? I look at the road atlas. If we go to Mobberley we will go near Manchester Airport and take a little winding road that will eventually bring us back to the motorway.

There's a police car – we overtake it, then it comes up behind us, its headlights flooding the interior of our car. They overtake us. They're also after the chess-players.

Earlier, I had seen a copy of a short story by Jonathan Coe. I was able to read the title but now I can't remember it. It took the form of an old Penguin Len Deighton paperback, exactly like *Billion Dollar Brain*, even with a picture on the cover of Michael Caine as Harry Palmer.

Billion Dollar Brain has a great opening line. 'It was the morning of my hundredth birthday.' Some might feel that Anthony Burgess improved on it with the opening line of *Earthly Powers* – 'It was the afternoon of my eighty-first birthday, and I was in bed with my catamite when Ali announced that the archbishop had come to see me' – but I don't. Burgess's narrator, Kenneth Toomey, is actually 81, whereas Deighton's unnamed narrator (who acquired the name of Harry Palmer only in the film adaptations) is not 100, which makes him an unreliable narrator and therefore much more interesting, but he is also wisecracking in the manner of Chandler's Philip Marlowe. Indeed, a couple of lines later, shaving in the bathroom mirror, he says, 'It was all very well telling oneself that Humphrey Bogart had that sort of face; but he also had a hairpiece, half a million dollars a year and a stand-in for the rough bits.'

Humphrey Bogart had a hairpiece? I'm glad I didn't know this when staying up late to watch Bogart films with my mum throughout the 1970s.

When I flick through my copy of Deighton's *Funeral in Berlin*, in the same Penguin edition as *Billion Dollar Brain*, I find a word redacted on page 232. A third of the way down the page we read, '"[redacted] Fireworks," I said.' When you hold the page up to the light you can see the word crossed out, apparently with black marker pen, is 'Brock's', the name of a prominent fireworks manufacturer. Five minutes later, thanks to Twitter, I know the whole story, which, it turns out, is also on Wikipedia. Brock's objected to being named in the context of a conversation about the dangers of fireworks and the possibility that vested interests prevented the government from controlling their sale. Brock's sued and won and in later editions the conversation has been removed. In some copies of the 1966 paperback, it seems, the name was redacted by hand. Author and artist Tim Etchells tweets a picture of his copy with the same word redacted, and you can see tiny differences between the pen strokes. Likewise Twitter account-holders Vintage Paperback Collector and The Deighton Dossier. Other Twitter users Peter Birks, Phil Marsden and Mr Tim have the same edition but with 'Brock's' intact. Cracabond Books, on Twitter, has one with redaction, one without. My afternoon is spent picturing a man in expanding metal shirt-sleeve holders and a green visor going through a pile of books – or piles of books, or a warehouseful of books – with a marker pen at some point in 1966.

My copy of Deighton's *Horse Under Water*, same series, was previously owned by Brigadier F Pocock.

Five of my eleven Raymond Chandler titles in green-spined Penguin Crime editions with covers designed by James Tormey (using colourised images from the films) bear the name of the same previous owner: Paul Griffiths. I wonder if it could be the same Paul Griffiths who is the author of two novels in my Picador collection, *Myself and Marco Polo* and *The Lay of Sir Tristram*, and indeed a chapbook in my Nightjar series, which, of course, are all signed by the authors. I compare the signatures. They're sufficiently different to place doubt in my mind, but then the Chandlers go back decades, whereas the Nightjar was only 2019 and signatures change over time. They also change over the course of an hour if you have to do 200 of them.

I check with Paul Griffiths. The Chandlers belonged to a different Paul Griffiths.

'There's a lot of us about,' he tells me.

I ask him about being published by Picador. What was it like?

'"Glow with pride" is the phrase, but internally this was a pretty chill glow. You're up there with your gods (didn't they have *More Pricks Than Kicks* by then? When being read, reread, it would always go back on the table face-down), but do you merit the place? Answer: no. The other thing is a snapshot visual image of a tall, slender man with dark, dark hair walking just behind me in a London street. Presumably we'd just had lunch, but all memory of that has gone. Peter Straus – a name I'd heard spoken only in tones of "Well, you know who this person is, don't you?"'

I knew who Peter Straus was in 1988. He was the editor of *20 Under 35: Original Stories By Britain's Best New Young Writers* (Sceptre), which was published in that year, when I was 25. I carried it with me everywhere for a while, reading it with forensic attention, looking for clues as to how I might inveigle my way into any subsequent volume. If Sceptre were to copy *Granta*'s approach with their *Best of Young British Novelists*, maybe they would do another in ten years' time, when I would be 35. Anxious times. I needn't have worried.

Two years later, in May 1990, Peter Straus moved to Picador, where his role was publisher. 'I was tasked with building up the almost non-existent hardcover list and maintaining the paperback brand,' Straus tells me. 'The first books I bought were *Cloudstreet* by Tim Winton, *American Psycho* by Bret Easton Ellis, *Understanding the Present* by Bryan Appleyard. Then new authors for Picador such as Pat McCabe, Colm Tóibín, John Banville, Helen Fielding, VS Naipaul. It was a magical time with wonderful colleagues. I was lucky to inherit such an amazing list from my great predecessors and we tried to punch above our weight. It meant and still means a huge deal. I have loads of terrific memories, but I don't know if you can print any of them.'

Straus left Picador in the summer of 2002 to join Rogers, Coleridge and White as a literary agent. In 2007 he became managing director.

My smallish collection of green Penguins more than doubled in size in 1999 when my friend and *Time Out* colleague Sarah Guy very kindly gave me two boxes of them. Crime and mystery novels by Margery Allingham, Nicolas Freeling, Dashiell Hammett, Michael Innes, Ed McBain, Georges Simenon and many others, they had belonged to Sarah's 'beloved' Uncle Paul. 'He died aged 41,' she tells me, 'and I inherited them when my aunt (his wife) died. He was a journalist, worked in various places (Fleet Street, Reuters, ITN) after starting out on local papers, and a big reader. I kept lots of his books, and I'm especially fond of his collection of Pevsner guides. He was Paul Stephen Guy – initials PS, my grandparents' little joke as he was born about 20 years after his two older brothers.'

Hammett and Chandler both got the Picador treatment. *The Four Great Novels* collected together Hammett's novels *The Dain Curse*, *The Glass Key*, *The Maltese Falcon* and *Red Harvest* in 1982, with *The Continental Op*, a collection of stories, following in 1984. Meanwhile, *The Chandler Collection Volume One* and *The Chandler Collection Volume Two* appeared in 1983 with three novels in each, and three short story collections were bundled together in *The Chandler Collection Volume Three* the following year. The covers of all five books were illustrated by Nancy Slonims, using collage and photomontage techniques.

On Monday 3 October 2016, in the Chorlton Oxfam Bookshop, I buy a Picador edition of Bruce Chatwin's *On the Black Hill* that I hope I don't already have. Next door in Red Cross I get a 1998 Picador edition of Hermann Hesse's *Siddhartha*, but I resist *The Chandler Collection Volume Two*, because my Salt author Neil Campbell has previously offered to give me his copy. A couple of months later we're short of players in my weekly five-a-side football game and, knowing from our conversations around editing his first novel, *Sky Hooks*, that Neil can play a bit, I invite him to join us and, somewhat slyly perhaps, offer him the chance to pay in Picadors. He brings volumes one and two of the Chandler. I sense he might not be altogether happy handing them over. This is more or less confirmed the next day when he says he thinks he'll pay cash next time. I offer to let him have them back, but I'm not sure he responded.

Two weeks later I'm in Mind on Stoke Newington Church Street in north London, where I find a couple of Picadors I don't have, Githa Hariharan's *When Dreams Travel* and Eoin McNamee's *Resurrection Man*, and one of those US Vintage paperbacks – Joe Connelly's *Bringing Out the Dead* – that I know Neil collects. I buy it for him as a present. It's almost Christmas, after all.

Back at the beginning of December 2016, on a Sunday, I went with my daughter, Bella, then 17, to Stockport Record and Book Fair but we couldn't find many books, so we called in at the Children's Society in Heaton Moor on the way back and I picked out Roger Penrose's *The Emperor's New Mind* (Vintage) with a gorgeous cover by Dennis Leigh (aka John Foxx). Queueing up to pay for it, I spotted writer and fellow Didsbury resident – neighbour, in fact, more or less – Adrian Slatcher ahead of us in the queue. Adrian is usually in front of me, I realise, on the weekend rounds of local charity shops and the tables outside Morten's, our excellent local independent bookshop, where they put out second-hand books. He said he'd been to Stockport and bought a bunch of books, among them three Picador Brautigans, including one I didn't have – *Dreaming of Babylon*. I checked the time. Bella and I could bob back to Stockport to see if any new stallholders had somehow turned up since we'd been there, or if we'd somehow missed some. They hadn't and we hadn't. It was a mystery, like the Brautigan novel, whose subtitle is *A Private Eye Novel 1942*. When I tweeted about it later, Adrian replied, kindly offering to give me *Dreaming of Babylon*. He said it was only fair as I'd previously given him a Slade LP, which was true. I told Bella about this and she said, 'What's an LP?'

Another writer gave me another Picador Brautigan. Mick Jackson, author of Picador title *The Underground Man*, which was shortlisted for the Booker Prize the same year I won the *Literary Review*'s Bad Sex in Fiction Award for my novel *The Matter of the Heart*, sent me a copy of *In Watermelon Sugar*. On a postcard he wrote, 'As you may have guessed, RB is pretty much my No. 1 guy, for his eccentricity and tenderness, but also his ability to make the world seem new and strange (and beautiful, often), a quiet transformer. I became pals with a Californian ten or so years ago who knew Richard. It was almost too much for me to hear him tell his Brautigan tales.'

Another copy of Hermann Hesse's *Siddhartha* turns up in the post. This one is the 1973 Picador edition, which manages to be only 119 pages long, in contrast to the 213-page edition I bought from Red Cross in Chorlton, which had a 70-page introduction. This new (older), shorter edition is a gift from David Rose, author, friend and enthusiastic supporter of my Picador habit. He will go on to send me David Grossman's *See Under: Love*, Walter Mosley's *RL's Dream* and EL Doctorow's *Lives of the Poets: A Novella and Six Stories*, one of which, 'The Foreign Legation', jumped straight into my Top 100 Short Stories with its opening two paragraphs, which are also its opening two sentences –

'After his wife left with all her clothes and the children's clothes and toys, Morgan continued to go to work and come home, though the house was empty and he had no one to talk to.

'In the evenings he stood at his windows with binoculars and watched the passage of his neighbors through their rooms.'

– and stayed there after I'd got to the end of the story and, indeed, after I'd read it a second time. David Rose, the author of *Vault* and *Posthumous Stories*, is also a great supporter of forgotten or unfairly overlooked writers. He introduced me – and others – to the work of novelist and short story writer David Wheldon, giving me copies of Wheldon's first two novels, *The Viaduct* (Penguin) and *The Course of Instruction* (Black Swan), which led directly to my pursuing him to become a Nightjar author and to Confingo Publishing's acceptance of a collection of Wheldon's stories, which will now, sadly, be posthumous stories, as Wheldon died, aged 70, in January 2021.

Some of my former students, who happen to have become published authors, among them Pete Lewis (if Pete Lewis hasn't become a published author by the time you read this, there's no justice in the world), Wyl Menmuir and Lucie McKnight Hardy, have given me Picadors. Richard Clegg gave me seven Picadors in exchange for one copy of my collection *Ornithology* (I know who got the better deal there and it's not the man from Oldham who went off to read mildly disturbing stories about owls, hoopoes and bee-eaters and even sent more Picadors after surviving the experience). Saxon Pepperdine sent me Knut Hamsun's *The Wanderer* in exchange for Julian Barnes's *Talking it Over*, and Chris Parker emailed me to say he had enjoyed

First Novel and the blog and to ask if he could send me a copy of Ethan Canin's *Blue River.* (I first wrote about my obsession with Picador in *First Novel*, actually my seventh, although at one remove as it was my narrator Paul Kinder who was collecting the white spines.) Novelist Stav Sherez sent me *Already Dead* by Denis Johnson, or did he send me *Already Dead* by Dennis Johnson? The parents of a prospective student attending an open day at Manchester Metropolitan University gave me a gift bag containing three Picadors with a red ribbon tied around them, and another prospective student, Rachel McIntyre, attended an interview carrying a copy of *Rat* by Andrzej Zaniewski, while Danny Rhodes sent me *The Rat* by Günter Grass through the post. Former publisher Patrick Janson-Smith turned up to a different kind of interview with three Picadors from his shelves. Gareth Evans has given me at least two dozen Picadors. I'll receive a text from Gareth on his travels in Newcastle or Norwich or Edinburgh: 'Picador charters kerouac biog got? gx.' 'Picador sam toperoff queen of desire got? gx.' 'Picador best of myles, flann o brien got? gx.' I've usually got them.

It would be ignoble of me to conclude this survey of 'other people's books', which began with a rant about books of mine that I had lent to people unknown and never seen again, without making mention of books I borrowed and never gave back. In my defence I will say that I resisted, in both cases, being loaned these books, but the lenders were most insistent. *Tony Buttitta's The Lost Summer: A Personal Memoir of F Scott Fitzgerald* (Sceptre) was pressed upon me by a young man I met at a weekend-long party in Suffolk in the early 1990s. I can't remember his name, only that he was startlingly handsome, with eyes like saucers and a curly cascade of chestnut hair. I can't remember if he gave me the book that weekend or later. I could probably find out who he was if I questioned some people carefully, but I'm slightly unwilling to do so, not because I want to keep the book, although it sits nicely in my collection of white-spined Sceptre paperbacks of the 1980s and '90s, but because I feared there was a shadow of vulnerability in the young man's beautiful eyes, a look of future tragedy. I hope not.

Some time in the mid 2000s, having moved from London back to Manchester, I came across a basement bookshop on Lever Street in the Northern Quarter. It felt like a temporary arrangement, something hastily thrown together, stocked only sparsely but with books chosen to appeal to me. There was a dog and a very tall young man, who told me he was Michael Butterworth's son. I knew Butterworth's name, associating it with underground publishing and Savoy Books, with people I had met in London like JG Ballard and Michael Moorcock, and with bookshops like this one. There was some unused space in the basement, which he encouraged me to consider renting. I could write there, he said. He wouldn't let me leave without taking a book, a US paperback of David Lindsay's *A Voyage to Arcturus*, which he said I must read. He wouldn't accept payment for it, suggesting instead that I return it at some point.

The next time I tried to visit the bookshop it was closed and didn't look like it was reopening. It never did. Before long, the space was cleared out and repurposed.

5

Some more favourite bookshops in London

Tuesday 21 May 2019

I'm in Any Amount of Books on Charing Cross Road. I'm there looking for the books of mine that I saw online that they have, with my inscriptions. But I can't find them. I look on two floors and can't find them. It doesn't look like Any Amount of Books. In fact, I forget which shop I'm in and have to look at a price label on a book to see Any Amount of Books printed there before I'm happy I know where I am. Ros goes off to ask for me and while she's gone I start to worry that I'm late for Novel Workshop and that I haven't read any of the work for it. I think of Mich, one of my students. Ros returns and gives me a soft caramel. It makes a mess. One of the bookshop staff comes to see me. Now I'm worrying about the mess. I go to the counter and ask about the books I'm looking for. I tell the staff the books have inscriptions. They're unable to find them.

In the early 2010s, in a new relationship, I started dividing my time, not between Gloucestershire and Tuscany, or between

New York and Malibu, but between south Manchester and north London. My girlfriend, Ros, lived in London, technically in Stoke Newington, in north London, but only five minutes' walk from the heart of Dalston, which is in east London. More to the point, she lived 0.9 miles from Church Street Bookshop in Stoke Newington, and only 0.7 miles from Dalston Oxfam.

In the last half a dozen years I've easily bought a score of Picadors – and loads of other books besides – from Church Street Bookshop. It's a wonderful little one-room shop with clearly laid-out sections, boxes of cheap books near the till, a small selection of classical CDs and a bookcase just inside the door for new stock, which is always a great feature because it makes you look at stuff you might not normally look at, just as deciding to collect everything published by a particular imprint gives you the opportunity to read things you might not otherwise. Had I not been collecting Picadors I might never have read Charles Palliser's *The Sensationist* and that would have been my considerable loss. *The Sensationist* is an invigorating and exhilarating lesson in entering scenes as late as possible and leaving them as early as possible. I read it in a single day (it's only 136 pages) in August 2016 and can't believe it's almost five years ago, it's that fresh in my mind. Not the story as such, but the memory of what it felt like and how excited I was by it. I want to read it again. I want, in fact, to reread it.

When I visit Church Street Bookshop on 20 December 2016 I find two Picadors – *The Forest People* by Colin Turnbull and *The Castle of Crossed Destinies* by Italo Calvino – and Rose Tremain's *Sacred Country* (Sceptre). The man behind the counter, whose name I won't find out for another four years, is playing an album by Keith Jarrett and Charlie Haden. I've always thought I didn't like Charlie Haden, because I heard one thing of his I didn't like, but I like this.

On 27 February 2017 I find two more Picadors – Duong Thu Huong's *Novel Without a Name* and Alain de Botton's *The Romantic Moment* – and, since Vesna Main has so strongly recommended her, I also get *The Collected Stories of Lydia Davis* (Penguin). There's no Keith Jarrett or Charlie Haden this time; it's Bill Evans instead.

I go in regularly when I'm in London. It's usually the Quiet Man, as I've started to think of him, because he never says much, beyond answering my customary question about what he's playing, and he's always playing jazz, usually Charlie Haden. Sometimes it's not the Quiet Man, but a slightly more ebullient, larger, chattier man – they're both probably in their 60s – who always plays classical. Had you shown me both men and told me one always plays jazz and the other always plays classical and asked me to identify them by their musical preferences, I might well have gone the other way.

On 12 February 2020, I pop in at two minutes to six. The shop is due to close, but the Quiet Man is talking to a customer who has come from Southend to pick up an order. The customer is talking about a hardback he says he ordered online from another bookseller. The copy never arrived. Lost in the post. 'When he realised what it was worth,' the customer says, setting his mouth in a way that clearly suggests what he thinks of an unreliable, even dishonest, bookseller. He asks the Quiet Man to look out for a hardback copy. He – the customer – says, 'You want something physically in your hands, don't you? It's the whole point of collecting.' Then he's asking for advice on how to get back to Stratford and then on to West Ham. I take advantage of the opportunity to join the conversation and, when the customer has gone, it continues. The Quiet Man's name is Tim Watson and he tells me he was one of four people who set up Skoob Books. After he left Skoob, he opened a series of second-hand bookshops, moving into the current premises in 1994. When I tell him about my collection, he says he's going to put up the prices of his Picadors. I tell him he always plays jazz and the other guy plays classical. He says he used to play classical sometimes, but now accepts that his role is to play jazz.

On Tuesday 20 June 2017, I walk past Church Street Bookshop without going in. It's probably the only time I've ever done that while it's been open, but I went in the previous afternoon, coming away with John Barth's *The Floating Opera* (lovely Penguin edition that in February 1970 belonged to H Shaw, excellent cover by Mike McInnery), Rupert Thomson's *The Book of Revelation* (for Bella, who is about to visit Amsterdam) and Jenny Offill's *Dept of Speculation* (because it's very short and Linda Huang's cover looks so good), and don't want the Quiet Man to think I'm weird going in again so soon. I see a man walking towards me who looks a lot like *Wish You Were Here* and *A Walk in the Park* author Travis Elborough. I've seen Travis in the 'hood before – can I say 'in the 'hood'? Maybe I just needed to put it in ironic quotes, and then wouldn't have needed to ask the question – and in fact there's no mistaking him in his cool black-framed glasses. Travis tells me he's just rescued a frog from his neighbour's cat. He's on his way back from Clissold Park, where he took the frog to release it into the pond. I could talk to Travis for hours, but time is getting on and the sun is beating down, so I take my own walk in the park (no sign of the frog, though, worryingly, a heron stands watchfully in the shallows) and then across Finsbury Park to the start of the Parkland Walk.

No one seems able to agree on the length of the Parkland Walk. It's variously described as 1.7 miles, 2.5 miles, 4 miles and even 4.5 miles long. This may be down to the fact that it's in two parts, north and south, but then why are there four given lengths, not two? The south part takes you, along the trackbed of a former railway line, from Finsbury Park to just south of Highgate tube, where I'm looking forward to paying a visit to the excellent Ripping Yarns, where, last time I was in, I chatted to book blogger and author Jen Campbell, who was working there. I've bought many books and back copies of *Ambit* from Ripping Yarns over the years. The old offices of *Ambit* were so close to Ripping Yarns you could have stood outside the bookshop, fashioned a paper aeroplane out of your manuscript and submitted it to Martin Bax by launching it across Archway Road. I would rather have done that than had to use Submittable.

When I reach the top of the south section of the Parkland Walk, I pass the Boogaloo, where Serpent's Tail used to hold readings, and cross Archway Road to enter, first, a Mind shop, which I remember has a particularly good selection of books. This, I'm pleased to see, is still the case. Once I'm able to tear my eyes away from the spines of two of my own books – my difficult second novel *Saxophone Dreams* ('not exactly beach reading,' BBC Three Counties radio presenter) and almost-but-not-quite-filmed fourth novel *The Director's Cut* ('You haven't quite managed to get what I most loved about the novel into the script,' Jeremy Thomas) – I find some gems. Among the Picadors there's a second novel from Julie Myerson, *The Touch*, which I can't remember ever seeing before in this edition, and Hermann Hesse's *Klingsor's Last Summer*. Additionally I am unable to resist a first novel, *I Hear Voices* (Abacus), by Paul Ableman, and a hardcover US first edition (fifth printing) of

Stephen Schneck's *The Nightclerk* (Grove Press), which starts, interestingly, mid-sentence, indeed mid-word. I've read something somewhere about this 1965 novel recently, but, annoyingly, can't remember what or where.

I worry about my memory some more when I leave the Mind shop and walk up Archway Road to look for Ripping Yarns. It's not where I thought it would be, so I walk back down past the Mind shop to the lower set of traffic lights. I know it's by a set of traffic lights, but not this low down, surely. I walk back up to the higher set of lights. I'm pretty sure that Handsome Mens Grooming is where Ripping Yarns should be. I feel disoriented and disgruntled – and not just on account of the missing apostrophe. A quick look at my phone tells me that Ripping Yarns closed in 2015 following a rent rise. I feel a sudden emptiness inside, a hollowing-out. Like the world needs another men's hair salon. I run my hand over my bald head and cross the road, then dive into Highgate Wood. I walk slowly along a path that runs parallel with Muswell Hill Road. Couples overtake me, men saying to women things like 'I think we need to take this to another level . . .' and 'Unless it comes from the artist himself, it's meaningless, decision by committee . . .'

Muswell Hill is sweltering. Last time I went shopping for books in Muswell Hill, Bridget O'Connor was still working behind the till in the Muswell Hill Bookshop. A friendly and vivacious bookseller, Bridget O'Connor was also a screenwriter and author of two short story collections in my Picador library, *Here Comes John* (1993) and *Tell Her You Love Her* (1997). She died in 2010 at the horribly young age of 49.

The Muswell Hill Bookshop, today, seems smaller, but I'm pretty sure it's a common phenomenon to remember things as being bigger than they are. In the Oxfam Bookshop it makes me smile to see, as it always does, Julian Barnes's 1989 novel *A History of the World in 10½ Chapters* shelved in History. In Fiction I select Colm Tóibín's *The Story of the Night* in Picador. I actually bought *The Story of the Night* last October from Dalston Oxfam for 99p, but this copy contains two inclusions: a folded-up *Pasatiempos* page from *La Vanguardia* Catalan newspaper dated 23 December 2011 on which the *difícil* sudoku has been completed, the *fácil* puzzle is part-completed and the *intermedio* grid remains blank, and a business card from a Soho café with two handwritten Miami phone numbers on the back.

I start walking down the hill towards Crouch End, setting and title of a 1980 Lovecraftian short story by Stephen King, and where, in 1983 and 1984, as the evenings drew in, I would occasionally sit in the front room of Clive Barker's raised-ground-floor flat on Hillfield Avenue, and he would say to me, 'If you don't leave my flat immediately I'm going to call the police.' Actually we would talk about Ramsey Campbell and Dennis Etchison and Arthur Machen and many others (Peter Straub had lived on the same road and King had stayed with him while they worked on *The Talisman* together). I divert on to the north part of the Parkland Walk and feel myself being taken in the wrong direction and so, at Cranley Gardens, return to street level and walk past the former home of mass-murderer Dennis Nilsen, who lived in the top flat at No. 23 from October 1981 to February 1983. Some years later, seeing a For Sale sign outside, I had made an appointment to view the flat. In 2020, I will write up this visit in an oblique way for a short story in my collection, *London Gothic*.

At the bottom of Cranley Gardens is Hornsey Parish Church with its second-hand Basement Bookshop that was recommended to me by writer and critic David Collard, whose regular Zoom salons 'A Leap in the Dark' and 'Carthorse Orchestra' gave writers, poets, artists and musicians something different to do on Saturday nights during lockdowns other than watching BBC4. The Basement Bookshop, though, is only open Saturday mornings and specifically only the first and third Saturdays of the month.

In Crouch End's reliably good Oxfam Books & Music I find a Corgi paperback of Arthur Machen's *Black Crusade* and, even more exciting, for a Picador collector, are a white-spined 1973 edition of Ken Kesey's *One Flew Over the Cuckoo's Nest*, which is usually seen in the orange wraparound cover of the later film tie-in edition, an edition of Ian McEwan's *In Between the Sheets* that *doesn't* have a nude model on the cover but *does* still picture an unmade bed (photographed by Tony Evans) instead of one of Russell Mills' lovely abstract compositions, and *The Beckett Trilogy* containing *Molloy*, *Malone Dies* and *The Unnamable* (cover by Russell Mills again).

I walk up Crouch Hill and then back down on to the south part of the Parkland Walk. When I reach Stoke Newington, the straps of my bag cutting ever more deeply into my shoulder, I look wistfully at Church Street Bookshop and wonder if 24 hours is long enough, but I have to acknowledge a simple fact: the book bag is full.

'I bet that orange spine annoys you!' says Mike Petty, former Picador editor, referring to the *One Flew Over the Cuckoo's Nest* film tie-in edition.

In 1996 I edited an anthology of football short stories for Mike Petty at Gollancz called *A Book of Two Halves*. It was the only 'best-selling' book I've ever had my name on, according to one definition I heard of 'best-selling', which is anything that sells more than 20,000 copies.

Almost twenty years earlier, in 1977, Petty had taken over the role of editor at Picador from Caroline Lasalle, who had been there since the launch in 1972. Petty had been at Jonathan Cape for the previous seven years. 'My actual commissioning experience was minimal,' says Petty from his home in Australia, 'but I'd been one of Cape's readers for a while, so was well used to being required to have opinions on books, assessing sales potential etc. Feeling it was time to move on – I was pushing 30 and wasn't getting anywhere at Cape – I'd been writing on spec to publishers I admired. Cape had supplied a fair number of books to Picador in the early years (Hoban, Hesse, Pynchon, Brautigan etc), so it made sense for Sonny Mehta to hire me after a surreal interview where we had to watch Geoffrey Boycott complete his hundredth century . . . slowly. I was pretty pissed by the time the interview actually started. He once admitted to me that I recommended myself because I was used to dealing with Tom Maschler, who Sonny found impossible. (The feeling was mutual.)'

It was Petty's dream job, if slightly unnerving. 'Sonny's phone call didn't help: "You've got the job. Don't fuck up." Suddenly I was in charge of the hottest paperback list in town. Already by then it had achieved cult status. I used to get letters from people who said they bought every book as it came out, and *One Flew Over the Cuckoo's Nest* had sold a million copies after the movie came out.

'Almost my first opportunity to fuck up was the Pan sales conference, where I gave a tremulous presentation of a whole season's list, most of which I hadn't had time to read. I can't remember what the book was, but after I'd finished with something rather literary, one of the reps said, "Well, that'll never sell on the fucking M4." Luckily the reps who worked more bookish areas gave me an easier ride.'

What was it like working with Sonny Mehta?

'Difficult at times – he could be very moody. At least he never made me cry, as he did at least one of my colleagues. I bought most of the books that appeared from '77 to '83, but he often came up with stuff himself. Sometimes he consulted me (Michael Herr, Clive James, Cyra McFadden, Hunter Thompson – Sonny and I had dinner with Hunter Thompson . . .), sometimes he didn't (Maxine Hong Kingston, Fritz Zorn). Some of my books were successful and/or got a lot of attention (not necessarily the same thing), and some sank without trace (*Mulligan Stew*, anyone?).'

Not only do I not have *Mulligan Stew* in my collection, I hadn't even heard of it and wasn't entirely sure whether *Mulligan Stew* was the title or the name of the author. It turns out to be the title, while the author was Gilbert Sorrentino. So, that's one to look out for.

'I was proud to bring to the list the likes of Calvino, Skvorecky, Musil, Peter Carey, Adam Mars-Jones, Cabrera Infante, Hugo Williams, Desmond Hogan, DM Thomas, Peter Matthiessen – and of course Salman Rushdie. I remember raving to Sonny about what a masterpiece *Midnight's Children* was, a great work of twentieth-century literature, we must publish it etc, and he merely said, "It's the best book by an Indian writer I've read this year."'

My copy of *Midnight's Children* came from Oxfam Books & Music Kentish Town. It contains an inclusion in the form of a street map of Dorking marked with a red pen, leaving two distinct dots, on Westcott Road and South Street, and four crosses over other roads or neighbourhoods. One day I'll go to Dorking and do a walk taking in the dots and crosses, while reading the book, and see what happens.

Petty continued to work with the likes of Tom Wolfe, Ian

McEwan, Russell Hoban and Bruce Chatwin. 'I snaffled García Márquez from Penguin when they went to sleep,' he adds. 'I kept John Calder afloat by buying paperback rights in Beckett and Burroughs when he had bills to pay.'

He left in 1982. 'I was headhunted by Chatto to work with Carmen Callil as part of a new regime. Swapping one tricky boss for another . . .'

Saturday 25 January 2020
Black Gull Books, East Finchley, North London.
Woman with dark hair and black coat: I've got some books to sell.
Bookseller: Uh-huh?
Woman: [. . .]
Bookseller: I can't buy anything today.
Woman: What do you mean?
Bookseller: I don't have any money.
Woman: I don't need money.
Bookseller: You can leave them there if you like. My colleague will look at them.
Woman: Leave them?
Bookseller: Yes, if you want to leave them.
Woman: Where shall I put them?
Bookseller: Just put them down there. I'll have a look.
Woman: Where?
Bookseller: Just down there so I can have a look, see if we want to buy them.
Woman: This one's new . . . I bought two of this one.
Bookseller: My colleague will look at them.
Woman: Tomorrow?
Bookseller: Probably tomorrow, if you want to leave your details?

Woman: Shall I leave you my name and number?
Bookseller: If you want us to be able to contact you. How else
    will we be able to contact you?
Woman: Should I list them?
Bookseller: Not for us. You can do so for yourself if you want
    to . . .
[Woman stands at counter for ten minutes making a list.]

Pages of Hackney on Lower Clapton Road is one of two lovely
bookshops in that borough – the other is Burley Fisher on
Kingsland Road – that sell mostly new books but have a stock
of second-hand books in a converted basement (and cheap-as-
chips selections in boxes out on the street), each with a busy
programme of events that took place on site pre-pandemic and
hopefully will again. In both of those Hackney basements you
get a strong sense of collections that have been carefully curated.
I'm sometimes a little surprised by some of the prices in Pages,
like when I spotted a PJ O'Rourke Picador, *Republican Party
Reptile*, for £8 only a day after I'd seen the same title in Notting
Hill Book & Comic Exchange for £1. Francis Stuart's *Black List,
Section H* (King Penguin) was another one: £8 in Pages, £3.50 in
Scrivener's in Buxton, where I eventually bought it. As for *The
Collected Short Stories of Conrad Aiken* previously owned by John
Sladek, £22 meant I didn't really consider it but perhaps should
have done. Still, I love the smell of new carpet in Pages, the
Agatha Christies, the French books, the spinner – not a Picador
spinner, like those I've seen in Abacus Books in Altrincham and
Halewood & Sons in Preston, but a spinner nonetheless. I love
the fact that the Picador edition of Nabokov's *Lectures on Literature* I found there contained an unused item of Kersti French's
personalised stationery, a postcard bearing her name, address

and telephone number. As a novice film reviewer excited to be attending press screenings in the early 1980s, I had recognised the bald head of Kersti's late husband Philip French often a few rows in front of me in the Camden Plaza or ABC Shaftesbury Avenue. Pages of Hackney is one of those slightly magical second-hand bookshops where I always find something, whether it's a gorgeous green Penguin edition of *A Kiss Before Dying* for former *Time Out* colleague, brilliant Nightjar designer and voracious reader John Oakey, who had asked me to look out for the Ira Levin novel, or a lovely slim 1968 Panther paperback edition of George Barker's 1950 novel *The Dead Seagull* for myself. The novel was inspired by Barker's affair with Canadian novelist Elizabeth Smart, whose 1945 work *By Grand Central Station I Sat Down and Wept* is the better-known and more widely read account of that relationship. I see its attractive Paladin edition often, although not, it seems, on my own shelves, so that's one to look for when bookshops reopen.

Friday 8 November 2019

Charity bookshop, Bethnal Green, London.

Woman customer 1: You've hurt your wrist.

Bookshop woman: Yes and no. It's not my wrist. It's my elbow. Golfer's elbow. I've never played golf in my life.

Woman customer 2: Bercitis!

Bookshop woman: Pardon?

Woman customer 2: Bercitis! It's like tennis elbow.

Bookshop woman: Golfer's elbow. It's slightly different.

Woman customer 2: It's a form of bercitis. I've literally just been diagnosed with it. It's a car accident. There's trauma and then these, like, they're like air bags. That's literally what it's like.

Bookshop woman: Right.

Woman customer 2: Anyway. I hope it gets better. [Leaves shop.]
[. . .]
Woman customer 1: Are you reading that?
Bookshop woman: Yes. Have you been watching *His Dark Materials*?
Woman customer 1: Ooh, yes.

Two miles south of Pages of Hackney is Jambala, on Globe Road, Bethnal Green. It is attached to and contributes to the charitable activities of the London Buddhist Centre around the corner on Roman Road and it is the only place where I have ever come across second-hand copies of Nightjar chapbooks – two of them on separate occasions. I bought them both as there are sometimes new Nightjar readers who wish they had been collecting the stories since the beginning. Simon Okotie, with whom I used to play football on Sunday nights at Westway Sports Centre in the 1990s and who will be a Nightjar author by the time this book is published, has been associated with the Buddhist Centre for some years, but this, I believe, is a coincidence.

When I visited Jambala on 2 July 2020 I was delighted to find Jen Campbell's *The Bookshop Book* (Constable) and Cecelia Watson's *Semicolon* (4th Estate). The latter is the only book I've ever seen about a single punctuation mark and, given the level of misuse of this specific one, I'd say it's much needed. Also interesting to see was *The Best of McSweeny's Volume 1* edited by Dave Eggers and containing a story by Dave Eggers; I didn't buy it. Those people who insisted *A Heartbreaking Work of Staggering Genius* was an ironic title or 'allographic paratext', I wonder if they still think that?

A short walk east along Roman Road brings you to the Regent's Canal and you can then walk beside the canal all the way down to Limehouse. The Thames Path will take you down the west side of the Isle of Dogs and around to the north entrance to the Greenwich Foot Tunnel. There is no better way to get to Greenwich, which boasts an excellent Oxfam Bookshop as well as Halcyon Books, and once you've walked to Greenwich you might as well keep going to Blackheath, where there's another Oxfam as well as the very fine Bookshop on the Heath run by former journalist Ian Irvine, who edited the *Talk of the Town* supplement distributed in the capital with copies of the *Independent on Sunday* from March 2003 to March 2004. Packed with features and columns on the arts, culture and London life, *Talk of the Town* also included new fiction in every issue, in the form mostly of new short stories and extracts from forthcoming novels. Unless we have at least one weekly magazine in this country regularly publishing new short stories, the claim that you often hear that the short story is finally being taken seriously in British culture is going to sound a little like the title of the Agatha Christie novel I see in the window of Bookshop on the Heath on 7 January 2018. *The Hollow*, in its Fontana paperback edition, has a characteristic Tom Adams cover featuring several eggs and a revolver lying on a red cloth in a wooden basket. There's often a splash of red on a Tom Adams cover, whether it's lipstick, nail varnish or blood.

I thank Ian Irvine for having printed one or two of my pieces in *Talk of the Town* and ask him about his career change. He says he gave up journalism as it seemed to him there was no future in it. I say it's great to hear someone suggest that second-hand bookselling does have a future. 'It's an undigitisable experience,' says Irvine. I buy the Agatha Christie and James T Farrell's *Studs Lonigan* (Picador Classics) with a cover by George Sharp that is very much in the manner of Edward Hopper, just as his cover for Joseph Heller's *Picture This* is very much in the manner of Rembrandt.

It's an hour's walk from Blackheath to Peckham. It's not the prettiest walk, along the A2, but if you've got your nose in a book, maybe that doesn't matter?

I don't actually know if it's called Books, or BOOKS, or BOOKS Peckham or Books Peckham – you see all four versions when it is written about, which is quite often – but Peter Willis's punk-style operation, which for four years was found at the end of a cobbled alley off Rye Lane in Peckham, has been one of the best second-hand bookshops in south London since it opened in 2016. Willis would post opening hours for the week ahead on his Instagram only once he got sight of his rota for his day job, and even then he might have to cancel plans in the event of rain, his premises being a cross between a shop and a market stall. On a visit there on 20 April 2018, I found three Picadors: Rudolph Wurlitzer's *Quake*, Gitta Sereny's *Into That Darkness* and David Black's *The Plague Years*, and something I'd been half-wondering if I might find since I started looking out for inclusions, in a wartime austerity hardback edition of Kafka's *The Trial*, tucked in at page 191, a message one might imagine an imprisoned or otherwise trapped character to have smuggled out of the nightmarish world of their dystopian novel and into our own. In this case, it was a piece of paper bearing the name Winston and a mobile phone number. It could only really have been better had it been *1984* rather than *The Trial*.

Quake is an astonishingly brutal short novel about the immediate aftermath of an earthquake that strikes Los Angeles. As you might expect of the period (first published 1972, in Picador 1974), the sexual politics are dubious and some encounters might feel slightly porny, but these take a back seat as violence largely takes over from sex. A people's militia attempts to take control, rounding up survivors randomly and either shooting them in the back of the head or herding them into a football stadium and then shooting them in the back of the head. I read it in a day, which I don't usually do. It's short, so short, indeed, that the wonderful US independent publisher Two Dollar Radio reissued it in an omnibus with Wurlitzer's 1970 novel *Flats* in 2011 and you're still looking at barely 200 pages.

BOOKS Peckham – that's what I'm going with – moved during the pandemic and will open in new premises, with a roof and everything, once it's legal and safe to do so. The new address is Maxted Road, but the entrance is on Oglander Road. You'll easily find it. But check his opening times for the week first.

Talking of the pandemic, I just managed to squeeze in a visit to the newly opened Ecstatic Peace Library before the first national lockdown and then another to its new premises at the Church Street end of Bouverie Road before new restrictions were imposed in the autumn of 2020. The Ecstatic Peace Library was founded by Edwin Pouncey – aka Savage Pencil – with Sonic Youth's Thurston Moore and Zippo Records' Pete Flanagan. Where those three names have been listed together in media coverage of the opening, Moore's would generally come first. I have moved the names around simply because Edwin Pouncey was once – 35 years ago – very encouraging to a young and wet-behind-the-ears short story writer, inviting him to his office at *Sounds* in Greater London House to talk about a supplement devoted to horror fiction and music.

I didn't buy anything on my first visit, but I did meet Pouncey, again, and was able to thank him for that early encouragement. On my second visit, to Bouverie Road, I discovered that Ecstatic Peace Library are big fans of Boris Vian. I'd never seen so many of his books in one place. I met Moore and Pete Flanagan's son Jim and bought a copy of Michel Butor's *Illustrations*, which doesn't contain any illustrations and doesn't have many words on its pages, leading me to suspect it may be poetry, and an issue of the always interesting *Transatlantic Review* (from 1975) including a story by Elspeth Davie. I'll buy anything with a story in by Elspeth Davie.

Friday 10 January 2020
Charity bookshop, north London.
Male volunteer: I'll be doing next Friday morning.
Female volunteer: Have you been away?
Male: Yes, the Alps.
Female: Was it good?
Male: A bit too much humping cases. We had first-class rail travel. Could have done without all the humping cases. Alice says she doesn't want to go on a rail holiday again.
[. . .]
Male: I've read that. [Pause.] I went to the same school, about five years before – 1966. You might see David Cameron. Look for a fat, smug face.

When my children were at primary school in south Manchester in the so-called noughties, their mum was working full time and so it was usually me taking them to school and picking them up at home time. I noticed another dad doing a lot of the dropping off and picking up, of his two daughters. He had the thickest, darkest eyebrows I'd seen on any man since Alistair Darling. We eventually got talking and he told me his name was Conrad Leyser. The conversation developed over time and I may have told him that I got through a lot of notebooks, because one day he presented me with a pack of four notebooks, 'Quartetto' by Fabriano, that he said he had bought for me when passing through an airport in Germany, possibly Frankfurt.

The notebooks have a design of overlapping spirals on the cover. In a pack of four, one has red spirals, one blue, one green and one black. One of those notebooks fits nicely in the back pocket of a pair of jeans, along with a Pilot V7 Hi-Tecpoint pen. I use the notebooks – and the pen – for recording ideas and thoughts, and things people tell me that otherwise I would forget. Back then, one of those notebooks would last me about six months. I got into the habit, when a notebook was full, of continuing to carry the old one at the same time as its replacement, as if I hadn't quite reached the point where I was happy to transfer the old one to the shelf at home where I stored them. This behaviour reminded me of that of a receptionist at a former place of work whose handbag was one day found to contain a great many greasy food wrappers. When asked why she kept them, she said she hadn't said goodbye to them yet.

Each time Conrad Leyser passed through Frankfurt airport, which he did with surprising frequency, he would buy me another set of notebooks, until I had so many lined up at home waiting to be used that, I worked out, given the rate at which I was getting through them, I almost certainly had enough to last me the rest of my life. I wasn't being conservative in my lifespan estimation; despite suffering from not-insignificant health anxiety, I allowed myself a good innings.

However, once I started using the notebooks to record overheard conversations – in pubs and cafés, trams, trains and on canal banks for that matter, as well as in charity shops and bookshops – I found that I started to get through them much faster, so that now I have another worry to add to what I consider to be reasonable concerns about the possibility of serious illness, which other people close to me prefer to characterise as hypochondria: I might have somehow tied my fate to the dwindling supply of notebooks. You might say, Well, you could buy more notebooks. I could, it's true, but what if it didn't work? What if, at the point where I declared that I had enough notebooks to last the rest of my life, I had somehow determined a future course of events?

Sunday 25 October 2020
Regent's Canal, Hackney, London.
Young woman with young male friend.
Young woman: So, are you going to get that book done?

6

French letters

Sunday 26 November 1995

I'm in London with a young writer, who I think is James Miller. He lives on the outskirts and is a proud champion of his area. We are in a bookshop checking it out. I'm giving it the only check I know – seeing if they have my book. But first I check the horror shelves. Very small selection. James is anxious to go because we've got a bus to catch. I want to have a look in the other sections. I go to do so and discover the other sections are in fact not part of the bookshop – I'm now in the Marks & Spencer food hall. I rejoin James. He's cross because we appear to have missed the bus. We run to the ramp – there's a ramp which doubles back on itself a couple of times. I jump down from section to section and run to jump on the running board of the orange-and-white bus. There's a small group of boys in blue shirts ahead of me and I think James must be one of them. But when I look again to check, he's not. He's waving to me from the bus stop, in a darker blue shirt than before. So I jump off and start walking back. The weather is beautiful – really hot and sunny. Suddenly it's not the outskirts of London, but of Paris. As I'm walking back under the shade of trees I see Dennis Etchison coming towards me. We stop and chat. He's very cheerful. I say, 'Are you having a good convention?' He says, 'Well, I'm just having a good time.' I say, 'Yes, that's what I meant.' His face is changing to a woman's, with orange lipstick and strange, jowly features. Somehow, though, she's attractive – in a *jolie laide* kind of way. And somehow she's still Dennis.

Peter Murphy of Bauhaus was not the only famous person I wrote to as a 17-year-old fanboy. I wrote to Leslie Halliwell, compiler of *Halliwell's Film Guide*, which had become my bible. I asked him about his exclusion of *The Texas Chain Saw Massacre* from the *Film Guide* and he responded that he supposed there was an argument to be made for including it and he would do so in the next edition. I wrote to Alain Robbe-Grillet. It would have been basically a fan letter with a question or two about his work in the hope of eliciting a reply, which duly came, beautifully handwritten, charming and generous, on a side of A4, which I photocopied and stuck to the front of my French folder. If my flat were to catch fire, it would be this letter I would be scrabbling around trying to find in the final minutes before failing to make it out alive.

Was it overweening ambition or foolish naivety that meant I included Robbe-Grillet – and Graham Greene and my all-time favourite novelist Derek Marlowe – on the invite list for the *Darklands* anthologies I edited in the early 1990s? Robbe-Grillet sent me another kind letter ('If I write anything in this genre, I will let you know immediately'), while Greene's secretary politely declined and Marlowe sent me an unpublished story.

When Robbe-Grillet came to the Institut Français in South Kensington on 27 March 2002 to sign copies of his latest novel, *La Reprise*, I was there. I waited in line for what seemed like years, but time must have been going backwards, because when I reached the front of the queue I heard myself babbling, stumbling and stuttering in embarrassing schoolboy French.

Six years later he was dead, at the age of 85.

I don't have all Robbe-Grillet's 12 novels. I have only eight of them, plus the short stories, the theory, two of the *ciné-romans* and one of the volumes of autobiography. I could go online and fill in the gaps, at some expense, but as with the missing Picadors, that doesn't appeal. Instead, I want to come across the ones I don't have, in second-hand bookshops, just as I came across a copy of *Le Voyeur* in Librairie Impressions on rue de la Tulipe in Ixelles on 9 June 2018, when Ros and I were in Brussels for a fiftieth birthday party, sadly neither hers nor mine, only I knew I already had a copy of *Le Voyeur*, with inclusions to boot (two torn halves of a club night flyer, 'girls FREE b4 11pm'). This copy was hardly any different. It wasn't signed, it contained neither an inclusion nor the name of a previous owner, it was probably a more recent printing and it had some marks on the cover, and marks on the covers of Minuit books often don't come off.

Certain books – certain books by certain authors or even all books by certain authors – have this effect. You see them, you want them, even if you already have them, even if you already have them in the same edition. That's important, too. So, certain editions of certain books by certain authors. I wouldn't buy a duplicate copy of one of the Penguin Modern Classics editions of Anna Kavan's *Ice*, for example, but I would buy another copy of the Picador edition, and not just for the Delvaux cover, although, now I think about it, partly for the Delvaux cover, so that I could add that copy to my minutely small but nevertheless growing collection of books with covers that feature works by Delvaux (Alice Thompson's *Pandora's Box*; a collection of works by Edgar Allan Poe, *Bizarre and Arabesque*, edited by Kay Dick; the October/November 1993 issue of *London Magazine*; the two Picador Anna Kavan titles).

Whenever I see any of the five Derek Marlowe novels reissued by Penguin in 1977 in matching white-spined A-format paperbacks (covers by Paul Wakefield), I buy them (and maybe give them away as presents). But you hardly ever see them. Indeed, I haven't seen the Penguin edition of *A Dandy in Aspic* for years, and that includes my copy.

Maybe I'm at that point with Robbe-Grillet, but only the Minuit editions. I might even be at that point with Minuit. Their books are beautiful artefacts and their authors always worth reading, among them the foremost practitioners of the *nouveau roman* – Robbe-Grillet, Natalie Sarraute, Claude Simon, Michel Butor, Robert Pinget, to a lesser extent Marguerite Duras – united by their rejection of the techniques of the nineteenth-century novel. That rejection appealed to me. I had not got on with Flaubert or, especially, Balzac. (Just as I had not enjoyed Dickens.) Zola (and Hardy) I liked, all that darkness and tragedy.

Working as a language assistant at a school in the nineteenth arrondissement in 1984 and 1985, I rented a studio apartment in rue Bouret, the same street the school was on. One of the teachers at the school, Jean-Bernard Piat, had translated two novels by an English writer called Robin Cook, who had been living in France for some time. *On ne meurt que deux fois* had appeared in 1983 and *Les mois d'avril sont meurtriers* in 1984, each appearing in French translation, from Série Noire, before they were published in English, as *He Died With His Eyes Open* and *The Devil's Home on Leave*, becoming the first two novels in the 'Factory' sequence, under the name of Derek Raymond. I met the author in a pub in Soho – either the Coach or the French, as they were known – after I returned to London and asked him what had happened to Robin Cook. 'That name's fucked,' he told me, referring to both the American thriller writer and the Labour MP.

Saturday 22 June 2019
Café Oto, Dalston, London. Indie book/record fair. Infinity Land Press table.
Guy with monocle on chain: Did Artaud like Schwob?
Guy with fiercely side-parted hair: Yes.

I am spending a few days in France – mid-July, 2017 – which is a good opportunity to be keeping an eye out for additions to my various small-but-growing French-language collections. Simenon novels in Livre de Poche. Nice editions of titles by Boris Vian/Vernon Sullivan, Marguerite Duras, Roland Topor. Anything I haven't already got by Alain Robbe-Grillet, Jean-Philippe Toussaint, Monique Wittig, Tanguy Viel or Jean Ravey in Minuit. In fact, anything I haven't already got in Minuit.

We're staying in the countryside near Bussières-Galant, nearest city Limoges, with one of my oldest friends and his lovely wife. On the first day we go for an hour's walk in country lanes and see three buzzards, a red kite, loads of jays and three black redstarts. At other times there are glimpses of a green wood-pecker, a barn owl, a heron and numerous great tits. As we sit out in the evening and watch dusk steal the light from the sky, a churring starts up that sounds a lot like a nightjar.

On a visit to the Dordogne town of Périgueux I leave my companions sitting outside a café to nip back to an alleyway we have just passed – rue de Berthe Bonaventure – and, at No. 9, one of the smallest second-hand bookshops I've ever been in. In fact, it's so small that as soon as you've entered, all you can do is turn around and go back outside again, and it's on the tables outside that I spot the familiar white cover and black and royal blue type of Les Editions de Minuit – *Forever Valley* by Marie Redonnet. I've never heard of Redonnet, but that only makes the find more exciting. The Minuit logo is an undisputable badge of quality and the books, which essentially all look the same, are beautiful, in that understated French way. I say something along these lines to the bookseller, who recommends another publisher, Editions José Corti, who he regards as highly as Minuit. He writes 'Editions José Corti' on the back of a flyer and slips it inside the book.

On the half-title page, I see later, are two names. The only one I can read is Nicole Kochmann. When I look up Nicole Kochmann I find a recording on YouTube of a Nicole Kochmann singing 'Ce que la vie fera de nous' accompanied on guitar and double-bass. It's a charming, slightly melancholic *chanson*, its air of melancholy no doubt enhanced by the passage of the years. A note on Discogs, where six copies of the album from which it's taken are available for sale, suggests it was recorded in the 1980s. So, Nicole and her accompanists will know now what life has thrown their way. Please don't tell me that Nicole Kochmann is a common name and it's unlikely to be her. As far as I'm concerned, it's her.

I will finally get around to reading *Forever Valley* in August 2020. Told in very simple, basic French, with short sentences and lots of repetition, it is nevertheless a very sophisticated short novel narrated by a 16-year-old girl living at a presbytery in a village called Forever Valley. Reaching – or approaching – the age of sixteen means she can go and work at 'le dancing', to which shepherds and customs officers come from the next valley down. They dance with the girls and then go upstairs with them. The narrator is also engaged in a personal project. She's realised that the village has no cemetery, unlike the village in the valley below, so she is looking for the dead she thinks must be buried somewhere in Forever Valley. She digs graves or pits (*la fosse* means both) around the church, but all she finds is either mud or clay or rock. The priest, meanwhile, who has occupied the role of guardian, is slowly becoming paralysed. He becomes equally obsessed with her search for the dead. We wonder why. Is there a sinister reason? Also, with her digging these pits or graves we're wondering who might end up filling them. It's a novel of light and dark with the qualities of a fable or fairy tale and having read it I really want to read the first and third novels in the trilogy, *Splendid Hôtel* and *Rose Mélie Rose* respectively. All three are available in English translations by Jordan Stump, published by US publisher Bison Books. Rather splendidly, Stump has translated the title of *Splendid Hôtel* as *Hôtel Splendid*.

If you want to return to London from one of the cities in the south of France that are served by Eurostar, you have to disembark at Lille in the north of France and go through security there and then reboard the same train. It's all a bit of a faff and frankly it's much more civilised to travel via Paris and spend a night there. This also means you can visit any number of wonderful *librairies d'occasions* like Le Livre à Venir on fashionable rue Oberkampf in the eleventh, where I find Jean-Philippe Toussaint's 2002 novel *Faire l'amour* in Minuit. When I said all Minuit books look alike I was of course ignoring their *'Double'* series of mass-market editions, which are smaller format and have photographic covers. I imagine that when Minuit introduced the *'Double'* collection, it was a bit like Dylan going electric, and it's true that I would generally prefer a Minuit first edition, but the photographic covers can be good and the small format fits more easily in a jacket pocket. I buy *Faire l'amour*, which has a cover picture of Tokyo at night taken by the author himself. It's the first in Toussaint's four-novel cycle *Marie Madeleine Marguerite de Montalte*.

I will read *Faire l'amour* exactly a year later. Marie, a fashion designer, and the narrator, her partner, have flown to Tokyo to mount an exhibition. They are in the process of splitting up. The narrator has packed a flask of hydrochloric acid. Their split is not going smoothly. First one and then the other disrupts the process. They both seem to find it hard to split up, yet impossible to remain together. The narrator describes in some detail what he does, where he goes. For most of the novel we infer what is going on in his head from what he is doing. He generally only tells us what he is thinking when he is thinking nothing. There's something compelling about the prose, about its lack of affect. The narrative just keeps going and you just keep reading. An English translation by Linda Coverdale appeared from US publisher the New Press, but most of Toussaint's work is available in English translation from Dalkey Archive.

We end up in our favourite bar, Les Pieds Sous la Table, on rue St Maur, in the eleventh. I am very much not normally a dog person, but Eugène offers most patrons a warm welcome. His owner is friendly, too; plus, she keeps a little library of free books in one corner of the bar. The idea is you bring a book, you take a book. Or take a book and bring one next time. I take *L'Evénement* by Annie Ernaux.

Spending a night in Paris, in a hotel where the black-and-yellow spines of Série Noire crime paperbacks decorate the bar, means we can spend most of the following day indulging the *flâneur* – and *flâneuse* – inside us. Actually, as soon as I write that, I think it's inaccurate. Where a *flâneur* strolls and observes the surrounding society, I usually walk at a fair lick with a book on the go, assuming daylight or good street lighting, and as long as it's not raining. If it is raining, I'll read a manuscript, which is disposable. And if I'm accompanied, I'll keep my book in my pocket. But does the *flâneur* – or *flâneuse* – have a destination in mind? We do.

In Librairie l'Atelier, which seems to have three outlets on rue du Jourdain in the twentieth, one of them devoted to second-hand stock, the shelves go up to the high ceiling. There's a ladder, but don't try to use it, as I did, unless you don't mind a telling-off. I sometimes find rows and rows of serious-looking leather-bound books intimidating, but being on the lookout for certain authors or certain imprints gives me a way in. It opens up what otherwise might feel like a forbidden space. In contemporary fiction I find a first edition of Jean-Philippe Toussaint's 2013 novel *Nue* in Minuit. It's the final part of the *Marie* cycle and it's only €5, which is not bad going. Toussaint, a Belgian, sent his first novel, *La Salle de bain* (1985), to Minuit, who accepted it and have been his publisher ever since.

I'm grateful to my teachers at school and university, in particular Barry Packham and Roger Huss, without whose patience and encouragement I wouldn't be able to read Redonnet or Toussaint in their original language.

Thursday 17 June 2010
Driving in West Hampstead. Looking for a turning on the right but they are all dead ends. Eventually take one. The sky darkens

dramatically. Is it night or thick black cloud? City lights ahead of me. It's Paris. Like a painting by Van Gogh.

I'm in some kind of shop and I'm naked. No one is reacting but I know it's not a good idea to be naked, in a shop. I grab a long-sleeved white top and put it on – and grey pants.

On the Métro. It's busy. You choose your destination once you're on the train. Mine will only let me travel one stop. That's OK. I'll walk.

I get off and see a party of people turning up in a car outside a hotel. One of them is publisher and author Jane Johnson. I climb over from the back into the front of their car, where there's a white woollen hat. Somehow time has looped over on itself.

Around 1998, a senior editor from Transworld asked me to read a French novel, *Pharricide* by Vincent de Swarte, and write them a report. They wanted to know if they should consider buying the translation rights to it. I read it quickly. It's a short, extraordinarily powerful diary-form novel narrated by lighthouse keeper and amateur taxidermist Geoffroy Lefayen. Asked to look after the lighthouse at Cordouan (an actual lighthouse off the west coast of France) for six months, Geoffroy agrees on condition that he's allowed to do the job on his own. Furthermore, 'I pray to God no one comes to the lighthouse during those six months,' he writes in his diary.

I loved the novel, which is very dark and brutal but also has a strange humanity about it. I sent in my report, advising that they should acquire the rights and let me translate it. Eventually I was told they weren't going to pursue it, but Cordouan had got into my head, the way it gets into Geoffroy's, and I started mithering publishers, asking them if they would be interested. Nobody was. Years went by. I did an event with Meike Ziervogel of Peirene

Press and thought they would be the ideal publisher. I wrote to Meike. She sent me a link to a blog post in which she had written about *Pharricide*, describing it as 'an incredible piece of literature' but adding, 'I won't publish it. It won't sell in this country.'

In the meantime, I had made contact with the author and told him of my wish to translate the novel. He was pleased. I felt a strange kind of kinship with De Swarte. We were born in the same year and we had both written first novels (in his case his first novel for adults) that skulked in the queasy borderlands between horror stories and literary fiction. When I heard in 2006 that De Swarte had died, at the age of only 42, the sense of loss I felt was out of proportion to the single exchange of correspondence that had existed between us. One or two of the stories in his posthumously published collection, *Pharanoïa*, are extremely difficult to read. He knew what was around the corner and didn't shy away from the subject in his fiction.

I was delighted when Confingo Publishing offered to publish a translation of *Pharricide*, although it did mean I had to get on and do it. It turned out I was as slow a translator as I am a writer. And it wasn't easy, but it was much easier than it would have been without the help of my bilingual former MA creative writing student Sonya Moor, who, luckily for me, fell for the book in a big way when she read it, even taking a trip out to Cordouan (from her home in Paris) to soak up the atmosphere. The English translation of *Pharricide* was published in 2019 and, in 2021, it was runner-up in the TA First Translation Prize.

The senior editor from Transworld was John Saddler, who is now my agent and remembers the story differently, but I suspect only as a way of characteristically avoiding taking credit.

Every time we go to Paris, I go – or try to go – to Le Jargon Libre, another second-hand bookshop in the twentieth. It looks great, through the picture window, through the glass door. Overflowing shelves, piles of books on every surface. Every time I go, it's closed, even when the note in the window says it should be open. There's a mobile number. I compose a quick text, imagining the owner to be near by, in a café, in his apartment. Perhaps he'll come down if he knows he's got a customer. Every time, the response comes: he's closed until the 28th, he's away for two weeks, he didn't get away in the summer. On my most recent visit to the pavement outside his door, he was away seeing Georges Ibrahim Abdallah in Lannemezan prison in the deep south-west of France. Arrested in 1984 and given a life sentence for murder in 1987, Abdallah has had several requests for parole turned down since he completed the minimum portion of his life sentence in 1999. The Palestine solidarity groups who meet regularly to march to the gates of the prison regard him as a political prisoner, the oldest such in Europe.

Paris's second-hand English-language bookshops, such as the Abbey Bookshop and the San Francisco Book Company, are lovely but expensive: £8 for Bruno Schulz's *The Street of Crocodiles* in Picador? (I will find it for £2 in Marylebone High Street's Oxfam Bookshop on the day of the anti-Trump march in London, the route passing close enough to Marylebone High Street to allow a detour. The following day I will remarry and on our honeymoon I will read *The Street of Crocodiles*, which, with its birds, old books and maps, and tailor's dummies, is right up my alley.) Shakespeare & Company has second-hand books in among the new stock, but prices are high and so is the footfall, what with it being a key stop on the tourist trail.

Might it be useful to enquire into the reasons behind the

human need for favourites? Is it even a need? What is my favourite second-hand bookshop in Paris? (Probably Librairie l'Atelier, although I'll be heading straight back to the two Oxfam Bookshops at the first post-pandemic opportunity, having discovered them only on my last visit in 2019.) What is my favourite second-hand bookshop in Brussels? (Definitely Librairie Impressions, although I never miss a visit to Galerie Bortier.) I don't have a favourite child – the very idea is preposterous. I don't have a favourite friend; there's no such concept, although, from early childhood, we have our best friends. It's easy to imagine how a second-favourite child might feel at being so designated. What about a friend who is not a best friend? Do they know and accept that they are 'just' a good friend or a very good friend? I like Le Livre à Venir on rue Oberkampf in Paris. I like the proprietor. He's never scolded me for climbing a ladder (he doesn't have one). I admired the patient way he dealt with two visitors who, when I was last there, were trying to persuade him to turn his bookshop into a café. I hope they have not returned and been successful. How would Le Livre à Venir feel if it knew it was only my second-favourite second-hand bookshop in Paris? I doubt it would be bothered, if it were possible for it to feel anything. Why is it important to me not only to have a favourite bar in Paris, but to identify it? I seem to want the proprietor of Les Pieds Sous la Table to welcome us back, saying, It's great to see you again. This is obviously your favourite bar in Paris. But I have to settle for Eugène not barking at me.

Wednesday 18 January 2016

On a bus with Leone Ross. Later we enter a bookshop. We're doing something for the proprietor, possibly judging a competition. The owner is French. Leone speaks to her in French. I speak to Leone in French. I ask her, When did you learn to speak French? I feel self-conscious speaking in French. She asks me, in English, if I have had my Remembrance Day service yet. I don't know what she is talking about. She says children had been marched to the front of the class for crying. I gather she's a teacher and she appears to think I am one too.

7

Black spines & anomalies

Tuesday 29 July 2003
[In Fuji-Hakone Guesthouse, a ryokan, in mountains near Hakone, Japan.]
Rupert Thomson turned up somewhere. I wanted to introduce him to my companion. I held his arm and was calling him 'R', but he slipped off to the toilets. When I found him in the toilets, his hair was sleek and black.

My first Picador Classics purchase was *My Madness: The Selected Writings of Anna Kavan*. It cost £4 but pre-dated my keeping of records, so I could have bought it anywhere. It has a cover illustration by Louise Brierley, who did other covers for Picador, including a lovely series of Angela Carter titles. The Picador Classics look was characterised by strong use of black and white blocks or bands, with type reversed out, and generally smaller illustrations, and, of course, the black spine, with white type, and the Picador Classics logo. The list was launched in 1987 with Aragon's *Paris Peasant*, which I found in Tin Drum Books in Leicester, and seven other titles including Henry de Montherlant's *The Girls*, which graced the shelves of the lovely Greenhouse Books in Cheadle until I removed it.

In October 2018, when I first visited Greenhouse Books, tucked away in a little arcade just off one of the suburb's two shopping streets, it was owned by Chris and Lorraine Witty. Chris happened to be a student of mine on the MA at Manchester Met. Between them, Chris and Lorraine sold hot drinks and homemade cake and, of course, books. I found another Picador Classics title that day, William Faulkner's *The Sound and the Fury*, which I thought I already had, but perhaps only in regular Picador. I bought it anyway, since it had an inclusion (some notes about the book, including the N word, which I gather appears several times in the text, but I can't check because it turned out I didn't already have the Picador edition and, oddly, my Picador Classics copy now seems to have vanished).

Chris Witty also sold me Chekhov's *The Duel and Other Stories* in my preferred Penguin Classics series – A-format, black spine. I'm not a particular fan of Chekhov – *takes cover* – but everyone else is and so I will persevere, and the collection contains a story entitled 'Murder'. It will have to be very good indeed to come close to the William Sansom story of the same title.

In September 2020, Greenhouse Books was taken over by Janet Penny, whose son, Beats fan and open-mic poet Jonathan Wilson, now manages the shop and vegan café. I went along on the first day of new business and bought another Faulkner, *Soldiers' Pay*, in Picador Classics, and a Penguin edition of Lisa St Aubin de Terán's 1992 novel *Nocturne*, for my small collection of books either called *Nocturne* or including the word – because it's one of my favourites – in the title. I haven't read *Nocturne* yet, but I read Antonio Tabucchi's *Indian Nocturne* (Vintage), bought from House of Hodge, about a man pursuing a missing friend across India. I enjoyed it, but not as much as the same author's *Vanishing Point*, with its mood of gently persistent existential enquiry, which I'm slightly embarrassed to admit I bought online, during lockdown. 'Faldini has the face of someone who has spent his entire life addressing letters to distant countries while looking out across a landscape of derricks and containers.' The translation is by Tim Parks. I read it while walking on the Fallowfield Loop in south Manchester and it cheered me up.

Chris and Lorraine Witty now live in Brittany and are still selling books via Instagram and eBay under the name Book Folk France.

My first ever visit to Southend – 4 July 2017 – and my first impressions are not encouraging. I get off the train and walk down the pedestrian shopping street to the sea front, which is a mess of contradictions. Grand buildings with trashy signs, a supposed amusement park, and a famous landmark that may be the longest 'pleasure pier' in the world but looks short on charm and costs two quid to go on. I'll save my £2 and buy an extra book with it, because the reason I've come to Southend is for the Bookshop Experience.

Away from the front and drifting westwards, Southend takes on a more attractive character. Indeed, it becomes Westcliff-on-Sea. The burble of blackbirds, hum of bees on buddleia, clink of china from tiny wrought-iron balconies. London Road, when I reach it, may be slightly less blissfully suburban, but it doesn't take long to reach No. 307. As soon as I enter the Bookshop Experience, I know I'm in luck. I'm immediately taking books off shelves. Paul Bowles – two Abacus collections, *A Thousand Days For Mokhtar* and *Call at Corazón*, in the same series, with excellent photographic covers, as two titles I already have. Calvino's *The Literature Machine*, in the Brothers Quai (sic) series of covers from Picador (a separate series is credited to the Brothers Quay). And then – *increasing heartbeat* – I spot an early Sceptre paperback of Siri Hustvedt's first novel, *The Blindfold*.

I love *The Blindfold*. My edition is later and features a woman's midriff in a crop top that has always felt wrong to me. I like this earlier, uncredited cover with its blindfold, its disembodied eyes, Chrysler Building and 109th Street sign. Next, a King Penguin edition of BS Johnson's best-known novel, *Christie Malry's Own Double-Entry*, that, as with *The Blindfold*, I hadn't even known existed. Finally, I can't quite believe it, but, yes, there, under K, a copy of the white-spined Picador edition of Kafka's *The Trial*, which I have only seen once before, in the home of writers David Gaffney and Sarah-Clare Conlon.

When I saw it at the Gaffney-Conlon residence, I was tempted to become a book thief. *The Trial* exists in many editions, from different publishers, with different covers. This Picador cover, by Steven Singer, has the distinction of having previously been, to me at least, invisible. Normally, if there's a Picador I know I want, I don't order it, as previously discussed. In the case of *The Trial*, however, I weakened. Having seen it in the wild, having even handled it, I couldn't resist and did go online and did order, off eBay, what appeared to be the same edition. When it arrived it was a Picador Classics edition. The same translation, by Douglas Scott and Chris Waller, but in the black spine of Picador Classics, with a cover illustration by Peter Till. The search for the white-spined edition would continue, but, my lesson learnt, only in the real world.

I'm now carrying half a dozen books and I'm not even half way through the fiction. I'm almost relieved to find the second half of the alphabet a little quieter. I find a lovely A-format Penguin edition of David Storey's *This Sporting Life*, cover by Allan Manham, to go alongside *Flight into Camden*, *A Temporary Life*, *Pasmore* and others.

At the till is Celeste, the loveliest, most charming woman I can remember meeting in a second-hand bookshop, and I don't say this only because she knocks the odd 50p off prices that are already very reasonable (£1–£3). We chat about the shop, about its owner, Andy, who is off somewhere taking care of business online, about there being good days and bad days, about how they hope to attract more passing trade – and I say I hope they do. I say that when I write about the shop I will mention the glass cases full of Celeste's beautiful handmade jewellery and Celeste tells me I don't have to and I say that I will anyway. I'm just turning reluctantly to go when I see something that I haven't seen, outside of my own home, for about thirty-five years (Skoob having discontinued theirs): a dedicated Picador bookcase.

I get down on my hands and knees – and only partly because these shelves are near to the floor. I start again. *The Lay of Sir Tristram*, second novel by Paul Griffiths, whose first novel, also in Picador, I already have. Stefan Heym's *The Wandering Jew*. *Five Black Ships* by Napoleón Baccino Ponce de León – I almost leave this because it's covered in sticky-back plastic, as *Blue Peter* presenters used to call Sellotape, but it's only 50p and, like so many others of these books in my arms, I've never seen it before. Kenzaburo Oë's *Nip the Buds, Shoot the Kids*, which Celeste tells me she's read after Andy recommended it. Caryl Phillips's *The European Tribe*. A John Cowper Powys novel, *After My Fashion*, that not only have I not seen before but Powys-lovers had not seen before 1980, despite its having been completed (and put aside) in 1919. Then, another white spine that I already have in the black of Picador Classics – Erich Maria Remarque's *All Quiet on the Western Front* – and a book I remember seeing somewhere but for some reason not buying, *Letters From a Faint-hearted Feminist*, 'introduced' by Jill Tweedie. And finally, José Saramago's *Baltasar and Blimunda*.

Am I imagining it or has a slight nervousness crept into Celeste's demeanour? Are her fingers searching under the counter for the panic button? Who is this raving lunatic? Why does he insist on showing her a picture on his phone of what he claims is his collection of more than 700 Picadors? She tots up the figures, knocks 50p off the Napoleón Baccino Ponce de León, which, you'll remember, only cost 50p to begin with. She says Andy has more Picadors where these came from and I'm already looking forward to making another visit to the Bookshop Experience, which turns out to be well named. Andy certainly has some gaps to fill on his shelves now, while my bag is full and I still have to walk a mile or so to the next shop on my list, not to mention four miles across the mudflats to Benfleet, if I'm to stick to the plan recommended by Gareth Evans, who advised me to come out here in the first place.

Luckily – and I don't often say this – the next shop is closed, but it looks good, so I'll drop in on my next visit. I realise that the home of *The Canal* author Lee Rourke is between where I am now and Leigh-on-Sea, where I will pick up the path across Hadleigh Marsh; it would be rude not to photograph his house and post it on Twitter with the message, 'Daddy, that strange man is outside the house again'. Having done so I descend to sea-level, then climb back up over the railway, and strike out across the marsh. The path meanders and time seems to slow down. I take numerous pictures of Canvey Island in honour of my former *Time Out* colleague Lesley McCave and, indeed, of

Lee Rourke, whose *Vulgar Things* was set there and who has, I see, responded to my tweet: 'HOLY SHIT!!!!!!!' he writes.

The sun comes out from behind the clouds and goes back in. To the right, toy trains pass beneath the castle on the hill. Crows and gulls commingle on the mudflats to my left. I stop and try to identify the call of a bird hiding in a bush some thirty yards distant. *Chup chup chup chup-chup-chup.* It shows itself: black head, white collar, brown and white body. I step off the path, telling myself I don't have time for this. I have to be back in London for a reading at Burley Fisher at 7pm. But what am I reading from, what am I promoting? My new collection, *Ornithology*, uncanny stories about birds. A bird call to me is a siren, drawing me from the path. I move closer and, as the black-headed bird flies off to a bush further away, I am reminded of a line in TH White's *The Goshawk*, which I bought in a Picador Classics edition from Bob's last year, for £4, but a James Marsh cover is worth £4: '. . . if you saw a bird . . . it had already seen you.' I follow it from bush to bush for a while and do what experience has taught me to do if immediate identification is impossible: make notes and check later.

On the train from Benfleet I try the RSPB online bird identifier: 'No matches found. Please try fewer search options.' I imagine it was an exotic migrant blown off course, stranded here. Tomorrow there will be armies of men with binoculars and telephoto lenses parking in the narrow lane by the cockle sellers at Leigh-on-Sea. When I get home and check the books I see that what I saw was a resident bird, after all, a reed bunting.

Wednesday 24 July 1996

I have to warn my mum that TV cameras have arrived to film my two brothers. It's possible that even in the dream I know I don't have any brothers. I go down to the basement bathroom where she's standing by the sink. I explain about the cameras – Melvyn Bragg is here, for example. Mum says she knew. She stands facing me in a black and white tiger-skin dress, which switches to a blue-green woollen dress that emphasises her incredibly narrow waist – I encircle it with my hands easily. I tell her she has to eat more (I also tell her she's switched dresses, which she denies).

Sitting with Mum watching fish being unloaded from a trawler – in some kind of indoor area. See loads of skate and monkfish and small flatfish. I'm saying she should eat a lot of this to build herself up. There's a bird among the catch. The captain fishes it out – it's an owl, but it's tiny. He says he wants to know how that got in there.

Standing with Jonathan Coe by the sea. He says a French film director, Patrick Norbert, wants me to provide a quote for him. He's sitting on a rock by the sea. He made films of Liz Jensen's books, says Jonathan. He made *Egg Dancing* and is doing *Darwin's Paradox*.

It's July 2017. Driving back to Manchester from an event in the Lake District gives me an opportunity to call in at two of the best second-hand bookshops in the north-west, if not the country. I can't remember what took me to the Carnforth Bookshop the first time I visited it, but I have now been several times. It's easily accessible both by road (just off the M6) and by rail (David Lean filmed *Brief Encounter* in the town's station, which, despite having been somewhat heritaged up, is still lovely).

The Carnforth Bookshop sells new books on the ground floor and second-hand books upstairs. The first book I find is a Picador, Christopher Hope's *Signs of the Heart: Love and Death in Languedoc*. On the back is a sticker with, on it, the name of the bookshop I'm in and the price, £6.99, which is the book's RRP. So, either a customer bought it, read it and sold it back to the shop, or it simply migrated up here from the ground floor. I pick out two other books – Thomas Healy's boxing memoir *A Hurting Business* (Picador) and Gordon Burn's novel *Alma Cogan*. It's inexplicable that I have never bought *Alma Cogan* – you see it often enough – when I think about how much I loved *Fullalove*.

The Carnforth Bookshop is tidy and well ordered. Yes, there are a lot of rooms, but you won't get lost, unlike six miles down the road in the Old Pier Bookshop in Morecambe. Twenty-six years ago, the owner, who calls himself Mr Bookshop on the shop's Facebook page, put a couple of shelves up in his mother's cafe. A quarter of a century later Mr Bookshop presides over an interior space designed by MC Escher. But the Old Pier Bookshop is not only a work of art; it's also a warm and welcoming shop packed full of reasonably priced books. While chaos might be your first impression, you soon start to spot some vestigial signs of category separation, but wherever gaps had been left, they have been filled with, it seems, random books, perhaps what was to hand, or what would fit the space. You wonder what would happen if they were all removed.

From scattered locations within the maze-like funhouse I find three Picadors – Andre Dubus's *Broken Vessels*, Eric Newby's *The Last Grain Race*, Hermann Hesse's *Demian* – and one Picador Classic, Hesse's *Siddhartha*. But that's not all. Three 1970s Penguins – two Andrea Newmans and a Françoise Sagan – and a Hardy Boys novel, *The Mystery of the Samurai Sword*, which I see is number 58 in Franklin W Dixon's series of children's novels about brothers Frank and Joe Hardy and the various scrapes they get into. This makes me think about my impulse to collect these books. I've got about ten Hardy Boys books. Maybe one or two have been mine since I was a child and I enjoyed reading the Hardy Boys' adventures. The others I've bought mainly in recent years. I have no intention of rereading them. And there are at least 58. It doesn't make any sense. It's not rational.

A similar thing is going on with Hermann Hesse's *Siddhartha*. Once I buy this Picador Classics edition, I will own three copies of the 1922 novel, the other two being the 1973 and 1998 Picador editions. If I am ever going to read *Siddhartha*, I hardly need three copies (the same translation features in each). But I can justify the retention of each one according to the parameters of my process. If the collecting impulse itself is irrational, the ways in which I am pursuing my aims are, I think, perfectly rational. If I am going mad, I am at least doing it in an ordered way.

If the Old Pier Bookshop represents the collecting impulse, the Carnforth Bookshop is an analogue for my modus operandi. I wouldn't want one without the other; I need both.

Saturday 22 February 2020
Faversham Literary Festival, Kent.
Two attendees, older ladies.
First lady: Melvyn Bragg was supposed to be coming, but he's not coming now.
Second lady: Oh. Well, I'm off to the toilet now and then I'm off for the bus.

Broadhurts in Southport is wonderful, of course, with its many rooms on numerous floors, its obvious serious commitment to bookselling, the smell of books everywhere, but apart from among the Agatha Christies and back issues of *London Magazine*, I never seem to find very much that I want. When I visited Southport in October 2016, it was Freshfields Animal Rescue charity shop that surprised me.

The space was large, extending back into the gloom, with shelving on the walls and free-standing units, and plastic crates that slid out from under the lowest shelves. I started looking at the books, but there was a quality to the manager's voice that made it hard to ignore as he talked to his volunteers. I slid the black Picador Classics spine of William Faulkner's *Sanctuary* out from between, say, Michel Faber's *The Apple* (unusual and perhaps even unique by beginning with ten pages of extracts from the author's fan mail) and, possibly, the prize-winning *Charlotte Gray* by my fellow Bad Sex laureate Sebastian Faulks, into my left hand, where it was joined by Jean Rhys's *Voyage in the Dark* (Penguin, one of a lovely series of illustrated covers by Faith Jacques). Three times I heard the manager say he was going outside, but he never made it. I added another Picador Classics title, Frederick Rolfe's *Hadrian the Seventh*, to the pile. Walking by me, the manager said not to miss the 'emergency' department, at the far end of the room and around the corner. And would I like a cup of tea? Yes, please. In the 'emergency' department – stacks of unsorted books on shelves, on the floor, piled this way, that way – I found two Picadors, Louise Erdrich's *The Beet Queen* and Robert McLiam Wilson's *Ripley Bogle*.

Working out what to charge me as he looked at the prices in the front of the books, the manager said he wouldn't have put Faulkner in Classics, which were £1 dearer. 'Only Penguin count as classics,' he said. 'But then there's Morrissey's *Autobiography . . .*' We laughed, although I hadn't thought it was funny at the time. 'Virago Classics,' he went on, 'only five per cent of those really were classics.'

Harsh words. My first Virago, *Winter Hunger* by Ann Tracy, was given to me – lent to me, really, but I did at least offer to return it – by Sue Zlosnik, head of the English Department and a very genial and agreeable boss when I started working at Manchester Met, or MMU as we were allowed to call it then. My second Virago, and the first one I bought (from Oxfam Dalston), was *F/32: The Second Coming* by Eurudice. I bought it partly for its inscription ('From me to you at winter solstice Moo Dec '97 with much love to ya'), partly for its inclusion (a Christmas card made out of a three of spades playing card, 'No. 3 Triple Goddess') and partly for its attention-grabbing opening line, which I am not going to quote as I hope my mum is reading this.

Inspired by my former MA student Sue McLeod, who had a large collection, I graduated to collecting Virago Modern Classics. Popping into Oxfam Books & Music Islington one bright February morning in 2019 (in 'spring sunshine', according to my notes, suggesting winter had been going on long enough), I couldn't resist Stevie Smith's *Novel on Yellow Paper*. I love that title in the same way as I love the titles of David Pirie's *Mystery Story* (and indeed MJ Fitzgerald's short story 'Mystery Story'), Richard Rayner's *Murder Book* and M Ageyev's *Novel With Cocaine*, which appeared in Picador with one of Russell Mills' best covers – mostly white with a distinctly powdery texture . . . The fact that *Novel on Yellow Paper* contained an inclusion, a page from a hotel memo pad from the Golden Age of Athens, with an inner London phone number, plus international prefix, written on it in ballpoint, was a bonus.

Friday 29 December 1995
Hanging around Blackwell's bookshop on Charing Cross Road with a friend. We're dressed smartly, as if for some function. Blackwell's has become a Greek specialist bookshop, though they still have lots of books of general interest including, for example, *Counterparts*, because I've got a copy and it's in my dad's old blue and white canvas holdall. I think, I must contact Athina Lazou in Athens and get her to get all her friends to buy it here to boost my sales.

'The white spines were sacrosanct,' Jacqueline Graham writes to me in an email.

Jacqueline Graham joined Picador on 2 January 1978 as chief press officer. 'Titles were very different in those days. There were only four directors: managing, deputy managing, editorial and publishing. The editorial director was Sonny Mehta.'

The first Picador title Graham worked on 'big time' was *Dispatches* by Michael Herr, published as a Picador paperback original (Pan were not contractually allowed to publish hardbacks) in March 1978. 'Michael Herr came over and it became a bestseller.' Other paperback originals included *A Boy's Own Story* by Edmund White, *The Serial* by Cyra McFadden, *The Woman Warrior* by Maxine Hong Kingston and *The Wind Blows Away Our Words* by Doris Lessing. Graham also worked on paperback editions by a range of authors, organising tours for the likes of Salman Rushdie, Julian Barnes, Graham Swift, Toni Morrison, Michael Ondaatje, Bruce Chatwin and Clive James.

'It was an amazing time, most especially that first decade with Sonny. We were a small, very tightly knit team back then.'

I'm struck by those words – 'The white spines were sacrosanct' – both because they reflect my own feeling about the imprint and because there were times when the 'rule', as Graham puts it, was broken. There are what I call the anomalies and they appear as early as 1973 with John Gardner's *Grendel*, on which Michael Leonard's illustration extends from the front cover to the back, across the spine, against a white background with black type, at least, as normal. In 1974 along came Russell Hoban's *The Lion of Boaz-Jachin and Jachin-Boaz* with John Hurford's illustration of the eponymous animal against a pink and orange sky covering front, back and spine, requiring the Picador logo to be reversed out in white type, title and author remaining black. Dee Brown's *Bury My Heart at Wounded Knee* and Albert Goldman's *Ladies and Gentlemen, Lenny Bruce!!*, in 1975 and 1976 respectively, had wraparound covers and even changed the typeface on the spine. The logo on the Goldman was yellow against black.

I shelve my Picadors together, in white bookcases. I think they look pretty good. I also shelve my orange Penguins together, and I shelve my green Penguins together. I shelve my Picador Classics together. Each of these collections is a different colour, but I will push back, in politely expressed frustration, against suggestions that my book shelves are colour coded. Some people create a rainbow effect with their books. Maybe they start with red and shade into orange and then yellow and so on and that's fine, each to their own – indeed, some charity shops, like the RSPCA in Stoke Newington, have started doing it – but it's not for me. I shelve by imprint, as far as these collections are concerned. My other books are all over the place, but mostly alphabetical by author, obviously. Fiction, anyway.

The Picador bookcases – various sizes of Billy from Ikea – are deep and allow for double stacking of B-format paperbacks. It makes sense that the shadow collection should fill up some of that space behind, but that's also where the anomalies live, the ones described above and the rest: the wraparound early McEwans, the odd lilac-jacketed edition of Julian Barnes's *Before She Met Me* with atypical type on the spine, McEwan's *A Move Abroad* with blue band somewhat unnecessarily bleeding on to the spine (it stays off the back cover, so why stick it on the spine?). *A Move Abroad*, which bundles together an oratorio and a screenplay, also has that faint brown-flecked thing going on on the cover and spine that a few Picadors have. Maybe it's meant to resemble parchment, but it just looks a bit oatmealy to me and if there's a choice between an edition with it in evidence and an edition without it, or a copy on which it's thankfully faded away to near invisibility, then that's an easy choice to make. Barry Lopez's *Arctic Dreams* is another one where the spine is compromised by wraparound elements. The illustrations are by Russell Mills, who I'm a big fan of, but I can't condone the interference with the white spine. Next to Lopez in the main collection is Anita Loos with *Gentlemen Prefer Blondes*, and they're neighbours in the anomalies section as well because there's a back-to-back omnibus edition combining *Gentlemen Prefer Blondes* with *But Gentlemen Marry Brunettes*. The spine reads both ways, with two logos and titles running in opposite directions, so you can choose which way to shelve it. I choose to shelve it out of sight, for all its enjoyable novelty, in fact precisely for its enjoyable novelty.

Jonathan Schell's *The Fate of the Earth*, a non-fiction book about the very real – especially so in 1982 – danger of nuclear annihilation, was given an entirely black cover with white type, for understandable reasons, but it goes in the anomalies section, for, I hope, understandable reasons. Also sporting a black spine with white type and white Picador logo, not a Picador Classics logo, is the copy of Faulkner's *The Sound and the Fury* referred to earlier that I had been unable to find in either my regular Picador collection or on the Picador Classics shelves. This is why. This book has a few cousins among the main collection, Picador books sporting front cover designs lifted from the corresponding Picador Classics editions, but given white spines.

There are more, but I can sense the reader's patience wearing thin. So thin, perhaps, that not even a Mehta-textual joke can save the day. You probably don't want to hear about the first time I saw a Picador logo in horizontal rather than vertical orientation on the spine. You almost don't care that I couldn't believe my eyes. I was in one of the shipping containers at Sharston Books and my eyes alighted on a Picador spine. Title and author were new to me – *The Rules of Seduction* by Daniel L Magida – and so was the position of the logo. The book was lying flat, but the logo was standing up, on its end. It was all wrong. It wasn't only that it looked fake; it was a little disturbing. I found I didn't want to look at it and I certainly didn't want to buy it, so I left it. One of the many good things about Sharston Books was you could leave a book on the shelf and be fairly certain that if you changed your mind later you'd be able to go back and find it. I never shared one of those shipping containers with another customer. Although, you could never quite be sure that, in the meantime, Sharston Books wouldn't have turned into the version of itself that Conrad Williams conjures up in his short story, 'The Fold', in which CCTV collides with taxidermy, or the more benign manifestation explored in Neil Campbell's Manchester Fiction Prize short-listed story 'Needle in a Haystack', which had me in tears by the end with its vision of a world soon to be if not already lost.

The Picador logo is a thing of beauty, but let's take it apart. The meaning of the word – a person on a horse, armed with a lance, who supports the matador in a bullfight – is neither a bird (Penguin, Puffin, Pelican, Flamingo), nor any other kind of animal (Panther), but something created to help kill one. (The logo of Hutchinson, one of the UK's oldest imprints, is a bull.) The 'pica', in typography, is a unit of length measuring one-sixth of an inch, but the rules above and below the word, or either side of it when viewed vertically, are revealed, when you look closely, to be not just rules, but lances with sharp points.

I went back and bought Magida's *The Rules of Seduction* and thereafter would buy a Picador with an incorrectly oriented logo whenever I saw one. On 15 April 2017 in Oxfam Bookshop Chorlton I found a copy of *The Water of the Hills*, an omnibus containing two novels by Marcel Pagnol, *Jean de Florette* and *Manon of the Springs*, with a dodgy logo. The following month, I was in Edinburgh on my way back from leading a private week at Moniack Mhor, Scotland's creative writing centre and one of my favourite places on earth, where, under normal circumstances, I go every year with one of my favourite groups of people. In Edinburgh Books I saw another Pagnol with a horizontal logo, but I didn't buy it because the shop is one of those with signs up advising customers to leave bags (handbags excepted) at the desk. When I checked later, it was the same Pagnol, so I was glad I hadn't bought it. I also have Grass's *The Flounder*, Bulgakov's *The Master and Margarita*, Fowles's *The Magus* and Yeats's *Collected Poems*, all with naughty logos. In the case of all these books apart from the Magida, I have 'right' and 'wrong' versions.

I've got two Picadors without any logo at all: a 1977 edition of *Household Tales* by the Brothers Grimm illustrated by Mervyn Peake, and the 1979 edition (ninth printing) of McEwan's *In Between the Sheets* with unmade bed but no nude model.

For some reason I am more forgiving of spelling errors, which will be a surprise to any of my authors or students who might have read this far, but everyone makes mistakes. This book will no doubt contain a few. Research conducted at the University of My Flat has shown that if you are going to make a typo on a book cover it's most likely going to be either on the back, in the artist credit, or on the spine, in the author's name. It's very easy to miss a mistake on a spine if you are looking at it as part of a layout on a screen and giving it a quick check without turning it through 90 degrees. I feel certain Olivers (sic) Sacks would have taken a philosophical view regarding the minor error on the spine of *A Leg to Stand On*, while Dennis (sic) Johnson will have been mollified by the correction incorporated into the second printing of *Already Dead*. I have both copies of the Johnson, good and bad, but both live in the anomalies section thanks to the red band allowed to trail over the spine. Micheal (sic) Kelly's *Martyrs' Day* is the most entertaining, offering two spellings of his first name on the cover and changing it in the author biog to Matthew. 'Tonight, Matthew, I'm going to be . . .'

Thursday 1 October 1998

I had Charlie with me at work and took him with me when I was going to have lunch. I didn't have the buggy, but I thought he would sit on a proper chair and be good. I saw my former agent Clarissa Rushdie, who asked me to write a quote for a book by a Beat writer whose work I didn't know, but it was an opportunity to vent my spleen against the literary establishment. My sister Julie was looking after Charlie. I looked in his ear and saw that it was caked with mud and that little winged creatures were crawling out of it.

8

Names & inscriptions

Saturday 3 May 1997

[Night after Labour's staggering general election victory during which I stayed up all night, first at Kim Newman's, then Sarah Guy's, then drove down to Southbank to join in celebrations outside Royal Festival Hall . . .]

I was going out with a small group of men. Out on the town sort of thing. Somewhere in America. I was looking around for a brochure or some literature with the address of the place we were staying. I found something and started writing it down.

This switched from something that was happening – and that I was a part of – to a story or chapter of a novel written by a middle-aged man on an Arvon course. I thought it was OK, fairly promising, but his own comments on it clouded my judgment. He clearly thought it was very good indeed. 'It's got a lightness,' he said. The more he insisted it was good, the less convinced I became.

What author would not be pleased to board a train and see someone reading one of their books? The next best thing might be hearing from a friend that they saw someone reading your book. That happened to me with my novel *Antwerp*.

Then I found out, some months later, that the reader was a close friend.

The next best thing after that might be finding an inscribed second-hand copy of one of your books, ideally not a signed copy dedicated, by you, to another close friend, but one bought by a stranger and given to another stranger with a message, something like, maybe, *This is brilliant. You'll love it. I did*.

Shortly before moving from London back to Manchester, in 2003, I found a copy of my first novel, *Counterparts*, in the bookstalls on the Southbank under Waterloo Bridge, outside what used to be called the NFT and is now known as the BFI. In it is written, 'Anne, a book about desolation is probably not what you need right now, but I bought it a couple of weeks ago. How was I to know? Happy birthday. Lots of love, Steph xxx.'

How was I to know?

My copy of *The Silent Executioner* by Marcel Allain and Pierre Souvestre, published by Picador in 1988, was previously owned by Rowland Barker. This is unlikely to be Mrs Rowland Barker, donor of various objects to the British Museum and granddaughter of Frances Turner Palgrave, poet and compiler of *The Golden Treasury*, because the dates don't seem to quite work. In January 1977, WL St George became the owner of what is now my copy of Samuel Beckett's *Murphy*, with a John Holmes cover picturing the head of a blond man with matching gag growing out of the back of a rocking chair apparently made of stone, with grass for a cushion.

Richard Brautigan's *Trout Fishing in America* is inscribed, 'To Robert, Love, Drusilla xx 10.6.79.' A marriage notice appeared in the *Times* on 11 April 2009 announcing that Robert Broderick, 36, a partner in a private client law firm, would marry Drusilla Stacy Waddy, 35, a personal assistant and translator on 11 July. That would make Drusilla and Robert around five and six in 1979, so, again, it seems unlikely.

Trout Fishing in America includes a description of a second-hand bookshop that will remind readers who like to visit second-hand bookshops, which I'm guessing if you've got this far means you, of a certain kind of second-hand bookshop. 'The bookstore was a parking lot for used graveyards. Thousands of graveyards were parked in rows like cars. Most of the books were out of print, and no one wanted to read them any more and the people who had read the books had died or forgotten about them, but through the organic process of music the books had become virgins again. They wore their ancient copyrights like new maidenheads.' It reminds me of Halewood & Sons on Friargate in Preston. There are two second-hand bookshops on Friargate bearing the name Halewood, but I have never seen them both open at the same time, suggesting the possibility that the proprietor shuttles between the two. One is situated on a corner and is slightly further out of town. I visited in January 2017 and found only an Agatha Christie, *The Murder at the Vicarage*, with a Tom Adams cover, it should by now go without saying. The next time I'm in Preston, April 2019, it's the same branch of Halewood's that's open. There are even more books than last time. It will soon be impossible to move around in the shop. I remark on this to the owner. 'I just love books,' he says. I buy Kafka's *The Trial* in the 1970 Penguin Classics edition, with Lotte B Prechner's *Ruins* on the cover.

My copy of Bulgakov's *The Master and Margarita* complete with correctly oriented logo, a 1997 Picador edition, has, on the flyleaf, a postcode: TS18 5AW. If we assume that the book's former owner resided at this postcode – Greens Grove, Stockton-on-Tees – we can have a virtual wander up this charming cul-de-sac and think about where, precisely, the book might have lived. In one of the bungalows that line both sides of the western end of Greens Grove, perhaps, or, beyond the Sea Scouts' meeting hall in one of the bigger, detached houses at the eastern end of the road? At first it seems like there's not much to go on, but then, on a second pass – how could I have missed it? – stretched out on a window ledge, between net curtain and glass pane, in one of the bungalows on the north side of the road, his back arched in readiness for standing on his hind legs and striking a haughty pose, is Behemoth, Bulgakov's talking cat.

A William Burroughs Reader edited by John Calder was previously owned, in 1984, by N Hargreaves. I shelve my Beckett, Burroughs and Henry Miller 'readers' under B and M. I wonder if I ought to shelve them under C for Calder, who edited all three. Calvino's *If on a Winter's Night a Traveller* was given, as a birthday present, on 28 April 1986, to Ruth by someone with an illegible signature. In 1987, G Karam was the owner of the Elias Canetti omnibus *The Conscience of Words & Earwitness*, which came into my possession in August 2019 when I bought it from the wonderful Beckside Books in Penrith along with two Virago Modern Classics, *Bid Me to Live* by HD and *The Passion of New Eve* by Angela Carter. They always have a good number of Virago Modern Classics in Beckside Books. The Canetti is translated from the German by Joachim Neugroschel, who edited the Picador anthology *Great Works of Jewish Fantasy*, which has a great cover by Robert Mason.

I've got two Picador editions of Peter Carey's *Exotic Pleasures* with different covers. The Russell Mills is my favourite – a surreal landscape of orange earth, mauve rocks and a brown wall or shield with an eye peeping out of it – but it's the Andrzej Krauze-illustrated edition that was given to Kate by Anne with the inscription 'Something to read on the plane. Have a wonderful time – you truly deserve it. Much love'. I've also got two editions of Angela Carter's *Nights at the Circus*, with covers by Louise Brierley and Jean-Christian Knaff; I like both, but only one was given by Elizabeth to Catherine King for Christmas in 1985, and that's the Knaff.

Maybe this is a relatively safe moment to mention that I didn't really get on with Angela Carter's *Heroes and Villains*, one of Picador's first eight titles. I like Carter's short stories and this was my first of her novels. It's hardly long, but I found it a slog. Perhaps I just don't massively like post-apocalyptic novels, the world being created from scratch, the anything-goes approach to narrative.

Matt Simpson used to own *The Stories of Raymond Carver*, while Bruce Chatwin's *In Patagonia* was given to Barney by Davena for Christmas in 1994. Chatwin's *The Songlines* was Richard Clegg's. Paul gave Jill *Sweet Freedom: The Struggle For Women's Liberation* by Anna Coote and Beatrix Campbell for her birthday in July 1982. I was very happy to find *Stockhausen: Conversations With the Composer* by Jonathan Cott in Oxfam Books & Music Islington in April 2018, as it's an early Picador, from 1974, in good condition, and I had not heard of it or seen it before. It was previously owned by a Patricia Shaw. In 2011, possibly the same Patricia Shaw was inviting proposals for papers to be given at a conference at a London college celebrating Cornelius Cardew, a composer of experimental music and, between 1958 and 1960, Stockhausen's assistant.

'I wanted to get you a pack of cards,' writes Robert, on the inside front cover of Rachel Cusk's *The Country Life*, to an unnamed recipient, 'not MAGIC (however tempting) or playing cards, but "A Pack of Cards", the Penelope Lively short story collection. However, none of the bookshops I tried had it in stock so you've got this instead. She's one of my favourite contemporary writers. Hope you enjoy . . .'

Another early Picador, from 1975, was Salvador Dalí's novel, *Hidden Faces*. My copy was previously owned by a Marshall Ronald. In 2003, a painting worth £30m by another great artist, Leonardo da Vinci, was stolen from Drumlanrig Castle in Scotland. Among the five men accused of trying to extort money for the painting's return was a lawyer by the name of Marshall Ronald. No case was proven and Ronald later sued the Duke of Buccleuch for payment he insisted was due to him. His bid was unsuccessful.

I'd put money on it being the same Marshall Ronald. Maybe not £30m, but a couple of quid.

'Max,' wrote Oli, on the inside front cover of Alain de Botton's first novel *Essays in Love*, 'hope you enjoy this. I did. A lot. Take care.' That was dated 23.11.01. De Botton's second novel, *The Romantic Movement*, has the name of a former owner also on its inside front cover. 'Rosie Bain, Oct 1997.' There's a Rosie Bain listed in the Federation of Holistic Therapies directory. If holistic therapists aren't reading Alain de Botton, then I don't understand anything about the world and should probably book an appointment.

EL Doctorow's *Ragtime* was given to Chip at Christmas 1982 by his mum and dad. *The Waterworks*, by the same author, has what looks like a dedication on the title page: 'for biyi, Brixton, 1/2/98'. Could this be Biyi Bandele, whose novel *The Street*, in which the street is based on Brixton High Street, was published in 1999 by Picador? My orange-jacketed paperback edition came out the following year, by which time the white spine was more or less history.

I bought *The Novellas of Martha Gellhorn*, a 1994 Picador omnibus edition, from one of my favourite second-hand bookshops in Todmorden. OK, that's a joke. For clarity, I should have inserted a comma after 'bookshops', but, joking aside, there are two excellent second-hand bookshops in Todmorden, Lancashire, which is quite a thing, because just up the road in Hebden Bridge in West Yorkshire they no longer have even one (although they do have a new bookshop and some charity shops that sell books). Tod has Border Books and Lyall's, a few minutes' walk apart. It was in Lyall's I found the Gellhorn. The cover has the remains of a sticky label on it, and attempts to remove same have resulted in some loss of the top layer of the card, but, you can't tell until you look closely, because the cover painting – Willem de Kooning's *Door to the River* – is one of those rough-hewn abstract works that look slapdash even though they're probably not and it disguises the damage.

I started cleaning second-hand books years before the pandemic took hold. I use furniture polish and a duster. For stubborn stains and residue from sticky labels someone recommended Sticky Stuff Remover, which usually works, but a little of that goes a long way and attempts to apply just a small amount can lead to disaster. I've learned it's best to apply it to the duster rather than the book cover. Other solvent-based solutions are available.

Someone has added to Martha Gellhorn's author biog, in small, neat handwriting, 'Born St Louis, 1908. Married at one time to Ernest Hemingway. Mainly worked as a war correspondent,' which reminds me of the time many years ago when

I found a hardback edition of one of Derek Raymond's 'Factory' novels in Kilburn Library. A borrower had defaced the book throughout, writing angry comments in green ballpoint. The one that sticks in the mind as a warning against inventing names for bars in fiction is 'No such pub cunt head'. It's the thought of this reader coming across one of my books that has led me mainly to write a form of what in recent years has started to become known, rather annoyingly, as autofiction.

Germaine Greer's *Sex & Destiny: The Politics of Human Fertility* was acquired by Elizabeth Parker on 21 April 1988 in Melbourne. It came into my possession on 3 June 2017 along with *The Greenpeace Chronicle* by Robert Hunter and *Picture This* by Joseph Heller, at the New Broom Community Shop & Hub, Ullapool, where three-for-two was given a new spin as three-for-£2.

Woody Guthrie's *Bound For Glory* is another early Picador, from 1974. I would have a hard time tracking down former owner 'Geoff'; cover artist Graham Dean, whose oddly dream-like portrait of the author makes you want to stick on *Dust Bowl Ballads*, has a website stuffed with extraordinary paintings. On the inside front cover of Knut Hamsun's love story *Victoria*, Kenny writes to Dinah, 'Don't forget to keep a fire extinguisher by your side when reading this book . . .!?' I was happy when, on 10 February 2018, I discovered a second Oxfam shop in Bath. 'To Sue, for idle moments, love and best wishes, David. May 1985,' it says on the flyleaf of *The Selected Letters of Anton Chekhov*, which I found there. The inside front cover and flyleaf of Tama Janowitz's *A Cannibal in Manhattan* are covered in New York phone numbers. There's one for Albert's Printing, one for Wilson/Wenzel, two for Dennis and one for 2N, 30E 9th Street and University Place.

I can't believe I can't find any trace of Oriel Fawls Boyle who owned James Joyce's *Ulysses* in 1998. Next to *Ulysses* on the shelf is Carl Jung's *Man and His Symbols* with a name, Evelyn, and a mobile phone number. Was it her book or did she give her number to the book's owner, who reached for the first thing to write it on? What would Jung make of Paramount Books in Manchester, where I bought my copy of his book? Paramount Books feels like a link to the past. 'No mobile phones,' say a number of notices inside the shop. You wouldn't be able to hear yourself speak anyway, as there is usually fairly loud music playing, jazz or classical. The proprietor is pleasant and affable without being over-friendly. He pushes your change towards you on a tray that sits on the counter like a coin pusher arcade game next to a basket from which he will offer you a piece of fruit. Usually I will take a banana or an orange. On one occasion the choice included heads of garlic.

Lisa MacMaster writes her name boldly on the flyleaf of Arthur Koestler's *The Roots of Coincidence*. George Lamming's *Natives of My Person*, which I bought from Jambala in Bethnal Green in 2017, belonged to Alex Josephy in 1976. Probably not the same Alex Josephy as the poet, author of *Naked Since Faversham* and other collections, who actually does divide her time between London and Tuscany, but you never know.

Two of my copies of Ian McEwan's *First Love, Last Rites* have been written in. The Russell Mills cover opens to reveal 'Adam – Merry Christmas 1988, Love Vicky'. A revised 1991 edition with a cover designed by Kyle Burris and photography by Robin Cracknell was owned, in September 1997, by Craig David. That would make the singer-songwriter only 16 when he read McEwan's powerful debut collection. I was probably four years older than that.

It could be another Craig David.

Robin Cracknell's photographic covers for three of Robert McCrum's novels, which are separated from McEwan only by two different editions of AG Macdonell's *England, Their England*, I find moodily atmospheric. Cracknell's website reveals he also provided the cover image for the Vintage paperback edition of *Arc d'X* by Steve Erickson, whose name would be one of the answers I would give if asked why I prefer hanging around second-hand bookshops to visiting new ones.

Candia McWilliam's *A Case of Knives*, her first novel, has been signed by the author.

Gabriel García Márquez's *One Hundred Years of Solitude*, previously owned by 'Di-Di Wheatley-Beatley', appears to have been dedicated to her by the author on the inside front cover, signing on his author photo no less: 'To my Darling Diane, Gabriel Garcia Marquez xx.' Except that the author's actual signature, which can be seen online, for some reason looks more like 'GA Ball 2'. Diane has made a further intervention, adding a line to the author biog: 'And is currently writing another boring book!' On the last page of the novel, perplexingly, she has written, 'Artaud + Camus.'

Belinda Brittain staked her claim to ownership of Eric Newby's *Departures and Arrivals* in extremely neat pencil on 27 January 2000. Wanda Newby, married to Eric Newby, had already signed *Peace and War: Growing Up in Fascist Italy*, 'To Millard with best wishes', on 2 April 1992, when I bought it from Oxfam Original on Bold Street in Liverpool on 11 December 2016. My copy of *Black Water* by Joyce Carol Oates, I'm mildly surprised to see, is signed by the author to me, until I remember handing it to her and asking her to do exactly that, when we shared a platform at the Dublin

Ghost Story Festival and no one had to call security to ask me to leave.

Caryl Phillips's *Cambridge* and *The European Tribe* were owned by George Mason and Derek Brookfield respectively. Wendy Millyard owned Thomas Pynchon's *V.* Jonathan Raban's *Coasting* (Robin Cracknell's photography again) appears to have been owned by a mobile phone number beginning 07900. Derrick A Pike, who wrote his name in the front of Jonathan Schell's *The Abolition* in February 1985, is the author of *Thoughts of an Anarcho-Pacifist*, one copy of which is, at the time of writing, available via a popular online bookseller for £15. Jeremy Seal, meanwhile, has signed *A Fez of the Heart*, overwriting his own name on the title page.

Natsume Soseki's *Light and Darkness*, the Japanese author's last, unfinished novel, was given to 'aj' by 'jayne' on 16 September 1989, 'with all my love'. I bought it from Walden Books on Harmood Street in Camden Town, on New Year's Day 2017, along with two other Picadors, a Saint-Exupéry omnibus and MJ Fitzgerald's *Ropedancer*. Being realistic, I may never read *Light and Darkness* (almost 400 pages and still not finished) or the Saint-Exupéry, but I read *Ropedancer*, a short story collection, in April 2020 while enjoying 'outdoor recreation' or 'personal exercise', or whatever the government called going for a walk in the first national lockdown, and found that it contained some outstanding stories, in particular the opening story, 'Creases', about a man who folds up his girlfriend and puts her in a box when he's going away, and 'Mystery Story', and 'The Fire Eater', for its metafictional commentary on writing: 'Someone has to read these pages. I thought I wielded the power because I invent the story but in fact the life of my words, the neutral of Barbara and the fire-eater are mere conductors, potential light: I need you, to turn on the switch. Words and events are not enough, however live the words might be, however carefully manipulated the events. Without you neither Barbara nor the words are more than black decorating white, and I, struggling with both, am as useless as a plug without a socket. Someone has to read: I can play with the story, twist the copper hair this way and that, but you have the final word.' Brad Bigelow posts a very fine review of *Ropedancer* on his Neglected Books Page website.

I returned to Walden Books in January 2019, during which year proprietor David Tobin would celebrate his business's fortieth anniversary, to buy a first edition hardback of Giles Gordon's 1972 novel *About a Marriage* with an inscription: 'Ilsa, Mistress of my literary affections. What else? Love, Giles. 17 January 1974.' Ilsa, Gordon's widow Maggie McKernan and daughter Hattie Gordon both tell me later, will have been Ilsa Yardley, Gordon's agent for many years. In a moving obituary published online at BookBrunch, dated 3 October 2014, Penny Hoare and Angela Sheehan wrote of Ilsa Yardley, 'She did not do things by halves: she always offered champagne to her guests and she chain-smoked dozens of cigarettes a day.' Indeed, when I riffle through the pages of *About a Marriage* today, seven years after the death of its owner, there's still the faintest smell of cigarettes.

I don't know where I bought CK Stead's *All Visitors Ashore*, but I'm certain I did buy it somewhere, despite the inscription on the flyleaf: 'To Nick, Happy birthday 1986, Andrew.'

Notting Hill's Book & Comic Exchange is another shop that has been a regular haunt for many years, in spite of its level of customer service. If they ever close this place, where will I go to be made to feel about two inches tall? On 13 December 2016

I bought five Picadors: *Maiden Castle* by John Cowper Powys, *Night Beat* by Mikal Gilmore, *A Crooked Field* by Colm O'Gaora, *Awakenings* by Oliver Sacks and *Virtually Normal: An Argument About Homosexuality* by Andrew Sullivan. On the flyleaf of the latter I read, 'RODNEY ARCHER, LONDON, NOVEMBER '96.' I would put a ton on this being actor, playwright and former Spitalfields resident Rodney Archer, who died in 2015. There's a lovely short documentary on YouTube about Archer and his relationship with his eighteenth-century Fournier Street town-house, directed by Ed Beck and David Mead, entitled *Spirit of the House*.

Emma Tennant's *The Bad Sister* was the property of Lorna Tennent, who signed her name in green ink, in tiny, careful handwriting, in February 1984. I read *The Bad Sister* in April 2019 and didn't have a clue, for most of the time, what was going on. The main part of the novel is a long account by a character, Jane Wild, who is supposed to be mad. Wild's narrative veers from lucid to hallucinatory and is, of course, unreliable, but not in a good way. This edition has a great cover by Grizelda Holderness. There's another edition with a detail from Frida Kahlo's *The Two Fridas* on the cover, which is also great, but if you told me I could only keep one of them, I'd keep Grizelda Holderness.

A Chinese Anthology edited by Raymond Van Over was once owned by Peter Eastman, who adds, 'Troutbeck 1976,' on the inside front cover. Somewhat disappointingly, this is not the same Peter Eastman who is the author of *Advanced Buddhist Metaphysics: Exercises in Sceptical Spirituality*, published in February 2021. I felt sure that it would be.

Gregor von Rezzori's *The Death of My Brother Abel*, which Picador did after their edition of the same author's later novel *Memoirs of an Anti-Semite*, is another Joachim Neugroschel translation. My copy is inscribed, '10/12/86. Dear Omi, I hope you enjoy this book and the next year, lots of love, Daniel.'

I bought my copy of Edmund White's *The Beautiful Room is Empty* from the Book Palace in Canterbury on 13 October 2016.

The older couple who ran the shop were friendly and keen to chat. They asked how long it was since I'd last been to Canterbury. The late 1980s, I said, or early '90s. I had been using an optician, Alan J Drever, who operated from some kind of communal space in a civic-style building in Canterbury. I would buy old frames from Camden or Greenwich markets and he would get them glazed for me with flat prescription lenses, since he and I agreed that an old frame that would have had flat lenses in the old days wouldn't look right with convex lenses. The couple told me my optician was probably based in the Sidney Cooper Centre. That rang a bell, I said.

The shop had a great selection of books. I picked out a couple of Penguins – Robert Graves' *The Shout* and Edna O'Brien's *August is a Wicked Month* – and four Picadors – Tom Wolfe's *The Right Stuff*, Joseph Heller's *Picture This*, Norman Mailer's *Ancient Evenings* and Edmund White's *The Beautiful Room is Empty*. These added up to £10, but the man charged me £9.

Adrian Howells was born in Sittingbourne in 1962. He attended Borden Grammar School in his home town, then teacher training college near Wakefield. From a young age he had suffered bouts of depression. He did a range of work from panto to performance art, becoming close friends with Leigh Bowery. Offered a role at the Citizens' Theatre, Glasgow, he moved to Scotland. A decade on, he started developing a series of ground-breaking one-to-one shows combining aspects of theatre and performance. He would interact with audiences as his female alter-ego, Adrienne, although, as his practice developed, he allowed Adrian to return to centre stage. As a theatre maker and artist he was hugely admired and respected, and, as a teacher and mentor, greatly loved. He had continued to struggle with depression and on 16 March 2014 took his own life. He was survived by his parents and his brother Julian.

On the flyleaf of *The Beautiful Room is Empty*, in strong, confident capitals, is the name Adrian Howells.

9

Double acts

Thursday 3 April 2007
In a literary magazine, a letter or a review of something by Nicholas Royle. It confuses me and the other Nicholas Royle in a way that I find entertaining. The byline is Nicholas Royle (17 ½). I think, in the dream, I'll have to get in touch with him, get him to help us promote our book.

I knew there was another one, another Nicholas Royle, but he wrote completely different stuff, so it was all right.

At the end of the 1980s or the beginning of the 1990s I sent one or two stories to a lovely little magazine called *Sunk Island Review* edited by Michael Blackburn. I enclosed a stamped addressed envelope, but didn't hear back. Some time later, I received a letter from the other Nicholas Royle. It was strange, seeing the name typed at the bottom of the letter. It was my name and yet, suddenly, it wasn't. The signature was different. That should have made it less strange, but it made it stranger. I noticed that the large envelope in which he had sent his letter also contained my stories, the ones I had sent to Michael Blackburn. The other Nicholas Royle explained. By coincidence, he had also submitted some stories to *Sunk Island Review* at the same time. All the stories had been rejected and sent back to him. My address was on mine, which meant he could return mine to me and make contact.

The reason for my being in Canterbury, at the end of the last chapter, on 13 October 2016, was to talk to Danny Rhodes's creative writing students at Canterbury Christ Church University. I'm referring to Danny Rhodes the author of *Asboville*, *Soldier Boy* and *Fan*, not Dan Rhodes the author of *Timoleon Vieta Come Home*, *This is Life* and *When the Professor Got Stuck in the Snow*. I have never met Dan Rhodes, despite having been to Buxton many times, where I think he lives. I imagine he must visit Scrivener's, surely one of the ten best second-hand bookshops in the north of England. On a visit there on 12 February 2017, a snowy day in that part of Derbyshire, I bought Ovid's *Metamorphoses*, which I had been looking for, as previously discussed, and Francis Stuart's *Black List, Section H* (King Penguin), which I had seen in Pages of Hackney (also as previously discussed). The fiction shelves were well stocked with Picadors, although three of the four I bought were non-fiction – Stephen Brook's *Honky Tonk Gelato*, Bruce Chatwin's *Anatomy of Restlessness* and Leon Wieseltier's *Kaddish*. The fourth Picador was *The Stories of Tobias Wolff*, the second story in which, 'Hunters in the Snow', starts with a driver losing control of his vehicle in the snow: 'A truck slid around the corner, horn blaring, rear end sashaying. Tub moved to the sidewalk and held up his hand. The truck jumped the kerb and kept coming, half on the street and half on the sidewalk.' It was still snowing when we left Scrivener's and drove carefully out of Buxton. We passed one car in a ditch and another overturned with people climbing out of it.

'As for sharing author names,' Danny Rhodes writes to me, 'I share mine with Dan Rhodes, which has led to various minor misunderstandings over the years. It's like having a doppelgänger who is more respected, more successful, and effectively reminding you of this fact every now and again just in case you've forgotten.

'I received a congratulatory email from an old writer friend on the release of the *Granta Best of Young British Novelists* (issue 81, 2003), who thought it might be referring to me. It wasn't. That was quite depressing.'

In 1997 I wrote to one of the writers who would later appear in that list (not Dan Rhodes) to invite him to submit a story to an anthology I was editing for Quartet. He wouldn't have been on my list, but my editor at Quartet was a big fan of his work and begged me to try him. He wrote back saying he wouldn't be able to submit anything, he would only consider a commission and he was getting £900 to £1000 for stories at that time. I later bought a signed copy of his second novel (the only one I've read) from a charity shop to keep on a special shelf where I also keep copies of books by Harry Ritchie (see above).

'On the release of *Asboville*,' Danny Rhodes continues, 'I visited a university to deliver a workshop. Arriving, I was greeted by a professor who was clearly disappointed I was not the other Dan Rhodes writing under a pseudonym and effectively said as much. A strange evening.'

Danny Rhodes refers me to an entertaining paragraph on the 'About' page of Dan Rhodes's website in which Rhodes write about the names thing.

'For the record,' Danny Rhodes concludes, 'Dan Rhodes and I now follow each other on Twitter and he seems very nice.'

I'm sure he is, although I have no direct experience, whereas I can confirm that Danny Rhodes is very nice indeed.

As a young man I liked the Angry Young Men and associated writers. Maybe I liked them a little too much as I became, myself, an angry young man, at least as a reviewer of new fiction mostly for the *Guardian*, *Independent* and *Time Out*. I recall some of those reviews and feel myself shrivelling up inside. Even the good ones were embarrassing, but some of the bad ones were unforgivable, so it's to their great credit that one or two people have been gracious enough at least to appear to have forgiven me. I should probably be more forgiving of people who did to me what I did to others. Although I never stooped to personal abuse ('specky guy'), or not until it came to taking revenge in the next book.

Tuesday 8 May 2007

[Night after attending the other Nicholas Royle's 'Reality Literature' lecture at Sussex.]

The other Nicholas Royle and I did a project together, but it wasn't a book. It was a music project.

As previously noted, in my experience, the second most commonly seen Picador title in charity shops and second-hand bookshops is Andrea Ashworth's *Once in a House on Fire*. I wondered if short story writer AJ Ashworth, winner of Salt Publishing's Scott Prize for her debut collection *Somewhere Else, Or Even Here*, was aware of the ubiquity of her namesake's book.

'I deliberately decided to use the writing name AJ Ashworth because I didn't want people to think I was her,' Ashworth writes back. 'It hasn't worked, unfortunately. I've lost count of the number of times readers have messaged me to say how much they loved my memoir, *Once in a House on Fire*. They say such lovely things – about how it's moved them, affected them, had an impact on them – that I'm always sad to tell them it's not me. I've also had editors and writers who I've submitted work to, or worked with, ask me "Are you *the* Andrea Ashworth?" and then go on to say how wonderful the book is. A little part of me dies every time I have to say no and that I'm just *an* Andrea Ashworth instead.

'One fairly high-profile writer friended me on Facebook because she thought I was her. She then sent a message saying how wonderful the book is. I told her it wasn't me and that she could unfriend me again if she wanted, seeing as I was a different writer. She said no, and that I was a writer and that was good enough for her. A while after, I noticed she had actually unfriended me.

'I've had people buy me copies of the memoir because they think it's funny to see "my" name on it, but I've never been able to bring myself to read it. I know it will be brilliant – and knowing there's already one brilliant Andrea Ashworth out there makes me feel there can't be another, so I'd rather not know. I even delayed going after a PhD because I know she has one.'

In my case the opposite was true. Part of my motivation for finally deciding to pursue a PhD was the fact that the other Nicholas Royle had one. Also, I had started to feel like a fraud, examining PhDs at universities up and down the country, even if I always replied to invitations with a clarification: I didn't have a PhD myself and I would, as long as they agreed, focus mainly on the creative component. I was all set to attempt a PhD by publication when the pandemic hit and funding for staff to undertake PhDs was withdrawn.

'I don't want to embarrass her agent,' Ashworth continues,

'but I did submit my first novel to her a number of years ago – not because of my name but because I thought my work would be a good fit. She very nicely declined, but emailed me a few years ago asking me how life in LA was going and if I was going to send her some more work soon – my email address had obviously stayed in her contacts list and so when she wanted to email her client she got me instead. For a brief moment I felt like I'd arrived – life in LA, being asked about what I was working on. Of course I had to tell her she'd got the wrong Andrea Ashworth and she was very apologetic. But for a moment I had a glimpse into life as it could be.'

Monday 10 August 2009

I took Bella somewhere in south London. I was on my bike. She was on foot. On the way back – it was dark now, lots of lights, traffic, noise – I realised I'd got too far ahead. I'd lost her. I did a big turning circle in Victoria Station (no trains or buses, just a big empty shed) where I heard the other Nicholas Royle, as a uniformed security guard, call, 'Nick,' and tell me that he knew I'd stood a wet drink on a book in Waterstones, which was where he worked. I headed back to look for Bella, feeling panicky. I found her.

Towards the end of June 2020, in Coventry's Big Comfy Bookshop, I came across an old hardback novel I'd never heard of, *The Exhibitionist*, from a publisher I'd never heard of, Bernard Geis, by an author I had kind of heard of, Henry Sutton. Unless he had been a miraculous prodigy, I couldn't see my contemporary of that name and sometime fellow Serpent's Tail author having written a 400-page novel at the age of four. I contacted Henry Sutton to see if he knew about his namesake.

'Years ago, when I was starting out,' Sutton writes, 'friends would send me "Henry Sutton" novels such as *The Exhibitionist* or *The Voyeur*. Later, when I happened to be in New York interviewing Don DeLillo, his agent said to me, "Oh, you're the second Henry Sutton I've met." She used to represent Henry Sutton, who was in fact a classics academic and poet really called David Slavitt. Anyway, when I came to write *My Criminal World*, a novel about a struggling crime writer, it seemed logical that my protagonist should be called David Slavitt. Well, he'd nicked my name. I did contact him and sent him a proof. He got the joke. One of his more recent works was *Aspects of the Novel: A Novel*.'

Friday 28 July 2010

I am with the other Nicholas Royle at some kind of party. When he's leaving he goes to get a lift with someone. The car he's going to get into is full of strange metal pipework. There would be no room for a driver or passengers. The car turns into a glider/light aircraft with US military markings. It flies a little way and lands safely, albeit leaning to one side.

John Saul is a British novelist and short story writer. His work is subtle and nuanced and often innovative in form. I first came across his work in his 1999 collection, *The Most Serene Republic*, reissued by Salt Publishing in 2008.

John Saul is a bestselling American author of horror and suspense novels, none of which I have read.

The author of *The Most Serene Republic* writes to me: 'The fiction I write and the fiction written by the US author John Saul, resident in the Seattle area, could hardly be more different. Where this has clearly emerged is on the Internet, most notably in reactions to my novel *Seventeen*. Some (mainly US) buyers seemed to have leapt with pleasure at finding a hitherto undiscovered text by their hero, the US author, only to discover to their chagrin, not to say ire, that the tale before them was not at all about abducting children, skin burning or crushing some animal's skull. When *Seventeen* was available online, reviewers gave it either five stars or one, never something between. The one-star reviewers would inevitably trash my writing, either as being pretentious or on the lines of "not up to his usual". Of course it wasn't *his* at all. It didn't seem to occur to any of these disappointed buyers (I say disappointed, but they had at least donated to a good charity, which is where all the sales income went) that there might be a reason behind this – another author having the same name. "John Saul's Words Make Readers' Skin Crawl", as one magazine article was headed, gives an idea of what readers can expect – from the US author. Had prospective readers of *Seventeen* taken a few seconds to check, they might have realised they would be in for something quite different, indeed for someone quite different.

'Occasionally a photo of myself becomes attached to a book title of Seattle John Saul's or vice versa. Careless website presenters (probably algorithms) have even allowed our photos to appear alongside each other, the images ludicrously purporting to be of the same person.

'I've been surprised that no one has accused me of using his name. But no one has (been that) bothered.'

The formulation used by John Saul there, to denote the other John Saul, as Seattle John Saul, is one that some people have used for me and the other Nicholas Royle. We become Manchester Nicholas Royle and Sussex Nicholas Royle. We could also be Nicholas Royle (1963-) and Nicholas Royle (1957-), as in the British Library catalogue, but there's something insidiously disturbing about that hyphen, sticking out there untidily, an ugly stub, waiting for something (quite apart from the fact that it should really be an en-dash).

Saturday 17 March 2018
In a car behind the other Nicholas Royle at traffic lights in a city centre at night. I see an opportunity to cut in front of him and drop down to a lower level and so overtake him. I go for it, but then realise, when I need to accelerate, that I've slipped both legs into one leg of a pair of dark grey woollen leggings. I can't operate the pedals safely. I'm trying to get my right leg out and manage to do so and get ahead, but then, outside a shop, on the pavement, I see a lot of mess to be cleared up, like crumbs on a kitchen worktop. It might slow me down, but it has to be done. I do it and still remain, narrowly, ahead.

Robert Stone appeared on the first page of this book as he first appeared in my inbox, in connection with Nightjar Press, after placing an order. This was in 2017. Some time later, after placing several more orders, he enquired about submitting a story. This is definitely the recommended way in which to go about these things.

Robert Stone the American novelist and Picador author had died in 2015. My copies of his books came mostly from Oxfam bookshops, but also the excellent Bookmongers in Brixton, a LOROS Hospice charity shop in Leicester, the much-missed Lucky Seven second-hand book and record shop on Stoke Newington Church Street, and in a book swap with author, editor and publisher Ashley Stokes. Unless dying merely meant you moved to Ipswich, like a provincial variation on Will Self's short story 'The North London Book of the Dead', I was fairly confident the Robert Stone who was ordering Nightjar titles was another Robert Stone, now the author of around twenty short stories published in a variety of magazines and anthologies in print and online.

'When I was an undergraduate at UEA, 1981–84,' Robert Stone writes, 'I worked in the second-hand bookshop on the campus. This was run by a rather sexy non-student called Anita and she wanted volunteers to look after the shop for just an hour a week so that she could go and have lunch. It wasn't her sexiness that persuaded me to go in for this. There was no pay, but you could buy as many books as you wanted at cost price. That was enough.

'Anita might have got a bit annoyed with the number of books I bought. I used to go home for the weekend half way through each ten-week term, partly to see my parents but also because I had to take my books home in stages. I could barely carry what I bought after five weeks. Ten weeks' worth would have been impossible. I would fill a suitcase. Not only from Anita's shop. There were several really good second-hand shops in the city, some of which are still there.

'Anyway, one of the books I found on the shelves on my first day was a novel by Robert Stone called *A Hall of Mirrors*. Quite a burly hardback with a grey and white cover. I had started to write stories at about that time and even though I had not so much as sent one off to a magazine I still thought that this book might somehow be by me. There is something uncanny about seeing your own name and realising that those words do not refer to you. I was also reading Borges at this time. I had never even heard of Robert Stone. No internet, of course, and I was only about 19. I didn't know anything. I didn't buy that book. I never bought that book, nor did anyone else in all of the three years of my time in Norwich. If I was looking for a sign, the unadulterated unpopularity of writers called Robert Stone would not have been encouraging. I later saw another book by him in the new bookshop on campus. I can't remember what that one was called, but I think it was probably a Picador. I can't honestly say I reflected on the pertinence of that *Hall of Mirrors* title, Borges or not.'

While working on this chapter I have been reading Borges, his *A Personal Anthology*, another one of the first eight Picador launch titles. Normally I only read his fiction – indeed, his *Fictions* – but this collection offers stories alongside essays and poems. I would get a page or two into an essay and become so curious about the individual he was writing about that I would break off and look them up, only to find that they had never existed. I was, after all, reading a story.

'To this day I have only read one story by Robert Stone which, in fact, I thought was rather good even though it was not the kind of thing I usually like. I can't remember the title, but it might be quite famous. About a Vietnam vet who falls out with some bikers.'

Most of my copies of the other Nicholas Royle's books have been very kindly given to me by the author, and, in the case of a couple of them, signed and inscribed. Only one bears a pencilled price on the flyleaf, suggesting I paid £2.99 for *How to Read Shakespeare*. I have read more of them than Robert Stone has read books by Robert Stone, but it's not a competition. I just didn't want to give the impression that I amass these books without reading them. Luckily, I loved the novels, *Quilt* and *An English Guide to Birdwatching*, and I found the irrepressible and witty inventiveness of *The Uncanny* completely beguiling. I say 'luckily' because there will always be people who will think I wrote those novels, just as there will always be others who will think the other Nicholas Royle wrote *my* novels.

Sunday 23 September 2018

I'm in Scotland to kill another Nicholas Royle. I have to kill a man called James McAfree and this will somehow in turn kill the other Nicholas Royle, or another Nicholas Royle. I can't do it and yet it seems I've already killed one of them, the real one, I think. I feel sick. I'll be caught. How could I have thought it was OK? As I drift towards consciousness, I become more and more upset, as the feeling that I have actually killed someone becomes stronger and stronger.

On 28 November 2018, I found, in Oxfam Bookshop Chorlton, a Picador I didn't have, *The Letters of William S Burroughs 1945 to 1959*, edited by Oliver Harris.

I email my Manchester Met colleague, novelist Oliver Harris, author of the Nick Belsey crime fiction sequence and now the Elliot Kane series of espionage novels, to put the squeeze on him for content. I know he didn't edit the Burroughs letters, because he was only 15 when they came out and, while I know he's smart, he probably wasn't that smart at 15.

'I wish I could regale you,' he responds, 'with tales of ending up in Tangiers for a Burroughs conference, off my head on opium, before people realised the mistake they'd made. Alas, my anecdotes don't get any funnier than someone contacting me on Facebook asking if I'm that Oliver Harris or this Oliver Harris.'

In the case of me and the other Nicholas Royle, people don't tend to contact us to check. They just launch straight into what is generally a very tempting invitation to read this, or write that, or go there, and do that. The latest came from a Polish academic at the University of Warsaw asking me to write something about Beckett's *The Unnamable* for *Anglica: An International Journal of English Studies*. I do have two Picador editions of *The Beckett Trilogy*, one with a Russell Mills cover, the other bearing Avigdor Arikha's portrait of Beckett on the front cover and a Sussex University Bookshop sticker on the back, which is nice because that's where the other Nicholas Royle is Professor of English, having previously taught at the universities of Stirling and Tampere, but writing about Beckett for a journal would be a tall order for me. Which is not to say I am not occasionally tempted to accept an invitation to Finland.

The furthest I have gone as an imposter is to sign copies of *Quilt* at the Cheltenham Literature Festival. It was only one or two and it was either that or embarrass the organiser, who had thoughtfully provided some of my books as well.

When I confess this to Conrad Williams, the aforementioned author of *London Revenant, The Unblemished* and *One Who Was With Me*, among many other titles, he writes back, 'Ha! I did that as well. I wonder if it happened to him.'

I decided to find out. I approached the one I think of as the other Conrad Williams, via his colleague Juliet Pickering at the Blake Friedmann agency.

'The Other Conrad Williams,' the other Conrad Williams writes back to me, 'came to my attention painfully in the late '90s. My mental health doesn't like to think about it.

'I was still unpublished back then and working full time as a film/TV agent, repping scriptwriters. I wrote my first novel across three years of evenings and weekends in the early '90s, and sent it to publishers on the eve of my honeymoon. Responses were prompt and by the time I got back, the book had been shot out of the skies. My second book was written over five years, and this time it was very clear: if I didn't get it away, I'd be a failure and a loser.

'I was in my mid-to-late thirties when the tome went out to agents. Most of my literary friends were published by then and we had seen one new impostor after another take wing at the agency. It seemed that getting published was easy as pie for some.

'That second book didn't land an agent, and there began an 18-month period of fraught reckoning. I was in last chance saloon, balls absolutely against the wall. My conception of myself as a writer had a revolver to its head. Not that anybody else gave a damn; the sufferings of writers are a matter of jocular indifference and scented Schadenfreude to others. I was looking forward to enjoying the adage "It is not enough to succeed, others must fail", but was in danger of delivering on the wrong side of that pithy little headshot.

'It was around this time that I was commuting into work one morning and saw "HEAD INJURIES by Conrad Williams" in poster adverts all over the Underground. The sense of chagrin was instant and immolating, and I remember the holed-beneath-the-water-line feeling as I stood on the platform, the sense of being fortune's patsy and catamite. Not only had I not got published, somebody called Conrad Williams had. We writers pride ourselves on having something unique to offer. I no longer had my name, and although I knew this was not unprecedented, I felt withered and etiolated, ghosted, just not there.

'Worse was to come. I staggered into the office, reached for the to-do list: the in-tray brimming with the demands of clients, the petty admin, the ghastly contractual small-print, the sea of neediness, the sheer mediocrity of it, everywhere, limitless, and then the phone started ringing.

'Friends.

'Joyous, cheering, jubilant friends. They were so happy. I had done it. I had stuck to my guns, strained every sinew, won the prize. Half of London had seen the posters and thought the other Conrad was me. "We had our doubts," said one, "reckoned you might have been a bit of a duffer and a no-hoper, but you've proven us wrong. Well done, mate. You're a star. *Chapeau*."

'You can imagine their disappointment when I told them in a soft low broken voice that it wasn't me. It was . . . another . . . Conrad Williams. The groans of dismay were awful to hear. My humiliation was like a softening of the ego into shit.

'It did seem back then that I was being tested by malign fates and made to suffer more than other writers in some Christ-like preparation for my final redemption. I later got an agent for book two and had to go through the misery of 15 publisher rejections before the evil spell broke. Eventually I hired an editor and she told me to cut the first 65 pages and start the book right by the amputation scar. With her help I repositioned the exposition deeper in the story and suddenly we had a proposition that was beginning to throb with life.

'It went to auction and was eventually published as a lead title by Bloomsbury.

'*Sex and Genius* by Conrad Williams.

'During this frazzling time I hadn't dared to pick up *Head Injuries*, but in the early meetings with Bloomsbury I suggested I ought to change my name. I favoured "Conrad Renaissance", which had a certain je ne sais quoi. But the ladies at Bloomsbury, those vestals to literature with their ravishing coils of Pre-Raph-aelite hair, wouldn't hear of it. They really liked my name. Who is this other Conrad Williams, they said? We've never heard of him, they pleaded. It was difficult not to be flattered by their protestations and I thought, OK, I've got my identity back. It does make things easier to be who you are, and keeping my name had one big advantage. It would be a blunt two fingers to all the nay-sayers who thought I couldn't cut it.

'I'm glad to say that from then on, the existence of the other Conrad Williams stopped bothering me. I did dip in to one of his books, and it looked pretty good. The guy could certainly write. I saw some top reviews. It seemed to me that he did honour to the name and that we were both rather brilliant writers (if we say so ourselves, and I'm sure he's not going to disagree) and that as long as I wasn't letting him down, and he wasn't letting me down, it was OK. Our readerships were bound to be different, and if one or two accidentally strayed my way and read *The Concert Pianist* expecting a horror novel, I would get an extra sale. A few pages of Wigmore Hall ambience would permeate the reader's mind before he realised there were no amputations, body parts or screaming skulls, and what the fuck was Conrad doing?

'So gradually it became irrelevant and I came to like the idea of my parallel namesake out there, playing the same long game, book after book, joined to the same creative task, dealing with the same cycle, albeit more prolifically than me. We were in it together. His author photo and mine handsomely defended our joint patch on Google images, going toe to toe with the athlete Conrad Williams who was all over bloody everything. I liked his surly visage, the face of an author who has gazed deep into the human condition and needs to spit out the aftertaste. His book covers became companionable siblings to my titles online. I knew that if I ever met him, we'd have a good laugh and a good pint.

'There was one late and priceless humiliation that helped to make me the man I now am.

'I had been involved in a series of amateur celebrity piano concerts hosted by the concert pianist Lucy Parham at King's Place. Various fabled amateur maestros ranging from Alan Rusbridger to Ed Balls, Anneka Rice and Alistair McGowan, and yours truly, played easy classical pieces to a paying audience as a pre-Xmas charity gig. We were wittily compèred by Iain Burnside or Sean Rafferty and the whole thing was terrific adrenalin-rush laced with hilarity. I was a non-celebrity of course, only there because of my *Concert Pianist* book, but one of these concerts roughly coincided with the publication of *Unfinished Business*, my third. There was an opportunity to get a puff from Sean Rafferty in the onstage interview and as we sat in the green room beforehand I said to him, "Be a mate and mention my book", and he took the bait, jotting in his notebook and making a deal to tell the audience before I played.

'The only problem was that when Sean went online to mug up about me, he hit the other Conrad, mastered that brief, and then when I arrived nervously on stage and stood before a packed audience, he introduced me as the brilliant and prolific author of a dozen horror novels. "Ladies and gentlemen, I give you the incredible, the one, the only . . . Conrad Williams."'

10

Some more favourite bookshops around the country

Imagine a tour of Britain (my apologies to readers in Northern Ireland, and Wales beyond Hay-on-Wye), that increasingly *Debatable Land*, to misappropriate Candia McWilliam's 1995 Picador title. You might travel by VW microbus, like DR Davenport in Gurney Norman's *Divine Right's Trip*, or by actual bus. If you chose to go by train, you'd probably have to *Zig-Zag* a fair bit like Richard Thornley. There would be *Departures and Arrivals* and you might end up with a *A Book of Traveller's Tales* to rival Eric Newby's, as you went *Wandering* in the manner of Hermann Hesse, hopefully not on Moris Farhi's *Journey Through the Wilderness*. May you travel not through *The Broken Lands* of Robert Edric but *In the Land of Dreamy Dreams* with Ellen Gilchrist for company. Why not carry a copy of Knut Hamsun's *The Wanderer*, but maybe leave Keath Fraser's *Worst Journeys: The Picador Book of Travel* at home?

I get the train from London to Brighton. The date is Friday 26 May 2017. Poet Neil Rollinson wonders if I'd like to meet for a coffee. There's something not quite congruous about this earthy, northern wordsmith living on the south coast. We last saw each other a decade ago at Lumb Bank, when he was centre director and I was guest reader (if anyone from Arvon is reading this, doing the guest reader slot at any of the Arvon centres, but especially Lumb Bank, is one of my favourite things in the whole world and I haven't done it for a while and I'm always happy to be invited, even at the last minute). Rollinson is off to the South Downs, while I'm heading to Fiveways to visit Savery Books.

First, though, Preston Drove. Preston Drove is one of those evocative addresses that connect me so strongly to my past I feel as if I'm 25 again. In the mid-1980s I was constantly photocopying stories and sticking them in envelopes addressed to David Pringle, then editor of *Interzone*, which in those days was publishing Angela Carter, JG Ballard, M John Harrison and other writers I greatly admired. Pringle lived on Preston Drove, which I remember checking. Surely it was Preston Drive, but no, Preston Drove. And Pringle, of course, was constantly slipping my stories into the stamped addressed envelopes I supplied and returning them to me, until one day he didn't and I became, to my great and lasting excitement, for a few years at least, an *Interzone* writer.

I walk down Preston Drove and enact a small gesture of homage outside what was – and may still be – Pringle's address. No one calls the police.

Just around the corner, on Ditchling Road, is Savery Books. Two women browse the boxes of crime novels outside. 'Mum, have you seen this?' one of them says and when I enter the shop I hear another voice say, 'Mum, shall we put these railway books out tomorrow?' As I look over the stock I listen to these two conversations continuing between two different mothers and daughters, visitors to and proprietors of this lovely shop bursting with books. 'I put out two more Du Mauriers,' says one mother and, 'I've read that one, love,' says another.

I find some Picadors I don't have – Oliver Sacks' *An Anthropologist on Mars*, Hunter S Thompson's *Songs of the Doomed*, Alice Hoffman's *Practical Magic* and Richard Wright's *Black Boy* – and take them to the till. I ask how long the shop has been there. Twenty-five years, they tell me.

I walk down the hill towards the centre of Brighton. The English Channel is like a vertical blue wall. I think of Ballard's 'Now Wakes the Sea', with its brilliant opening line, 'Again at night Mason heard the sounds of the approaching sea, the muffled thunder of breakers rolling up the near-by streets.'

Another poet, Michael Kemp, and his wife Sooty, live close to Ditchling Road. Shouldn't they live in Kemptown? Outside the Studio Bookshop on St James's Street are shelves of books that appear to stay out in all weathers: £1 each and customers are invited to post money through the letter box if the shop is shut, but it's open, so I pay in person for the 1972 poetry pamphlet edited by Bernard J Kelly that I buy for Michael Kemp.

In Snoopers Paradise, a warren of stalls selling everything from beetles to books about the Beatles, I find more Picadors – the second volume of F Scott Fitzgerald's stories as well as *Torch in My Ear* by Elias Canetti and Marina Warner's *Alone of All Her Sex: The Myth and the Cult of the Virgin Mary*.

By the time I enter Brighton Books at the north end of Kensington Gardens, having visited the Oxfam Bookshop and Books For Amnesty, I am experiencing the beginnings of Collector's Fatigue, the surest sign of which is the faintest desire *not* to find any books to buy, but I can't resist either MJ Fitzgerald's *Concertina* or Haniel Long's *The Marvellous Adventures of Cabeza de Vaca*.

Saturday 11 July 2020

Oxfam Bookshop St Giles Street, Oxford.

Manager, 30s, and volunteer, 20s, both male. Volunteer has long hair, big mask.

Manager: How's it going?

Volunteer: Fine, fine. Just like a normal Saturday actually.

Manager: Really?

Volunteer: Well, a quiet Saturday rather than a busy Saturday. Just sold seventy-five quid's worth of books to one chap. Then twenty-five.

Manager: I'll get Theresa on the till if you like.

Volunteer: Fine, but I'm happy to keep going.

Draw a triangle connecting Bristol, Bath and Wells, and Bookbarn International lies right at the centre. It's less a barn, more a hangar, but is far from intimidating, as a warm welcome is guaranteed – from the counter just within and the café beyond. The 'new arrivals' shelves have as many books on them as some second-hand bookshops have in their entirety. Past these is where Bookbarn really begins, but don't venture in without a basket. A blue-carpeted walkway extends 50 yards, a seemingly endless wall of fiction on the right, while on the left are rows of non-fiction divided into subject areas. In some aisles the order breaks down; there are some empty shelves, but they won't remain that way for long, at least one wheeled trolley constantly within earshot. It's bookselling's equivalent of the painting of the Forth Bridge. If you've ever fancied collecting the *Penguin*

Modern Poets series, this would be a good place to start; they had eight of the 27 volumes on my visit in January 2018. At the end of one aisle a vivid splash of turquoise heralds a huge selection of Pelicans.

I found several Picadors: Caroline Blackwood's *The Last of the Duchess*, Christopher Tilghman's *In a Father's Place*, Jacobo Timerman's *Chile*, Myles Harris's *Breakfast in Hell*, Clive Sinclair's *Blood Libels* and Jonathan Schell's *The Abolition*.

I was pleased when my children went to university in Bristol because it meant fresh opportunities for me as well as for them. I wouldn't have wanted to miss Oxfam Bookshop Queen's Road, in particular, where I found Deirdre Bair's Picador biography of Samuel Beckett or the bookseller tucked away in St Nicholas Market who had a number of Agatha Christies in Fontana . . . One afternoon in and out of the charity shops on and around Whiteladies Road produced two Editions de Minuit titles – Marie Redonnet's *Diego* and Tanguy Viel's *Paris-Brest*.

My copy of Candia McWilliam's *Debatable Land* came from Oxfam Books & Music Crouch End, although there's been a copy in my local Didsbury Village Oxfam for about five years, which I'm thinking of buying as soon as they reopen just to get it off the shelf and so avoid future episodes of White Spine Disappointment. The Crouch End-sourced *Debatable Land* has an inclusion, a hotel registration slip in the name of Ashworth, who was booked in to stay three nights in August (no year given) in room 14 at The Chase at Ross-on-Wye. Had – let's assume it was AJ – Ashworth headed out of Ross-on-Wye on the A49, then cut across country on the B4348, she would have ended up in Hay-on-Wye, a small town mostly just over the Welsh border where there are one or two bookshops.

My most recent visit to Hay was on 2 September 2019 en

route to Abergavenny to meet Picador author Paul Griffiths, who was kindly meeting me half way to sign 200 copies of his Nightjar chapbook, *so this is it.* In Addyman Books I bought three Virago Modern Classics – Jennifer Dawson's *The Ha-Ha*, Dorothy Edwards' *Rhapsody* and Gertrude Stein's *Blood on the Dining-Room Floor.* Dawson writes convincingly about a severe mental health crisis, while Edwards' collection may be somewhat top-loaded, but the first two stories are quite outstanding. Here she is on Chopin's *Nocturnes* in 'A Country House': 'But I tell you they are the result of thinking of darkness as the absence of the sun's light. It is better to think of it as a vapour rising from the depths of the earth and perhaps bringing many things with it.' Stein's experimental crime novel, first published in 1948 and the title surely a nod to Cameron McCabe's *The Face on the Cutting-Room Floor*, may be a masterpiece; I'm going to have to reread it to make sure.

I don't feel I have to reread Adrian Mitchell's *The Bodyguard*, first published in October 1972 and another one of those first eight Picadors. It has its moments (and it hasn't put me off reading his later novel, *Wartime*, also in Picador). As the country is being torn apart by violence and revolution, the bodyguard – or BG – of the title, Len Rossman, is driving north with his mentor Finn, in Finn's Rolls-Royce. In an exchange of dialogue, Finn offers his assessment of northern cities (they are specifically on their way to Manchester): '"Those run-down, broken up cities rusting away, ruddy great iron buildings all black and stinking, windows broken, old bricks in every odd corner of the street, the kingdom of slumdom . . ."'

Thursday 21 November 2019
Oxfam Bookshop, Altrincham, Cheshire.

Two older female volunteers.

A: I found this in Literature.

B: What's that? Ooh.

A: That should be in Religion. Where's Religion?

B: Just round there.

[...]

A: Look what I found in Religion. What's that doing in Religion?

B: We've already got one of those in Fiction. Is it Gift Aided?

A: Yes.

B: I do like his fiction ones. The Bertie ones.

New Mills in the High Peak tended to close around 4.30pm, on a Saturday at least, even before the pandemic, so it's hard to predict how lively it will be in the future. But if High Street Books and Bele Bakery are both open, it's always going to be worth a visit. I have never left Bele Bakery with room in my belly or High Street Books empty handed. Martin Amis's *Dark Secrets* (a Panther reissue of *Dead Babies*), Brazilian author Autran Dourado's short story collection *Pattern For a Tapestry* (King Penguin) and Giles Gordon's memoir *Aren't We Due a Royalty Statement?* are among the treasures I've found there, and owner Adam Morris is always good value.

Wednesday 20 November 2019

Deansgate Waterstones, Manchester.

Bookseller with green hair and bookseller with brown hair in general fiction.

Green hair [as he picks up book from crime table]: What's this? Is it the first in a series?

Brown hair: I don't know. I can't take credit for it. If I could take credit for it I would. There'll be something to swop it out for.

Green hair: I dragged some Pullmans in here for you. What do
  you call it? Cross-pollination?

Five miles north-east of Rochdale – you can walk it along the
Rochdale Canal – is Littleborough, home of George Kelsall
Booksellers, where you'll find new books on the ground floor
and lots of second-hand stock upstairs. One name you'll find
represented in both parts of the shop is that of local author
Trevor Hoyle, author of three fascinating novels published by
John Calder between 1979 and 1994 and numerous works of
science fiction. George runs the business with his son Ben; their
welcome is warm.

Retired social worker Paul Hamer, who has taken over the
Clitheroe Bookshop, is chattier than his predecessor, who passed
away, Hamer tells me when I call in on 30 July 2020. Hamer
had tried to buy the business while the previous owner was
still alive. Only on his second attempt was he was successful.
The shop is clean and tidy, with lots of first editions in plastic
wrappers and everything divided into sections, but, within
sections, no alphabetical order. In a more disorderly-looking
shop that would be expected; in these surroundings it is oddly
unsettling. I leave with Gabriel Josipovici's 2014 novel *Hotel
Andromeda* (Carcanet) and a collection of Boris Vian's poems,
Je voudrais pas crever (10/18), which I read over the next couple
of days. If I'm going to not understand a bunch of poems, I
may as well not understand them in French. Poets tell me it's
all about the music in the language. The music in the language
comes across, in French, but I still didn't really know what the
poems are about, other than not wanting to die. I can relate
to that. *Je voudrais pas crever* was published, posthumously,
in 1962.

On the other side of the Forest of Bowland, Westwood Books in Sedbergh – England's book town, apparently – looks very promising. A large space over two floors. Central tables on the ground floor have remainder books, which are easy to spot and just as easy to ignore. Second-hand paperback fiction is off to the right. Lots of stock: thrillers, SF, general, literature. Tons of hardbacks and non-fiction in paperback upstairs along with a huge selection of classical CDs. There are comfy sofas and there's coffee.

Co-owner Mark Westwood told me, when I first visited in August 2019, that he and his wife Evelyn had been there 13 or 14 years, having come from Hay-on-Wye. 'Hay had become more of a festival town than a book town. Business is better here.' I found a Picador, Richard Wiley's *Fool's Gold*, but Westwood Books looked and felt like the real deal. Ownership has since passed to local couple Paul and Heather Thomas. I look forward to going back.

There's more of everything at Bookcase in Carlisle – stairs, rooms, books, CDs, even Picadors. Prices are a wee bit higher, too, but it doesn't stop the books piling up in my arms. Carlisle is also home to Paul Leith, artist and illustrator of most of Picador's Knut Hamsun covers. His website has a short film that shows him cycling around Carlisle in a bow tie and a hat like Monsieur Hulot and painting a mural and I immediately have a hundred questions I want to ask him, like, why did you do only six of those Knut Hamsun covers? Why not *Victoria* as well? Why did they get George Sharp to do that one? An email comes back. Paul Leith doesn't know, but kindly suggests we meet for a tea in Cakes & Ale, the café and garden attached to Bookcase, once it is safe to do so.

On Sunday 26 May 2019, I leave home at 4pm to drive to Wigtown, where I'll spend the night, en route to Moniack Mhor. A week among friends awaits, although I'm not fully prepared for the bits that are work. But, first, Wigtown. Scotland's book town. I book into my B&B and go in the Craft for a local ale, which isn't Belgian, but isn't bad. After half an hour I realise I've been sitting under a sign that says, *Jock's Weekly Special.* I leave. A man stares at me from a window. It starts to rain. There's an empty shop for sale. It is, strangely, very tempting. The last time I was here was with the England Writers football team, one of whose number was saying he'd have to get me into *Granta*, which, naturally, never happened. I met James Delingpole in somebody's kitchen. Politically suspect, even a decade ago.

On Monday morning I enjoy a full Scottish breakfast in Craigmount Guesthouse before heading to the bookshops. First stop The Bookshop. If I owned a bookshop I wouldn't call it 'The' something, because then no one knows whether to upper-case the definite article when writing about it. Upper-casing it looks ugly, but lower-casing it you worry someone might take offence. I guess you could do whatever you liked and leave it up to the subs or the editor or whoever you're writing it for. But what if you're writing it for someone who will have less interest in that kind of thing than you do? And you feel you have to get it right. I wonder if this is why shop-owner Shaun Bythell is a bit Dylan-Moran-in-*Black-Books* – by his own admission, in the first entry in his memoir, *The Diary of a Bookseller* (Profile), which I buy in The Bookshop, feeling I should, but also because I want to read it. I'm listening to him talking to some students about his book while I'm rooting through his paperback shelves. He's sending mixed messages about it. Perhaps, like me, he feels awkward talking about his work, one to one, or, in this case, one to two or three. I think there are three of them, and one of them is studying something I had no idea you could study. I've forgotten what it was now, but it was something kind of practical, more practical than creative writing. Anyway, they buy one, and I buy one, and I also buy three Kurt Vonnegut paperbacks in Panther – *Welcome to the Monkey House, God Bless You, Mr Rosewater* and *Mothernight*. I will read the first diary entry of *The Diary of a Bookseller* that night in bed at Moniack Mhor. I will note it definitely strikes a somewhat grumpy tone at the same time as making me snort with laughter and I will see it runs to 310 pages, which will strike me as far too long for this kind of thing. I would have thought 246 pages is the optimum.

I'm worrying about whether it's The Bookshop or the Bookshop when really I should be worrying about whether it's Bookshop or Book Shop. The sign and the book suggest two words, the website one word, so who knows?

I like the Old Bank Bookshop immediately, partly because the owners, Joyce and Ian Cochrane, are so friendly. The shelves I'm looking at are for dead authors, Joyce explains. But I can see books by Jonathan Coe, Emma Donoghue, Esther Freud, DM Thomas and others, none of them dead, as I'm writing these words. I end up being invited into the office for a photo. I ask for one in return. I buy only one book, John Haskell's *Out of My Skin*, which is new and a US edition. No UK publisher has acquired it, as far as I know, which is a shame as I loved *American Purgatorio*. I'll read *Out of My Skin* walking around Manchester parks during the first national lockdown in 2020.

The prose has the same relaxed gait as *American Purgatorio*. In fact, it's even more relaxed. It strolls along like Larry David doing a walk-and-talk. But it's about *another* actor-comedian. The narrator, having moved from New York to LA, meets a

Steve Martin impersonator and likes what he sees so much that he starts impersonating Steve Martin himself. It's very good on what it's like to have the sense of inhabiting someone else's skin. The narrator tries to have a relationship with a woman called Jane, but Steve, or being Steve, or more to the point not being Steve, gets in the way.

I enter Well Read Books and the enjoyable company of retired judge turned second-hand bookseller Ruth Anderson QC, who kindly drags loads of Virago Modern Classics out of the back room for me to inspect. We have a good conversation. I leave with a Penguin, Jean Rhys's *After Leaving Mr Mackenzie*.

The Open Book, sadly, is closed.

With its exposed spiral staircase, mezzanine floor and balconies, Leakey's, on Church Street, Inverness, achieves the remarkable feat of making the majority of its stock on at least three levels visible to the visitor from almost any location inside the premises. There's a woodburning stove in the middle of the ground floor and a large counter where you will find owner Charles Leakey busy making sales and graciously accepting compliments on his extraordinarily beautiful bookshop.

It was in Leakey's that I discovered that Tom Adams' covers for Fontana's Agatha Christie series were sometimes replaced, with new Tom Adams covers. That came as a surprise, the idea that someone decided the master's work could be improved on, if only by the master. There's no doubt, though, that the *Ordeal By Innocence* cover with the birds is better than the one with the snake and that the spider cover for *Appointment With Death* is a vast improvement on the one with the syringe. As for *Passenger to Frankfurt*, the one with the bubbles or the one with the spider? It's a difficult one to call.

Saturday 1 June 2019
Priory Books, Pitlochry.
Bookseller and well-dressed man in mustard jumbo cords.
Well-dressed man [buying map of Edinburgh]: I'm actually on
    my way to Loch Ness. I'm a collector. Can you tell?
Bookseller [smiles].

Favourite bookshop in Edinburgh? That's easy. Armchair
Books on West Port. On 7 June 2017, I find two Picadors –
Brenda Maddox's *George's Ghosts* and Malcolm Lowry's *Under
the Volcano* – plus William Burroughs' *The Place of Dead Roads*
in Paladin with an inclusion, a scrap of paper with sums on one
side and an eight-digit number on the other, probably a bank
account. The man in the shop says, of the Lowry, 'Fuck. This is
a great book. Heavy going, but great.' He talks about it having
the best description of anything he can remember reading
anywhere. 'The sound of a Mexican town being like the noise
made by a thirsty man in the desert.' I ask him why the prices
are not round numbers, but figures like £3.80 or £4.20. He says,
'I don't know, man. Above my pay grade.'

Saturday 5 January 2019
In a bookshop I picked up a book by somebody called Kendrick.
I knew that it was actually Jenn Ashworth. A man appeared
with a copy of the same book. He said, 'My name is Peter
Kendrick.' I said, 'You must be very proud,' assuming he was
Jenn Ashworth's father. He went to get all the copies there were
of the book. He was going to buy them all.

Seven months after I had that dream, my wife and I went on
holiday to Northumberland. Visiting Holy Island on a hot

day we were plagued by dense clouds of thrips and it was an enormous relief to escape up the coast to Berwick-upon-Tweed, where someone, possibly Paul Feeney, had recommended Berrydin Books. Second-hand books and an absence of thrips: the day had definitely improved. The owner told me he used to run the Barter Books outpost in Seahouses. When they closed it, he moved up the A1 and opened his own shop in Berwick. I came away with a Picador by Eric Newby that was new to me, *A Merry Dance Around the World*. It contained a couple of inclusions – Newby's obituary from the *Scotsman* and a typed sheet headed 'A Brief History About Symi'. Also, two Penguins: Iris Murdoch's *The Red and the Green* and Brigid Brophy's *Hackenfeller's Ape*.

A year later, having become a bit obsessed with Brophy's reviews in *London Magazine* from the early 1960s, and tweeting photographs of these to Brophy's daughter Kate Levey, I thought it was about time I read her fiction. *Hackenfeller's Ape* had a promising premise. A professor is interested in a pair of Hackenfeller's apes in London Zoo. He – and the Zoo – hope they will mate, but although the female, Edwina, is very keen, the male, Percy, is less so. Then a man called Kendrick turns up.

My copies of two of Giles Gordon's novels, *Girl With Red Hair* and *Enemies*, and one of his short story collections, *Farewell, Fond Dreams*, which I bought from the amazing Barter Books in Alnwick, are all signed and dated to 'Paddy and Dulan, with love'. Writers Paddy Kitchen and Dulan Barber, married in 1968, were friends of Gordon's. Barber appeared alongside Gordon in one or two anthologies and they edited a book together about jury service. My first edition of *Farewell, Fond Dreams* contains an inclusion, a postcard of St Mawes in Cornwall, sent to 'All' at an address in Holyport Road, London SW6. The sender writes about the view of Falmouth from St Mawes and says, 'I felt very sad not to be able to gather up an armful of mackerel at 4p each that they are selling in St Mawes harbour for P & P. Though I suppose they wouldn't recognise fish with heads & tails. Love, P.' I wonder if P is Paddy Kitchen, but the card is postmarked October 1974 and the book, published the following year, is inscribed on 24 February 1975. The postcard sits between pages 90 and 91, half way through the strongest story in the collection, 'An Office Meeting', in which two men (Perkins and Roberts, the narrator), in an office that belongs to neither of them, are joined by a third man who Perkins thinks is called Dangerfield. At first, Roberts thinks the third man looks like Dangerfield, then realises he is not Dangerfield, but Egerton, although he, Egerton, or Dangerfield, insists he is Dangerfield. Roberts understands less and less as the tension grows and grows. It's a superbly compressed piece of claustrophobic prose drama.

Barter Books, housed inside Alnwick's former railway station and boasting a model railway that runs above customers' heads as they browse, has to be seen to be believed. Last time I was there I only bought one book, Stevie Smith's *The Holiday* (Virago Modern Classics). Did that mean Barter Books would lose its allure for me? Or did it mean I was close to the point where I would have all the books I wanted? Could such a point exist? What if I do find all the Picadors? Will I go from collecting only those Virago Modern Classics that appeal to me, that I think I might read, to collecting all of them? Will I up my game in relation to the other, similar white-spined B-format imprints of the 1980s and '90s, Paladin, Sceptre, Abacus, King Penguin, Vintage? Will my reading tastes continue to broaden and evolve?

Rooting around on my shelves for my Quartet editions of BS Johnson to check something, I find my Quartet paperback of *The Angry Brigade* by Alan Burns. I read it years ago having bought it I don't know where. It opens at the title page, the flyleaf hugging the cover. I turn back to the flyleaf and see, for the first time, that it has been inscribed: 'For Paddy & Dulan, Love – Alan.' Under the title on the same page – maybe it's technically a half-title rather than a flyleaf – Burns has added, 'Published 21.1.74.' So maybe I do know where I bought it now. I go to another shelf where I know I have some other Alan Burns books that have been there for a number of years. Among them is a Calder & Boyars hardback first edition of *Babel*. On the flyleaf – and it is a flyleaf this time – we read, 'For Dulan and Paddy, with best wishes, Alan. 10.6.69.'

This lightning tour has not stopped at many Oxfam branches, but the fact is that wherever I go, if there is an Oxfam Bookshop or an Oxfam Books & Music, that's top of my list. I am aware of the argument that the success of Oxfam as a second-hand bookseller poses an existential threat to other second-hand booksellers, but the fact that if you buy a book from Oxfam you are joining the fight against poverty is also a compelling argument.

If branches of Oxfam have not figured as much in this chapter, maybe it's down to their essential similarity, and yet, as I know I've said before, individual managers and local conditions can make a big difference between one branch and another. York's Oxfam Bookshop Micklegate and Oxfam Bookshop Leeds in Headingley are both outstanding. Sometimes a general Oxfam shop can be as good as a specialist branch, as in Sheffield where the Nether Edge branch would hold its own in a competition with Oxfam Bookshop Glossop Road. In Birmingham I was surprised to find many more reasons to be parted from my money in Oxfam Bookshop Birmingham, in King's Heath, than in Oxfam Bookshop Moseley. While we're in the West Midlands, Oxfam Bookshop Coventry is always worth a look, but the big draw in Coventry is Gosford Books.

In Coventry in May 2018 to get another Nightjar author to sign her chapbooks, I gladly allowed Florence Sunnen and George Ttoouli to lead me out of the city centre to see if Gosford Books would be open. It wasn't. A year later, passing through, I tried again. Closed. And another year later, September 2020, delivering Nightjar orders in Coventry, I tried again, with low expectations, and this time Gosford Books was open. Well, half-open. Owner Rob Gill opened the door a crack and allowed me, quite rightly, not to come inside but to look through the crack. Stacks of books as far as I could see and that included in the window, into which space Gill obligingly climbed to extract books I thought I might not have and of course discovered when I got home that I did, apart from the last of Richard Brautigan's Picador titles, *The Tokyo-Montana Express*, which was new to me. It didn't exactly plug a gap, because I hadn't known there was a gap, and wouldn't have wanted to know there was a gap, but it added to the collection. I told Gill about my previous unsuccessful attempts to visit the shop. 'That's the point of second-hand bookshops,' he said. 'Being closed.' The pandemic, he added, had given him 'new opportunities to be obstructive'. I liked him – and his shop – enormously.

Wednesday 22 July 2020
Oxfam Books & Music, St Paul's Square, Bedford.
Older gentleman customer on his way out of shop chatting to

middle-aged shop manager waiting by door to welcome customers with squirt of hand-sanitiser.

Customer: Very few people know that Bedford Corn Exchange
was the headquarters of the BBC during the war. I don't
know why the Germans never worked that out. If you cross
off Scotland and Wales, Bedford is right in the middle of the
country, furthest from the sea. I don't know why Mr Hitler
never worked that out. Anyway, tell me to shut up.

Manager: No, no, no.

Customer: I was born in Sussex, right in the middle of the war.
Now, where was I going? Home. Cheers.

Manager: Take care.

As we approach London, we enter a golden triangle of Oxfam
bookshops, defined by Harpenden, Berkhamsted and St Albans.
In St Albans I found a surprising number of French books,
including a Simenon in Livre de Poche and two Becketts in
Editions de Minuit, and three Picadors, when, in August 2020,
it had got to the stage where I would very rarely find even one
that I didn't have. At Harpenden, which I visited partly because
of Nicholas Lezard's joke in his column in the *New Statesman* –
'Actually, these days, I can kind of see the point of St Albans, if I
squint really hard; but I'll never see the point of Harpenden' – I
found a well-managed shop, a selection that felt not just donated
but curated, specifically a literature loyalty scheme, excellent
black culture section and collection of vintage Penguins. It was,
I had to admit, better than St Albans. Among the books I went
away with was an edition of Stefan Zweig's *Selected Stories* with a
cover quote from Nicholas Lezard. The manager at Harpenden
said to me, 'You must have been to Berkhamsted.' I hadn't, but
I would soon put that right.

Overflowing shelves. Books on the floor. Old wooden book-cases. These things definitely make a difference. In the end, in Berkhamsted, I had to stop myself buying. I could have gone on all day. It's like eating too many chocolates. I walked away with *Wayward Girls and Wicked Women*, the first of three Virago Modern Classics, this one edited by Angela Carter, the other two being Brigid Brophy's *The King of a Rainy Country* and Jane Bowles's *Two Serious Ladies*; Kurt Vonnegut's *Deadeye Dick* (Paladin); Brigid Brophy's *The Finishing Touch* (GMP); *The Gift of Stones* by Jim Crace, a Picador but with an illustration on the spine that knocks it into the long grass of the anomalies section; finally, a Picador for the main collection, Richard Bausch's short stories, *Aren't You Happy For Me?*, with a cover by the Senate (or The Senate?), which, like the Senate's Don DeLillo covers for Picador, looks more like a cover for a pensions brochure or company report than for a work of fiction, but then maybe pensions brochures and company reports *are* works of fiction.

The Angela Carter anthology has an inclusion, a postcard of Philip Wilson Steer's *The Beach at Walberswick*, sent from Andy with love to Helen: 'Thank you for a lovely weekend. Here's a reminder as an antidote to the London madness.'

11

Other people's memories

Sunday 28th February 1999

I was with Russell Celyn Jones at some kind of literary function and we were both naked. Up to us came Peter Porter, who I knew was a friend of Ron Butlin's. I quickly became embarrassed by my nakedness.

'My first novel, *Soldiers and Innocents*, was sold to Picador from Jonathan Cape in late 1989,' Russell Celyn Jones tells me. 'But my editor, Tom Maschler, neglected to tell me or my agent. The good news was broken to me six months later by John Saddler at a party, then an editor at a rival paperback house who had tried to buy the title from Cape. When I met my new paperback editor, Peter Straus, I was needing a place to live and straightaway he offered me his spare room. I didn't take up his unexpected and generous offer but did have lunch with him. Walking into the restaurant on Fulham Road, opposite the Pan Macmillan offices, he introduced me to Picador author Michael Herr, who was having lunch with his agent, Abner Stein. I confessed to Herr that I'd reviewed his latest book, Walter Winchell, and he thanked me. Michael Herr thanked me! Towards the end of our lunch, Abner Stein joined us for a drink. He compared my first novel being published by Cape and then Picador to getting two As at A-level. I've never had a better and more apt compliment since.'

I met Russell Celyn Jones a few years later, when we were both published by Penguin. I don't remember if we met first at a Penguin event or at Lumb Bank, where either we were co-tutoring or one of us was a guest reader. I do remember that everybody kept their clothes on.

'Picador was the most glamorous curator of the world's greatest writers,' Jones continues, 'and to have come from nowhere to be part of it felt unreal, to me at least. I was over-whelmed, and naïve – until the book came out. The cover design was problematic to get right, which delayed the paper-back edition by six months, and its short length was crammed into a short number of pages, to look insubstantial. Straus has spoken subsequently of his regret for not publishing me strongly enough. Yet, if I knew then what I know now, I would have sold all my subsequent books to him. He fought off the threat to Picador's existence, posed by vertical publishing, by setting up the Picador hardback list to rival them all.'

Sunday 8 February 1998

At a convention in New Orleans. On a panel with John Clute. I see an opportunity to respond to the bad review he gave me for *The Matter of the Heart*. 'You upset me very much indeed,' I say. Michael Marshall Smith is in the room. I feel him backing me up. At the end of the panel, they show a film. Clute comes to sit near me. I get up and leave the bar and the hotel. It's humid. I find myself in a lane with big houses and overhanging trees. See a row of wooden huts with bunk beds – holiday units for rent. From inside one looking out I see a red-covered map with a woman's name on it. The windows won't open, so I go outside to see if I can get it. A man's face looms up. Other men appear. One introduces himself as Harry Hill, but he means Harry Ritchie.

A few years later, Mick Jackson, a debut author with his novel *The Underground Man*, was surprised to find himself being published in hardback by Picador.

'It's easy to forget,' says Jackson, 'but when Picador started publishing paperbacks they looked and felt different to other books – more generously proportioned, in a way that made your traditional Penguin paperback format seem a little mean by comparison.'

The difference between A-format and B-format is no more than a couple of centimetres, but a couple of centimetres can make all the difference. So can who you sign.

'I got into Picador books through Richard Brautigan. He was (and remains) a sort of household god to me. In the late '70s and early '80s Picador had their own carousels/spinners in bookshops and I remember heading straight over to them. Initially, I'd be looking to see if they had any new Brautigans, but without realising it I came to see Picador books as cool, because they'd publish writers like Robert Coover and Michael Herr and Russell Hoban – a lot of US writers but also something a little more leftfield, a little weird. Years later, when my agent told me it looked like we might have an offer from Picador for *The Underground Man* I was a bit baffled. I didn't realise they published fiction in hardback. I think they made the offer in December '95 but didn't publish it till January '97, so it seemed like a long, long wait for it to come out, but it also gave me time to revise and polish it.'

Jackson remembers having lunch with the jacket designer and she told him about her idea for a wraparound that would unfold to reveal hidden images, which would reflect some of the content of the novel. They went to town over the book's presentation and Jackson feels that this was a gamble that paid off because it did well and was shortlisted for the Booker and couple of other prizes.

'In those days they didn't release the Booker longlist, but everyone in the industry knew who was on it. There were about thirty books on the longlist, which had to be whittled down to six. I knew they were going to announce the shortlist live on Radio 4 on *Kaleidoscope*.'

It was on late in the afternoon, but Jackson had promised to drop some bookshelves round at his in-laws' in Essex and so was in traffic on the M25 when the programme started.

'*The Underground Man* is about an eccentric Victorian who builds a network of tunnels under his estate and as the Booker judges were introduced on the radio I was going down into the Dartford Tunnel and the reception on the radio slowly died away. I crawled through the tunnel, thinking, Great! I'm going to be down a tunnel when the rest of the world gets to hear if my book about tunnels has been shortlisted for the Booker. I finally emerged on the north side of the Thames and a few seconds later they began to announce the shortlist. I think mine was the fifth or sixth novel to be named, by which point I was convinced I'd missed the boat. It'd be easy now to come over all blasé about it, but believe me, having my first novel shortlisted for the Booker was a very big deal for me. I had to pull the car over onto the hard shoulder to try and keep it together. For a couple of seconds back there I completely lost it and was most definitely a danger to other people on the road.'

Jackson enjoyed his time at Picador. 'The editor-in-chief, Peter Straus, was a lovely, charismatic (and very funny) guy. I got the impression everybody loved working for him. Some of the staff at Picador told me that when they came back after being on holiday Peter would grill them about what they'd been reading. You got the feeling he genuinely cared about books and publishing and it seemed to permeate the whole place.'

One of the perks of having a publishing deal and going in for meetings with your editor or your publicist is that you might come away with a few books. 'I love Jonathan Raban's writing so I'd get the bound proofs of whatever book of his was due to be published. *Bridget Jones's Diary* came out around that time and was a big, big seller. I got hold of a copy and really enjoyed it and happened to say as much at some event or other.'

Helen Fielding's *Bridget Jones's Diary* is another of those Picadors one sees a lot in charity shops and second-hand shops, after *Last Orders* and *Once in a House on Fire*.

'I remember one or two people being rather dismissive of it, which I thought was odd because for several years Helen Fielding must've pretty much been paying everybody's wages at Picador.

'I imagine a lot of the people who worked at Picador back then are now elsewhere. They moved their offices from Victoria to Kings Cross soon after I left. My editor, Jon Riley, moved to Faber and I basically followed him. Peter Straus became an agent. But Picador certainly got behind my first novel and I owe them a great deal for that.'

Friday 10 July 2020
Oxfam Bookshop, Chorlton, Manchester.
Two young female volunteers, one in glasses and mask by door,

other in mask and gloves at till, and customer, male, glasses, floppy hair, backpack. Other customers entering.

Customer: I've been looking forward to getting back to looking at books and stuff.

Volunteer on till: Yeah.

Volunteer by door: Do you want to take a basket? Just so we know how many people are in the shop. Anything you pick up and don't buy put in the box.

New customer: I don't want a basket.

Volunteer by door: Just so we know how many people are in the shop.

New customer: Oh. OK.

Customer: It's bizarre how many things that you do that you miss.

Volunteer on till: Yeah, exactly.

Volunteer by door: Do you want to take a basket? Just so we know how many people are in the shop. Anything you touch and don't buy please put in the box.

Customer [picking up book – Picador edition of Hermann Hesse's *Klingsor's Last Summer* – from pile of books volunteer has already rung up]: Oh, I've read this. I think.

Volunteer by door: Could you wait outside, please, just for one minute?

Customer: Yeah. Do you mind if I reject this one?

Volunteer on till: Sure.

Volunteer by door: Do you want to take a basket? Just so we know how many people are in the shop. Anything you pick up and don't buy put in the box.

Customer: I'll put it in this box.

Volunteer on till [to Volunteer by door]: Do you know how you . . .?

Customer [picking up book not yet rung up]: I think they're the
    same price. [Picking *Klingsor's Last Summer* out of quaran-
    tine box again] Oh, no. This is two ninety-nine.
Volunteer on till: That's nineteen ninety-four. Paying by card?
Customer: Er, yeah.
Volunteer by door: Do you want to take a basket? Just so we
    know how many people are in the shop. Anything you pick
    up and don't buy put in the box.

It seemed like a new development at the time, Jane Solomon's
debut novel, *Hotel 167*, not only coming out as a paperback
original, but having the words A PICADOR PAPERBACK ORIGINAL
running across the bottom of the front cover and the top of the
back cover. Everything about *Hotel 167* seemed bold. Protagonist and antagonist: young woman versus psychiatrist. Subject
matter: cutting with blades, unusual sexual activities, fantasy
versus reality. Not only was the novel named after an actual hotel
on the Old Brompton Road, but I imagined the colour scheme
of the front cover – green title, red background (photograph by
Andrew Thompson) – to have been inspired by its red brick
and mint-green masonry paint. Even the decision to publish it,
when it didn't seem quite ready, was surprising. Maybe, in 1993,
I was easily impressed, but I was even impressed by the brevity
of the author biog: 'Jane Solomon is twenty and lives in Chelsea.'
(Short author biogs were in for new Picador authors in the early
1990s. Phillip Baker's for *Blood Posse* the following year was even
shorter: 'Phillip Baker is thirty-seven.')
    Solomon was impressed, too. 'In the 1990s, the Picador head-
quarters were in a modern building on Cavaye Place, all tinted
windows, open-plan design, track lighting, boxes of freshly minted
books everywhere, a place of subdued glamour to a young writer.'

By chance – or design? – the novel was published during an important year for Picador. 'I remember the swish literary party for the imprint's twenty-first anniversary: silver helium balloons, a grand cake, white wine and canapés, unstructured jackets, sequins and black Lycra, and many famous faces like Oliver Sacks, Julian Barnes and Ian McEwan, with whom, as a fellow Picador writer, I was supposed to have a group photograph taken. How I wish I had, but instead, rather than stand up with them against a wall and be shot, I hid.'

It was a difficult time for Solomon. She told Andrew Billen, in an interview for the *Observer*, that shortly after writing the novel she was admitted as a psychiatric in-patient.

'Many of the opportunities my lovely publicist organised for me seemed impossible at that time, since I couldn't even take a bus and panicked in supermarket queues; they included appearing on the *Good Morning* sofa with Anne and Nick, featuring in a documentary by Magenta Devine and writing a weekly column in the *Mail on Sunday*. Instead, I managed about half a dozen newspaper interviews, a couple on the radio, and one underwhelming appearance on Sky TV.'

It seemed to me, having just had my own first novel partly about cutting with razor blades published by a one-man operation, Preston-based Christopher Kenworthy's Barrington Books, after it had been turned down by all the publishers in London, that everything was in place to make *Hotel 167* a smash hit.

'Although my novel was reprinted once,' Solomon tells me, 'I had failed to fulfil the publicity requirements that might have put it on the best-seller list. And so, Picador, perhaps reluctantly, raised their lance. As a Taurean, maybe I should have been more prepared. They severed their contract with me and my second novel was removed from their upcoming list, although it had already been assigned an ISBN, and I was duly paid. I have now completed ten novels and a book of poetry, but my lucky break came at the wrong time and, apart from some poems published in the *Spectator*, only *Hotel 167* has so far made it to the printed page.'

Wednesday 4 October 2006

I met someone who'd been given the job of science fiction book reviewer for *Time Out*. He was a very, very short person. So short he was just a head, with a pointed nose, sitting on top of a pair of wellington boots. His legs were inside these and he could walk. He wore some kind of hat.

It was daunting – too daunting – for Jane Solomon to have to stand side by side with famous Picador authors (and be photographed), but it's the names of those who have gone before that so often attracted new writers to the imprint. For short story writer Kate Pullinger, having arrived in Britain from Canada only a few years before her collection *Tiny Lies* appeared from Picador, it was Michael Ondaatje.

'Getting my paperback on to the Picador list, after hardcover publication with the then independent Jonathan Cape, felt very significant and important as it wasn't a given – hardcovers didn't always get into paperback then. I was an avid reader and Picador was an imprint that I looked for on the shelves of bookshops. They were publishing many of my favourite writers in the 1980s, including the great Michael Ondaatje – imagine having your book with the same logo as Ondaatje!'

Andrew O'Hagan, author of *The Missing*, looked for the same logo in the bookshop.

'I misspent my youth in the bookshop of the Third Eye Centre in Glasgow, half-way up Sauchiehall Street,' he tells me.

'The shop was full of strange smells – the smell of real coffee, for instance, coming from the cafe just beyond the bookshop, and the sort of cooking that seemed odd at the time, involving lentils and possibly herbs. In the middle of the shop there was a revolving bookstand. It was dedicated to Picador, and it had, for me, a very powerful magic. Here were the best writers. It had Kafka and Rimbaud. It had Tom Wolfe and Germaine Greer. Something about those white spines and the word "Picador" (underscored and super-scored) made me want to write. In time I came to be on that revolving shelf with my first book, *The Missing*. It was a lovely paperback, white all over and kind of fearlessly blank on the cover, and I was never prouder than when I saw it in that shop, which had changed by then, as we all had. Nowadays, with same-day-delivery, we sometimes forget the journeys we used to make to expand our capacity for wonder. Postcard Records, Harrington jackets, Picador Books. The idea that you could save up and make the journey and choose one – and holy fuck, that it could choose you – was a commonplace dream of the beautiful world.'

Saturday 2 January 2010

I was due to meet author Riddley Walker. [I had a nagging, vague doubt about the name, but he was an author, wasn't he? Wasn't he the author of *All the Little Animals*, the adaptation of which had been Jeremy Thomas's first film as director?] But I realised this appointment would clash with an already agreed trip on Eurostar to France or Belgium. Which should I do? I wanted somehow to do both, and as the dream neared its end [as I drifted towards consciousness] it did get easier to see how this might be possible. [The author of *All the Little Animals* was Walker Hamilton.]

꿏

The appearance in Picador of his collection, *Taking Doreen Out of the Sky*, was, for Alan Beard, a dream come true.

'Ever since I became aware of Picador books I wanted to be published by them,' the Birmingham-based short story writer tells me. 'Still a teenager (just), I bought their early anthologies, *The Naked i* and *The Existential Imagination*, and lapped them up. Then they published and introduced me to my still-favourite author Henry Green, with the magnificent three-novel volume *Loving – Living – Party Going*. (I re-bought this in Hay as my copy fell apart years ago – one of the problems of Picador.) Then they published three collections of Raymond Carver in one volume. And the Beckett trilogy (me and my mate loved Beckett so much we started a mag called *Malone Lives*, circulation six, issues four). Cormac McCarthy. Doris Lessing's *Memoirs of a Survivor*. Russell Hoban's *Riddley Walker*. Foreign literature in translation from Hamsun's *Hunger* to Hedayat's *Blind Owl*. Calvino, Márquez, Schulz. And they also gave short stories their due, publishing McEwan's collections, Graham Swift, Denis Johnson, Joyce Carol Oates. So many. I was writing stories and wanted so much to be published by Picador, to join my favourites.'

I so much wanted Penguin to publish my first novel, *Counterparts*, that I submitted it to them at least twice. I had already submitted it once and had it rejected when Mike Petty, rejecting it for Bloomsbury on 13 February 1989, said it might be worth my while trying Tim Binding at Penguin. I did as Petty suggested; Binding declined on 8 May.

'I belonged (still do) to a writers' group, Tindal Street Fiction Group, and in 1997 some members wanted to start a press and used my collection (I was the one ready to go, so to speak) as a dry run: commissioning a cover, liaising with printing firms, launching, marketing and so on. Joel Lane, who had recently joined the group, wrote the blurb. So successful were they, the book garnered reviews in the *Times*, *TLS* and *Time Out* among others. Your review in the latter suggested the book should "sail under the flag of, say, Faber, Picador or Quartet". Shortly after, I received offers from three or four firms but all except Picador wanted a novel as well. No chance of that. There was no debate anyway, this was my dream come true: my stuff was to appear in the famous white-spined imprint.'

I know exactly how Beard felt. After the Berlin Wall came down in November 1989, prompting a rewrite of the ending of my novel, I think I might have sent the new version to Penguin, but I have no record of any further correspondence until Fanny Blake wrote to welcome me to Penguin in 1994. They had finally taken it on after its first publication by Barrington Books and, I think significantly, after the appearance of a couple of good reviews by Jonathan Coe and Roz Kaveney, in the *Guardian* and *TLS* respectively. The prospect of joining the same imprint that had published Anthony Burgess, Graham Greene and Derek Marlowe was almost too exciting. How could the reality ever match up to the expectation?

'Picador published *Taking Doreen Out of the Sky* in 1999 as it stood, using the group's page proofs. They kept Joel's blurb but missed out the magazine credits (annoyingly). A new cover – at first I didn't like it (not urban enough) – which I now love. No launch, no promotion (although it was included in a library leaflet) and unsurprisingly it sold few copies, despite good reviews. It was subsequently pulped (without telling me). Second-hand copies still exist. I have several copies of both the

Tindal one (paper still perfect) and Picador (paper browning) and put them next to books I love (Alice Munro, Joy Williams) on my shelves to see if they can absorb some kudos by proximity.'

Wednesday 13 December 2006

I went in a bookshop and asked for a book on Manchester City manager and ex-player Stuart Pearce. I was handed a thick hardback. I thought, Great, but then looked at it. It was about polo. I thought, Maybe it's got something in it about Pearce, but I checked the index and there was nothing. I challenged the two assistants, who maintained it was an appropriate choice. I laughed. I showed them the index and told them how ridiculous this was. I said, This is great. A new kind of bookshop. You go in, ask for a book on X, they give you a book on Y. They didn't see what was funny about that.

I arrange to meet retired publisher Patrick Janson-Smith at an independent coffee shop in Notting Hill on 8 March 2018.

My agent, John Saddler, has taken a keen interest in my research for this book. He had some no doubt very wise ideas about what I should do and how I should do it. I should, for example, fly to New York and interview Sonny Mehta and write that up and put it at the end of the book. The quest narrative – to find and acquire all the white-spined Picadors – reaches its climax by going all the way to the source.

That wasn't really the approach I wanted to take and chose instead to meet Patrick Janson-Smith, who had rejected something of mine at some point, but quite rightly and very nicely, and who, more to the point, had worked with Sonny Mehta.

I arrive outside the coffee shop five minutes early feeling vaguely nervous. A couple of doors down is the reassuring fascia of an Oxfam Bookshop I somehow have not only never visited, but didn't even know existed. I'd normally want more than five minutes, but if I wait till after the interview it'll be awkward. Janson-Smith and I are bound to stand on the pavement outside the coffee shop and he'll walk one way and I'll more or less have to walk the other. I'm told he has a flat in Holland Park, so he's going to walk south, past Oxfam. I'll have to walk north. Unless I say I want to go in Oxfam, in which case he'll probably come in with me. If that happens, we will inevitably stand looking at the books together and it will be like standing at the urinals next to someone you know and finding yourself unable to go. I'm not quite sure what exactly that feeling will translate to in terms of looking at books in a bookshop, but I don't think I want to find out.

Before I know it, I've only got a minute left. I dart into Oxfam and spot *Last Orders* – of course – and David Malouf's *An Imaginary Life*. I'm holding them both in my hand, but there's a man at the till and in the set of his shoulders I can see he's going to be a while. I look at the time; I'm a minute late. I put the books back and leave the shop and arrive in the coffee shop a little bit flustered and apologising for being late. Janson-Smith stands up and we shake hands. My immediate impression is of a comfortable, relaxed man, tall, well dressed, youthful and pleasant. He goes to get me a cup of green tea and I sit down and when he returns I see that we're each wearing jackets from Old Town, an ice-breaker probably neither of us expected and we spend the first ten minutes discussing their various different styles. He asks me if my jacket is a Borough and I tell him it's a Stanley. I'm sure he says his is a Marshalsea, but later I wonder if it's a Medway.

Janson-Smith reaches into his bag and brings out three

Picadors – Alan Bold's anthology of erotic verse, *Making Love*, Bruce Chatwin's *What Am I Doing Here* and Clive James's *Unreliable Memoirs*. He tells me they're for me and, like an idiot, I tell him I've already got them, but how could I let him think I didn't already have the Chatwin and the James? You see them all the time. Not like *Last Orders* and *Once in a House on Fire*, but not far off. I pick up *Unreliable Memoirs* and flick through it and tucked in at page 69 is a boarding pass in the name of Mr Janson-Smith. British Caledonian Airways. Now I want these books. Janson-Smith tries to remember where he was going, but can't.

We talk about Paladin and Granada and Abacus and Black Swan. We talk about Herbert Van Thal's *Pan Book of Horror Stories* and Michel Parry's *Mayflower Book of Black Magic Stories*.

'Dear old Michel,' says Janson-Smith. 'I haven't been in touch with him for years.'

I say I've a horrible feeling he might be dead. (Parry died in 2014.)

We talk about Bill Bryson's *Notes From a Small Island*. 'Everybody told me I was mad to pay him £300,000,' says Janson-Smith. 'I knew what I had. The *FT* even went as far as to say, "Transworld have lost their marbles." Anyway, three million copies later . . .'

We talk about Octopus and Mayflower and Corgi ('Bloody stupid name').

'I wanted to publish in B format, having seen what Flamingo and Abacus and Picador, in particular, were doing. I remember Sonny saying to me, "What are you doing queering our pitch? I said, "Sonny, I'll be doing things very differently." Black Swan started in '83.'

What about Picador, though? Was it distinctive?

'Absolutely. Sonny had immaculate taste and they just pub-lished books that people seemed to want to read. Very early on. And they sort of grew and grew and they've kept the standard up. At the moment Picador is at the top of its game. They've got some very bright editors. I think Picador is a terrific list. I was quite horrified, though, by how few I had.'

He has fewer now.

'Well, yes. But that was all I could find. I've got a lot more books in the country.'

I think it's a shame that they abandoned this look. The white spine, black lettering.

'Yes, but people do. They don't think.'

We step outside and I say I'm going to have a look in the Oxfam Bookshop. He tells me he was in there just the other day. We stroll for a few yards and come to a halt. With a handshake we say goodbye. Janson-Smith walks on towards Holland Park and I enter the Oxfam Bookshop to see if *Last Orders* and *An Imaginary Life* are still there.

Having bonded with Patrick Janson-Smith over Old Town jackets, I was grateful for another element of my wardrobe the day I met Alberto Manguel. I had been invited to take part in an event at the British Library, 'Word Houses: Dictionaries, Archives, Libraries and Beyond', on 10 June 2019. Part of the reason I accepted the invitation – and the main reason why I became more and more nervous as the event drew nearer – was that among the individuals taking part would be Alberto Manguel, something of a hero of mine as the editor of *Black Water: The Anthology of Fantastic Literature*. We were not on the same panel, but he would be around and I might have an op-portunity to meet him. I would tell him how much *Black Water* had meant to me, how it had helped form me as both a reader and a writer, and I would see him looking over my shoulder for someone, anyone, to save him from this boring conversation.

Luckily, it didn't go like that at all. He was gracious and charming and enormous fun. He pointed at my sky-blue shoe-laces and pulled his trousers up off his shoes to reveal his own laces, which were the exact same shade of blue.

Of the novels among the first eight Picadors, I leave the longest till last. *The Lorry* (also known, in a later edition from another publisher, as *A Necessary Action*, although, since *The Lorry* is a literal translation of the Swedish title, *Lastbilen*, I can't see any reason for changing it) by Peter Wahloo (also known as Per Wahlöö, which, as it is his real name, seems fair enough) is a tense and gripping suspense novel set in Franco's Spain. Former German soldier turned amateur artist Willi Mohr is living outside a small town, sharing basic accommodation with a Norwegian couple. Much of their time is spent in a bar down at the harbour or driving between bar and house after having had too much to drink, or, occasionally fishing or swimming in the company of two local men who are brothers. When the Norwegians go missing, Willi Mohr, formerly passive and apa-thetic, takes action.

There are some extraordinarily tense and powerful scenes, whether involving two characters in a police interview room or four in a small boat. I can't help wishing the author had restrict-ed the point of view, either throughout or just within scenes, but I probably need to get over my objection to head-hopping. For me, *The Lorry* is the best of the six novels among the eight Picador launch titles. The Dalí painting on its cover may have little to do with the content of the novel, apart from its Spanish village setting and beautiful blue sky (the same blue, incidentally, as Alberto Manguel's shoelaces – and mine), but it works brilliantly both as a cover in the general sense and as a cover specifically for that book, because of its mood.

Mood was very important to the Radical Illustrators group, a loosely formed movement from the early 1980s of, mostly, graduates of the Royal College of Art. Several contributors to issue 38 of *Illustrators* magazine, dubbed *Radical Illustrators*, have become familiar names to me since I started reading the artist credit on the back of Picador Books, including Robert Mason, Andrzej Klimowski, Ian Pollock, Liz Pyle and Brothers Quay. This fits with art director Gary Day-Ellison's use of a particular word to describe himself and his colleagues: 'I would characterise Picador as maverick passion. Passion for writing, passion for art direction, passion for publishing. We were all mavericks at Picador.'

The maverick tendency could perhaps explain the anomalies. 'Every now and then,' Day-Ellison tells me, 'inconsistencies in the format were dropped in. For variety. Humanity. Anti-OCD sometimes, to break things up at others. Sometimes the book told us. For example, Jonathan Schell's *The Fate of the Earth* I wanted to be totally matt black with all the information, including title and author, on the back. For drama relevant to the content. I had to compromise on that one, sadly.'

Among the artists Day-Ellison commissioned, and a key contributor to *Radical Illustrators*, was Robert Mason, whose Picador covers number at least a dozen and in many cases, notably those for *Great Works of Jewish Fantasy*, Mike Nicol's *The Powers That Be* and Angela Carter's *Black Venus*, as well as a striking series of covers for three John Fowles novels, might be described as authentically surrealist.

'You did not meet the authors in question,' says Mason.

'Seems a little sad, in retrospect, but I think the theory was to keep cover ideas within a small number of people. I *always* read books before doing cover work, and was astonished to find that this practice didn't always apply to some fellow illustrators. It could be problematic, mind you: if given a juicy commission involving several books (e.g. Robert Musil [for Picador Classics]) the initial deadline – sometimes a month or two – might have seemed generous. But one could find oneself still reading with a week to go. One of the nicest things about the freelance illo's life, though, was that it supplied constant new reading material.'

How did doing a job for Picador compare with working for other publishers?

'Working for Picador was a pleasure, and felt like a privilege. Only Penguin, especially King Penguin, came close in that, latter respect. Presentations (to the art director only, back then) were very informal and decisions quickly made. I would take an A3 sketchbook with perhaps half a dozen possible directions, but with a couple developed more than the others. Obviously roughs were drawn in proportion to cover size, but they might be very understated, with handwritten notes to suggest possible ways forward. Gary Day-Ellison might have to do plenty of reading and "filling in the gaps". Sometimes he might home in on a peripheral sketch and ask me to develop that, as opposed to the major imagery. I didn't mind that, at all; there was always a reason. Colour in roughs would be quickly/washily applied; there was an understanding that things would firm up when taken forward.

'A lot was taken on trust, and in retrospect it was an amazingly trusting process, overall. I only did one "turkey" for Picador, and that was towards the end of my time working for them, when I think that other voices were becoming involved in decision-making. Generally, you felt you were working as part of an "elite" – silly word, but . . .

'Probably needless to say, but when Gary left, the atmosphere changed totally; I didn't do too much for Picador beyond that point but the working process was less interesting. One became less autonomous, and I recall having to (diplomatically) refuse to carry out some very banal art direction, and push such suggestions in more interesting directions.'

Interestingly, Day-Ellison says that 'Picador was a writers' imprint'. He goes on: 'Classy, diverse and ground-breaking. The editors were quiet, literary chaps: Mike Petty, Tim Binding and Geoff Mulligan. And always the classy publicist and press officer Jacqueline Graham. I was in the right place at the right time and loved it.'

Day-Ellison's cover artists and illustrators clearly loved working for him, among them Grizelda Holderness, who agrees with Mason about the nature of the relationship.

'It was about trust. Gary Day-Ellison trusted us to do the very best we could, and we did. We gave him our best. A joy! And laughed a lot too. Always. However serious the book or circumstances. I delivered my pictures on my motorbike, usually (probably always) late and in trouble, packed safe in mount board and cardboard and strapped over my shoulder like a huge sail, hoping it wouldn't be too windy that day. Sometimes I was forgiven!

'At that time,' she adds, 'approval didn't have to go through a hundred committees, or, if it did, he didn't burden us with it.'

I wonder if Holderness ever met or conferred with Emma Tennant, through whose door on Blenheim Crescent in Notting Hill I once, in 1998, unknowingly pushed a copy of Derek Marlowe's second novel, *Memoirs of a Venus Lackey*, in a lovely if slightly naughty Panther edition (cover photograph by Richard Stirling). Having constructed a twelve-and-a-half-mile walk past all of Marlowe's former London addresses for the *Time Out Book of London Walks*, I was delivering a copy of one of the author's books to each one, with a note inviting them to keep the book on their shelves. When I got home from the walk, it was to a message from Emma Tennant, who had been acquainted with Marlowe and was saddened to hear of his death, but happy to learn she was living in the same building where he had rented a bedsitter in 1964.

'Sadly,' Holderness tells me, 'I never spoke to Emma Tennant. I was always too shy. And then she went and died. So I don't know if she liked the pictures or not. I will always regret being too much of a scaredy-cat to ask.'

Nor did Holderness get to meet Norman Mailer.

'*Ancient Evenings* was a huge responsibility. I delved into Egyptian hieroglyphics. Eventually, the nearest thing/translation I could find for "Ancient Evenings" was: "The things we do before bedtime" or "All Activities Before Bedtime", which I thought was really funny. And profound! Wonderful! So that's what it says on the book. (I don't know if anyone else in the world would know that.) They printed it a bit too yellow, which completely broke my heart. And why I have not been able to read it since. One day. It should have been beautiful deep and light subtle gold ochres. But printers do their best, too, however much I've cursed them.'

Holderness has a rule: 'As an illustrator, my rule was and is: you never give away the secrets of a book on its cover. You have to unravel it. Find, if you can, the little kernel of it, what it's about (like unravelling a golf ball), and then make something. Hopefully, for the author – only imagined, and a whole distance away – it's something OK, and earns her or him some money – or at least something that might invite someone in, to hear a story. Stories, our stories, the most important things in the whole wide world! More precious than gold.'

In the end, that's what it's all about.

I often wonder when I'm walking down the street reading whatever I'm reading – most recently it was Jamaica Kincaid's 1984 Picador short story collection *At the Bottom of the River* – how many other people in the world are walking down the street right now reading the same book. If I think it might be zero, I wonder instead how many people in the world are reading Jamaica Kincaid's *At the Bottom of the River*, right now, whether walking down the street or not, or how many people in the world are reading anything by Jamaica Kincaid right now, and if I imagine there might be a few, or a few dozen or a few hundred, or even a few thousand, I feel a sort of connection with them. And that's why I think stories are important, whether they're by Jamaica Kincaid or any other writer and whether you read them walking down the street or curled up in a chair or lying in the bath or in bed or whatever, that's why Grizelda Holderness might be right: they might be the most important things in the whole wide world.

In the end, as I said, that's what it's all about, and it's that line that made me think of all that, because I wondered, as I typed it, how many other books might have concluded with those words. One or two? Dozens? Maybe even hundreds?

In the end, that's what it's all about.

Acknowledgements

I would like to thank the following: AJ Ashworth, Virginia Astley, Alan Beard, Geoff Bird, Anne Brichto, Bill Bulloch, Michael Caines, Neil Campbell, Richard Clegg, Jonathan Coe, David Collard, Austin Collings, Sarah-Clare Conlon, Ailsa Cox, Gary Day-Ellison, Claire Dean, Rae Donaldson, Simon Donoghue, Kris Doyle, James Draper, Tim Etchells, Gareth Evans, Adele Fielding, Samuel Fisher, David Gaffney, Rob Gill, Mike Goldmark, Wayne Gooderham, Jacqueline Graham, Paul Griffiths, Sarah Guy, Chris Hamilton-Emery, Jen Hamilton-Emery, Oliver Harris, Hilaire, Grizelda Holderness, Roger Huss, Ian Irvine, Mick Jackson, Patrick Janson-Smith, Liz Jensen, Russell Celyn Jones, Ella Joyce, Sue Joyce, Nigel Kendall, Paul Leith, Pete Lewis, Conrad Leyser, Nicholas Lezard, Emma Liggins, Patrick McGrath, Rachel McIntyre, Lucie McKnight Hardy, Robert Mason, Wyl Menmuir, More Maniacs & everyone at Moniack Mhor, Adam Morris, Dave Mundy, Emma Oakey, John Oakey, Andrew O'Hagan, Simon Okotie, Scott Pack, Chris Parker, Janet Penny, Saxon Pepperdine, Mike Petty, Alex Preston, Juliet Pickering, Kate Pullinger, Cathy Rentzenbrink, Danny Rhodes, Helen Richardson, Barbara Robinson, Nick

Rogers, David Rose, Bella Royle, Charlie Royle, Jean Royle, Joanna Royle, Julie Royle, Nicholas Royle, Kate Ryan, John Saddler, John Saul, Nicholas Shakespeare, Tim Shearer, Stav Sherez, Harry Sherriff, Adrian Slatcher, Jane Solomon, Yuka Sonobe, Robert Stone, Peter Straus, Tim Watson, Chris Witty, Chris White, Catherine Wilcox, Conrad Williams, Conrad Williams, Janet Zmroczek. Special thanks to my wife, Ros Sales, and apologies to those people I am bound to have forgotten.

Main collection

This is a list of the B-format Picador paperbacks published between 1972 and 1999/2000 that I have collected between 1982 and 2021, excluding 'anomalies' and Picador Classics, not a list of all the books Picador published during those years.

Chinua Achebe, *Anthills of the Savannah*

Kathy Acker, *Blood and Guts in High School, Plus Two* • *Empire of the Senseless*

Renata Adler, *Speedboat*

M Ageyev, *Novel With Cocaine*

Tariq Ali, *The Nehrus and the Gandhis: An Indian Dynasty* • *Redemption* • *Shadows of the Pomegranate Tree*

Marcel Allain & Pierre Souvestre, *Fantômas* • *The Silent Executioner*

Woody Allen, *Complete Prose*

Guido Almansi & Claude Béguin (eds), *Theatre of Sleep: An Anthology of Literary Dreams*

Brian Appleyard, *Understanding the Present*

Aragon, *Paris Peasant*

Jean-Claude Armen, *Gazelle-Boy*

Andrea Ashworth, *Once in a House on Fire*

Deirdre Bair, *Samuel Beckett*

Phillip Baker, *Blood Posse*

Russell Banks, *Affliction*

Don Bannister, *Burning Leaves*

John Banville, *The Untouchable*

Julian Barnes, *Before She Met Me* • *Birchwood* • *Cross Channel* • *Flaubert's Parrot* • *A History of the World in 10 1/2 Chapters* • *Letters From London 1990–1995* • *Mefisto* • *Metroland* • *The Porcupine* • *Staring at the Sun* • *Talking it Over*

Anthony Barnett, *Soviet Freedom*

Andrew Barrow, *The Man in the Moon* • *The Tap Dancer*

Fergus Barrowman (ed), *The Picador Book of Contemporary New Zealand Fiction*

Jonathan Bate, *The Cure for Love* • *The Genius of Shakespeare*

Richard Bausch, *Aren't You Happy For Me?*

Martin Bax, *The Hospital Ship*

Alan Beard, *Taking Doreen Out of the Sky*

Samuel Beckett, *Company* • *More Pricks Than Kicks* • *The Beckett Trilogy* • *Mercier and Camier* • *Murphy* • *A Samuel Beckett Reader* • *Watt*

Sybille Bedford, *As it Was* • *A Legacy*

William Bedford, *All Shook Up*

Louis Begley, *The Man Who Was Late* • *Wartime Lies*

Gavin Bell, *In Search of Tusitala*

Marina Benjamin, *Living at the End of the World*

Tim Binding, *A Perfect Execution*

David Black, *The Plague Years*

Caroline Blackwood, *Great Granny Webster* • *The Last of the Duchess*

Amy Bloom, *Come to Me*

Alan Bold (ed), *Making Love, the Picador Book of Erotic Verse* • *Mounts of Venus: The Picador Book of Erotic Prose*

Dermot Bolger (ed), *Finbar's Hotel* • *The Picador Book of Contemporary Irish Fiction*

Jorge Luis Borges, *The Aleph and Other Stories 1933–1969* • *A Personal Anthology*

Scott Bradfield, *Animal Planet* • *The History of Luminous Motion* • *What's Wrong With America*

Richard Brautigan, *The Abortion: An Historical Romance 1966* • *A Confederate General From Big Sur* • *Dreaming of Babylon: A Private Eye Novel 1942* • *The Hawkline Monster* • *Revenge of the Lawn* • *Sombrero Fallout: A Japanese Novel* • *The Tokyo-Montana Express* • *Trout Fishing in America* • *In Watermelon Sugar* • *Willard and his Bowling Trophies*

Miles Bredin, Blood on the Tracks

Harold Brodkey, *Stories in an Almost Classical Mode*

Stephen Brook, *Claws of the Crab* • *The Double Eagle* • *Honky Tonk Gelato* • *LA Law* • *Maple Leaf Rag* • *New York Days, New York Nights* • *Winner Takes All*

Peter Currell Brown, *Smallcreep's Day*

Rebecca Brown, *The Children's Crusade* • *The Haunted House* • *The Terrible Girls*

Jan Harold Brunvand, *The Vanishing Hitchhiker*

James Buchan, *Frozen Desire*

Andrew Buckoke, *Fishing in Africa*

Mikhail Bulgakov, *The Master and Margarita*

James Lee Burke, *The James Lee Burke Collection*

William Burroughs, *Cities of the Red Night* • *Interzone* • *My Education: A Book of Dreams* • *Queer* • *The Western Lands* • *A William Burroughs Reader*

Robert Byron, *The Road to Oxiana*

James M Cain, *The Five Great Novels of James M Cain*

Carmel Callil & Colm Tóibín, *The Modern Library: The Two Hundred Best Novels in English Since 1950*

Italo Calvino, *Adam, One Afternoon* • *The Castle of Crossed Destinies* • *Cosmicomics* • *Difficult Loves* • *If on a Winter's Night a Traveller* • *Invisible Cities* • *The Literature Machine* • *Marcovaldo* • *Our Ancestors* • *Mr Palomar* • *Time and the Hunter*

Elias Canetti, *Auto da Fé* • *The Conscience of Words: Earwitness* • *The Human Province* • *The Play of the Eyes* • *The Tongue Set Free* • *The Torch in my Ear*

Ethan Canin, *Blue River* • *Emperor of the Air*

Marie Cardinal, *The Words to Say It*

Peter Carey, *Bliss* • *Exotic Pleasures*

Angela Carter, *Black Venus* • *Heroes and Villains* • *Love* • *Nights at the Circus*

Justin Cartwright, *Look at it This Way* • *Masai Dreaming*

Raymond Carver, *Fires: Essays, Poems, Stories* • *In a Marine Light* • *The Stories of Raymond Carver*

Philip Casey, *The Water Star*

Richard Cavendish, *The Black Arts*

Raymond Chandler, *The Chandler Collection Volumes I, II & III*

Lesley Chamberlain, *Volga, Volga*

Ann Charters, *Kerouac*

Bruce Chatwin, *Anatomy of Restlessness* • *In Patagonia* • *On the Black Hill* • *The Songlines* • *Utz* • *The Viceroy of Ouidah* • *What Am I Doing Here*

Amit Chaudhuri, *Freedom Song*

Susan Cheever, *Home Before Dark*

Catherine Chidgey, *In a Fishbone Church*

Carolyn Chao & David Su Li-Qun (eds), *The Picador Book of Contemporary Chinese Fiction*

Lindsay Clarke, *Alice's Masque* • *The Chymical Wedding* • *Sunday Whiteman*

Nik Cohn, *Ball the Wall* • *King Death*

Nick Coleman & Nick Hornby (eds), *The Picador Book of Sports Writing*

Billy Collins, *Nine Horses* • *Taking Off Emily Dickinson's Clothes*

Matthew Condon, Usher

Evan S Connell, *Mrs Bridge and Mr Bridge* • *Son of the Morning Star*

Anna Coote & Beatrix Campbell (eds), *Sweet Freedom: The Struggle for Women's Liberation*

Robert Coover, *Pricksongs & Descants*

Alain Corbin, *The Foul & the Fragrant: Odour and the Social Imagination*

Graham Coster (ed), *The Picador Book of Aviation*

Jonathan Cott, *Stockhausen: Conversations With the Composer*

Jim Crace, *Arcadia* • *Continent* • *The Gift of Stones*

Margaret Craven, *I Heard the Owl Call My Name*

James Crumley, *The Collection* • *The Mexican Tree Duck* • *One to Count Cadence*

Rachel Cusk, *The Country Life* • *Saving Agnes* • *The Temporary*

Salvador Dalí, *Hidden Faces*

Guy Davenport, *Eclogues*

Robyn Davidson, *Tracks*

Miles Davis with Quincy Troupe, *Miles: The Autobiography*

Annabel Davis-Goff, *Walled Gardens*

Simone de Beauvoir, *The Second Sex*

Ralph de Boissière, *Crown Jewel*

Alain de Botton, *Essays in Love* • *Kiss and Tell* • *How Proust Can Change Your Life* • *The Romantic Movement*

Sebastian de Grazia, *Machiavelli in Hell*

Napoleón Baccino Ponce de León, *Five Black Ships*

Don DeLillo, *The Day Room* • *Great Jones Street* • *The Names*
    • *Running Dog* • *Underworld* • *White Noise*

Margriet de Moor, *Virtuoso*

Christine de Pizan, *The Book of the City of Ladies*

Robert S de Ropp, *The Master Game*

AK Dewdney, *The Planiverse*

Farrukh Dhondy, *Bombay Duck*

Michael Dibdin (ed), *The Picador Book of Crime Writing*

Annie Dillard, *An American Childhood* • *Pilgrim at Tinker Creek*

Isak Dinesen, *Letters From Africa 1914–1941*

EL Doctorow, *The Book of Daniel* • *Lives of the Poets: A Novella
    and Six Stories* • *Loon Lake* • *Ragtime* • *The Waterworks* •
    World's Fair

Christina Dodwell, *In Papua New Guinea*

Paul Driver, *Manchester Pieces*

Helena Drysdale, *Looking For George*

Andre Dubus, *Broken Vessels* • *Selected Stories* • *Voices From the
    Moon and Other Stories* • *We Don't Live Here Anymore: The
    Novellas of Andre Dubus*

Patricia Duncker, *Hallucinating Foucault* • *James Miranda Barry*
    • *Monsieur Shoushana's Lemon Trees*

Friedrich Dürrenmatt, *The Assignment* • *The Execution of Justice*
    • *The Novels of Friedrich Dürrenmatt*

Umberto Eco, *Foucault's Pendulum* • *Misreadings* • *The Name
    of the Rose* • *Travels in Hyperreality*

Robert Edrich, *The Broken Lands*

Jennifer Egan, *Emerald City*

Evan Eisenberg, *The Ecology of Eden* • *The Recording Angel*

Bret Easton Ellis, *American Psycho* • *The Informers* • *Less Than Zero* • *The Rules of Attraction*

Hans Magnus Enzensberger, *Europe, Europe*

Louise Erdrich, *The Beet Queen* • *Tracks*

Clifton Fadiman (ed), *The World of the Short Story*

Nureddin Farah, *Maps*

Moris Farhi, *Journey Through the Wilderness*

William Faulkner, *Intruder in the Dust* • *Light in August* • *Soldiers' Pay*

Leonard Feather, *The Jazz Years: Earwitness to an Era*

Helen Fielding, *Bridget Jones's Diary* • *Cause Celeb*

Frances FitzGerald, *Cities on a Hill: A Journey Through Contemporary American Culture*

F Scott Fitzgerald, *The Price Was High Volumes I & II*

Mary Anne Fitzgerald, *Nomad: One Woman's Journey into the Heart of Africa*

MJ Fitzgerald, *Concertina* • *Ropedancer*

Richard Flanagan, *The Sound of One Hand Clapping*

Kathryn Flett, *The Heart-Shaped Bullet*

Michael Foot, *Debts of Honour*

John Fowles, *The Aristos* • *The Collector* • *Daniel Martin* • *The French Lieutenant's Woman* • *A Maggot* • *The Magus* • *Mantissa*

Keath Fraser (ed), *Worst Journeys: The Picador Book of Travel*

Carlos Fuentes, *Christopher Unborn* • *Constancia and Other Stories for Virgins* • *The Old Gringo* • *The Orange Tree*

William Gaddis, *Carpenter's Gothic*

Mary Gaitskill, *Because They Wanted To*

Virginia Gay, *Penelope and Adelina*

Martha Gellhorn, *Liana* • *The Novellas of Martha Gellhorn*

Nikki Gemmell, *Cleave*

Jean Genet, *Prisoner of Love*

Amitav Ghosh, *The Calcutta Chromosome*

Ellen Gilchrist, *In the Land of Dreamy Dreams*

Mikal Gilmore, *Night Beat*

Charles Glass, *Money for Old Rope* • *Tribes With Flags*

Tania Glyde, *Clever Girl*

Peter Godwin, *Mukiwa: A White Boy in Africa*

F Gonzalez-Crussi, *The Five Senses* • *Three Forms of Sudden Death* • *Notes of an Anatomist*

Philip Gourevitch, *We Wish to Inform You That Tomorrow We Will Be Killed With Our Families*

Linda Grant, *The Cast Iron Shore*

Richard E Grant, *By Design* • *With Nails*

Günter Grass, *Cat and Mouse* • *Dog Years* • *The Flounder* • *From the Diary of a Snail* • *The Rat* • *The Tin Drum*

Alisdair Gray, *Lanark: A Life in 4 Books* • *Something Leather*

Spalding Gray, *Gray's Anatomy* • *Impossible Vacation* • *Monster in a Box* • *Swimming to Cambodia*

Henry Green, *Loving – Living – Party Going* • *Nothing – Doting – Blindness*

Germaine Greer, *The Madwoman's Underclothes: Essays and Occasional Writings 1968–1985* • *Sex and Destiny: The Politics of Human Fertility*

Kate Grenville, *The Idea of Perfection* • *Lilian's Story*

Paul Griffiths, *The Lay of Sir Tristram* • *Myself and Marco Polo*

David Grossman, *The Book of Intimate Grammar* • *See Under: Love* • *Sleeping on a Wire* • *The Smile of the Lamb* • *The Yellow Wind*

Güneli Gün, *On the Road to Baghdad*

GI Gurdjieff, *Meetings With Remarkable Men*
Woody Guthrie, *Bound For Glory*

Erich Hackl, *Aurora's Motive*
Dashiel Hammett, *The Continental Op* • *The Four Great Novels*
Knut Hamsun, *Growth of the Soil* • *Hunger* • *Mysteries* • *Victoria*
   • *The Wanderer* • *Wayfarers* • *The Women at the Pump*
Max Handley, *Meanwhile*
Ron Hansen, *Mariette in Ecstasy*
Githa Hariharan, *When Dreams Travel*
Myles Harris, *Breakfast in Hell*
Oliver Harris (ed), *The Letters of William S Burroughs 1945–1959*
Jim Harrison, *Dalva*
Andrew Harvey, *A Journey in Ladakh*
Stratis Haviaras, *When the Tree Sings*
Thomas Healy, *A Hurting Business*
Roy Heath, *The Murderer*
William Least Heat-Moon, *Blue Highways* • *Prairyerth*
Sadegh Hedayat, *The Blind Owl*
Christoph Hein, *The Distant Lover*
Joseph Heller, *Picture This*
Lillian Hellman (ed), *The Selected Letters of Anton Chekhov*
Michael Herr, *Dispatches* • *Walter Winchell*
Hermann Hesse, *Autobiographical Writings* • *Demian* • *The*
   Glass Bead Game • *If the War Goes On* • *The Journey to the*
   East • *Klingsor's Last Summer* • *Knulp* • *Rosshalde* • *Siddhartha* • *Wandering*
Stefan Heym, *The Wandering Jew*
Carl Hiaasen, *The Carl Hiaasen Omnibus*
Francis Hitching, *Earth Magic*
Russell Hoban, *Kleinzeit* • *The Medusa Frequency* • *The Moment*

Under the Moment • *Pilgermann* • *Riddley Walker* • *Turtle Diary*

Alice Hoffman, *Fortune's Daughter* • *Practical Magic* • *Second Nature*

Desmond Hogan, *A Curious Street* • *The Leaves on Grey* • *Stories*

Andrew Holleran, *The Beauty of Men*

Christopher Hope, *Darkest England* • *The Love Songs of Nathan J Swirsky* • *Me, the Moon and Elvis Presley* • *Serenity House* • *Signs of the Heart*

Chenjerai Hove, *Ancestors*

Bohumil Hrabal, *I Served the King of England*

David Huggins, *The Big Kiss*

Keri Hulme, *The Bone People*

Robert Hunter, *The Greenpeace Chronicle*

Duong Thu Huong, *Novel Without a Name*

G Cabrera Infante, *Three Trapped Tigers*

Mick Jackson, *The Underground Man*

Clive James, *Brilliant Creatures* • *Brrm! Brrm!* • *The Crystal Bucket* • *Falling Towards England* • *Flying Visits* • *From the Land of Shadows* • *Glued to the Box* • *May Week Was in June* • *Other Passports: Poems 1958–1985* • *The Remake* • *The Silver Castle* • *Snakecharmers in Texas* • *Unreliable Memoirs* • *Visions Before Midnight*

Kay Redfield Jamison, *An Unquiet Mind*

Tama Janowitz, *A Cannibal in Manhattan* • *The Male Cross-Dresser Support Group* • *Slaves of New York*

Humphrey Jennings, *Pandaemonium*

Carsten Jensen, *Earth in the Mouth*

Diane Johnson, *The Life of Dashiell Hammett*

Russell Celyn Jones, *Soldiers and Innocents*
Nicholas Jose, *The Custodians*
James Joyce, *Ulysses*
Carl Jung, *Man and His Symbols*

Franz Kafka, *The Trial*
Firdaus Kanga, *Heaven on Wheels* • *Trying to Grow*
Ryszard Kapuscinski, *Another Day of Life* • *The Emperor* • *Shah of Shahs*
Frederick R Karl & Leo Hamalian (eds), *The Existential Imagination* • *The Naked i*
Mary Karr, *The Liars' Club*
Anna Kavan, *Ice* • *Sleep Has His House*
Michael Kelly, *Martyrs' Day*
James Kelman, *A Chancer* • *A Disaffection* • *Greyhound For Breakfast*
Ken Kesey, *One Flew Over the Cuckoo's Nest*
Tracy Kidder, *House*
Jamaica Kincaid, *Annie John* • *At the Bottom of the River* • *Lucy*
Maxine Hong Kingston, *China Men* • *The Woman Warrior*
JK Klavans, *God, He Was Good*
Seymour Kleinberg (ed), *The Other Persuasion*
Arthur Koestler, *The Act of Creation* • *Bricks to Babel* • *The Case of the Midwife Toad* • *The Ghost in the Machine* • *The Heel of Achilles* • *Janus: A Summing Up* • *The Roots of Coincidence*
Peter Kravitz (ed), *The Picador Book of Contemporary Scottish Fiction*

B Kojo Laing, *Search Sweet Country* • *Woman of the Aeroplanes*
George Lamming, *Natives of My Person*
George Lamming (ed), *Cannon Shot and Glass Beads*

John Lanchester, *The Debt to Pleasure*

Lewis H Lapham, *Money and Class in America*

Ring Lardner, *The Best Short Stories of Ring Lardner*

Mark Lawson, *The Battle for Room Service* • *Bloody Margaret*
• *Idlewild*

Mitchell Leaska, *Granite and Rainbow*

Denis Leary, *No Cure For Cancer*

Peter Lennon, *Foreign Correspondent: Paris in the Sixties*

Doris Lessing, *The Memoirs of a Survivor* • *The Wind Blows
Away Our Words*

Kathy Lette, *Altar Ego* • *Foetal Attraction* • *Girls' Night Out* •
The Llama Parlour • *Mad Cows*

Norman Lewis, *An Empire of the East* • *A Goddess in the Stones*
• *I Came, I Saw* • *Norman Lewis Omnibus* • *Voices of the Old
Sea* • *The World, the World*

Simon Leys, *The Death of Napoleon*

Frances Liardet, *The Game*

Edward Limonov, *It's Me, Eddie*

Haniel Long, *The Marvellous Adventure of Cabeza de Vaca*

Anita Loos, *Gentlemen Prefer Blondes*

Barry Lopez, *Desert Notes & River Notes*

Herbert R Lottman, *Albert Camus: A Biography*

David Wong Louis, *Pangs of Love*

John Livingston Lowes, *The Road to Xanadu: A Study in the Ways
of the Imagination*

Malcolm Lowry, *Under the Volcano*

TJ Lustig, *Doubled Up*

Patrick McCabe, *Breakfast on Pluto* • *The Butcher Boy* • *Carn* •
The Dead School • *Mondo Desperado*

Anthony McCarton, *Spinners*

Cormac McCarthy, *All the Pretty Horses* • *Blood Meridian* • *Child of God* • *Cities of the Plain* • *The Crossing* • *The Orchard Keeper* • *Outer Dark* • *Suttree*

John McCrone, *The Ape That Spoke*

Robert McCrum, *The Fabulous Englishman* • *In the Secret State* • *Mainland* • *The Psychological Moment* • *Suspicion*

AG Macdonell, *England, Their England*

Ian McEwan, *Black Dogs* • *The Cement Garden* • *The Child in Time* • *The Comfort of Strangers* • *First Love, Last Rites* • *The Imitation Game* • *In Between the Sheets* • *The Innocent*

Cyra McFadden, *The Serial*

Patrick McGrath & Bradford Morrow (eds), *The New Gothic*

Craig McGregor (ed), *Bob Dylan: A Retrospective*

William McGuire & RFC Hull (eds), *CG Jung Speaking: Interviews and Encounters*

Ben Macintyre, *Forgotten Fatherland*

John MacKenna, *A Year of Our Lives*

Mary Mackey, *McCarthy's List*

Norman Maclean, *A River Runs Through It*

Robert McLiam Wilson, *Manfred's Pain* • *Ripley Bogle*

Thomas McMahon, *Loving Little Egypt*

Eoin McNamee, *The Last of Deeds & Love in History* • *Resurrection Man*

Candia McWilliam, *A Case of Knives* • *Debatable Land* • *A Little Stranger* • *Wait Till I Tell You*

Brenda Maddox, *George's Ghosts*

Norman Mailer, *Ancient Evenings*

Janet Malcolm, *Psychoanalysis: The Impossible Profession*

Thomas Mallon, *A Book of One's Own*

David Malouf, *The Great World* • *An Imaginary Life*

Alberto Manguel (ed), *Black Water: The Anthology of Fantastic*

Literature • *Other Fires: Stories From the Women of Latin America* • *White Fire: Further Fantastic Literature*

Michael March, *Description of a Struggle*

Leslie A Marchand (ed), *Lord Byron: Selected Letters and Journals*

Greil Marcus, *The Dustbin of History* • *Invisible Republic*

Gabriel García Márquez, *The Autumn of the Patriach* • *Chronicle of a Death Foretold* • *In Evil Hour* • *Innocent Eréndira* • *Leaf Storm* • *No One Writes to the Colonel* • *One Hundred Years of Solitude*

Edward Marriott, *The Lost Tribe*

Adam Mars-Jones, *Lantern Lecture*

Joanot Martorell & Marti Joan de Galba, *Tirant Lo Blanc*

Katinka Matson, *Short Lives*

Peter Matthiessen, *The Snow Leopard* • *The Tree Where Man Was Born*

Ved Mehta, *Daddyji/Mamaji* • *The Ledge Between the Streams* • *Sound-Shadows of the New World* • *Vedi*

Pauline Melville, *Shape-Shifter*

Henry Miller, *A Henry Miller Reader*

Karl Miller, *Dark Horses*

Adrian Mitchell, *The Bodyguard* • *Wartime*

Timothy Mo, *An Insular Possession*

George Monbiot, *No Man's Land*

Paul Monette, *Nosferatu the Vampyre*

Oscar Moore, *PWA: Looking Aids in the Face*

Susanna Moore, *In the Cut*

Frank Moorhouse, *Grand Days*

Toni Morrison, *Beloved* • *Jazz* • *Playing in the Dark* • *Song of Solomon* • *Sula* • *Tar Baby*

Walter Mosley, *A Little Yellow Dog* • *RL's Dream* • *The Walter Mosley Omnibus*

Ruchira Mukerjee, *Toad in My Garden*
Robert Musil, *The Man Without Qualities I, II & III*
Alvaro Mutis, *Maqroll*
Julie Myerson, *Sleepwalking* • *The Touch*
Jan Myrdal, *Report From a Chinese Village*

Vladimir Nabokov, *The Enchanter* • *Lectures on Literature*
Tom Nairn, *The Enchanted Glass: Britain and Its Monarchy*
Tonya Nelson, *Family Terrorists and Other Stories*
Joachim Neugroschel (ed), *Great Works of Jewish Fantasy*
Eric Newby, *The Big Red Train Ride* • *A Book of Travellers' Tales*
    • *Departures and Arrivals* • *The Last Grain Race* • *Love and
    War in the Apennines* • *A Merry Dance Around the World* •
    On the Shores of the Mediterranean • *Round Ireland in Low
    Gear* • *A Short Walk in the Hindu Kush* • *Slowly Down the
    Ganges* • *A Small Place in Italy* • *Something Wholesale* • *A
    Traveller's Life*
Wanda Newby, *Peace and War: Growing Up in Fascist Italy*
Ernest Newman, *Wagner Nights*
Charles Nicholl, *The Fruit Palace* • *The Reckoning*
Mike Nicol, *The Powers That Be*
Ann Nietzke, *Windowlight*
Christopher Nolan, *Under the Eye of the Clock*
Gurney Norman, *Divine Right's Trip*

Joyce Carol Oates, *American Appetites* • *Because it is Bitter, and
    Because it is My Heart* • *Black Water* • *Foxfire* • *What I Lived
    For*
Flann O'Brien, *The Best of Myles* • *The Dalkey Archive* • *The
    Hard Life* • *The Poor Mouth* • *The Third Policeman*
Bridget O'Connor, *Here Comes John* • *Tell Her You Love Her*

Kenzaburo Oë, *Nip the Buds, Shoot the Kids* • *A Personal Matter*

Colm O'Gaora, *A Crooked Field*

Timothy O'Grady, *Motherland*

Andrew O'Hagan, *The Missing*

Michael Ondaatje, *The Cinnamon Peeler* • *The Collected Works of Billy the Kid* • *Coming Through Slaughter* • *The English Patient* • *Handwriting* • *In the Skin of a Lion* • *Running in the Family*

PJ O'Rourke, *Age and Guile* • *The Bachelor Home Companion* • *Eat the Rich* • *Give War a Chance* • *Holidays in Hell* • *Parliament of Whores* • *Republican Party Reptile*

Whitney Otto, *How to Make an American Quilt*

Dennis Overbye, *Lonely Hearts of the Cosmos: The Quest for the Secret of the Universe*

Marcel Pagnol, *My Father's Glory & My Mother's Castle* • *The Time of Secrets and the Time of Love* • *The Water of the Hills*

Charles Palliser, *The Sensationist*

Tony Parker, *Russian Voices*

Karen Payne (ed), *Between Ourselves*

Roberto Pazzi, *Searching for the Emperor*

Mervyn Peake, *A Book of Nonsense* • *Letters From a Lost Uncle*

Emily Perkins, *Leave Before You Go*

Caryl Phillips, *Cambridge* • *Crossing the River* • *The European Tribe* • *The Final Passage* • *Higher Ground* • *A State of Independence*

George Plimpton, *Truman Capote*

Susan Power, *The Grass Dancer*

John Cowper Powys, *After My Fashion* • *Autobiography* • *The Brazen Head* • *A Glastonbury Romance* • *Maiden Castle* • *Owen Glendower* • *Weymouth Sands*

David Profumo & Graham Swift (eds), *The Magic Wheel: An Anthology of Fishing in Literature*

Kate Pullinger, *Tiny Lies*

Michael Pye, *Maximum City*

Thomas Pynchon, *The Crying of Lot 49* • *Gravity's Rainbow* • *Slow Learner* • *V*

Joe Queenan, *If You're Talking to Me, Your Career Must Be in Trouble* • *The Unkindest Cut*

Jonathan Raban, *Arabia* • *Bad Land* • *Coasting* • *Foreign Land* • *For Love and Money* • *Hunting Mister Heartbreak* • *Old Glory* • *Passage to Juneau*

Richard Rayner, *The Blue Suit* • *The Elephant*

Peter Reich, *A Book of Dreams*

Wilhelm Reich, *Passion of Youth: An Autobiography 1897–1922*

Erich Maria Remarque, *All Quiet on the Western Front*

David Remnick, *King of the World*

Darcy Ribeiro, *Maíra*

Daniel Richler, *Kicking Tomorrow*

Angelo Maria Ripellino, *Magic Prague*

Max Rodenbeck, *Cairo*

FR Rolfe, *Hadrian the Seventh*

AL Rowse, *The Case Books of Simon Forman*

Damon Runyon, *From First to Last* • *On Broadway*

Salman Rushdie, *The Jaguar Smile* • *Midnight's Children* • *Shame*

Robert Sabbag, *Snowblind*

Oliver Sacks, *An Anthropologist on Mars* • *Awakenings* • *The Island of the Colour-blind & Cycad Island* • *A Leg to Stand On* • *The Man Who Mistook His Wife For a Hat* • *Migraine*

- *Seeing Voices*

Antoine de Saint-Exupéry, *Wind, Sand and Stars & Flight to Arras*

Saki, *The Best of Saki*

Julie Salamon, *The Devil's Candy*

James Salter, *A Sport and a Pastime* • *Dusk and Other Stories*

José Saramago, *Baltasar and Blimunda*

Jonathan Schell, *The Abolition*

Karel Schoeman, *Another Country*

Bruno Schulz, *Sanatorium Under the Sign of the Hourglass* • *The Street of Crocodiles* • *The Fictions of Bruno Schulz*

Ingo Schulze, *33 Moments of Happiness*

Jeremy Seal, *A Fez of the Heart* • *The Snakebite Survivors' Club*

Gitta Sereny, *Albert Speer: His Battle With Truth* • *Into That Darkness*

Stan Sesser, *The Lands of Charm and Cruelty: Travels in Southeast Asia*

Bob Shacochis, *Easy in the Islands* • *The Next New World*

Idries Shah, *The Exploits of the Incomparable Mullah Nasrudin* • *The Pleasantries of the Incredible Mullah Nasrudin*

Nicholas Shakespeare, *The Dancer Upstairs* • *The High Flyer* • *The Vision of Elena Silves*

Neil Sheehan, *Two Cities: Hanoi and Saigon*

Elaine Showalter, *Hystories*

Eileen Simpson, *Poets in Their Youth*

Clive Sinclair, *Blood Libels* • *For Good or Evil* • *The Lady With the Laptop*

Iain Sinclair, *Conductors of Chaos: A Poetry Anthology*

Mark Singer, *Funny Money* • *Mr Personality*

Josef Skvorecky, *The Bass Saxophone* • *The Engineer of Human Souls* • *Miss Silver's Past* • *The Swell Season*

Giles Smith, *Lost in Music*

Lee Smith, *Fair and Tender Ladies* • *Family Linen* • *Oral History*

Paul Smith, *Annie* • *The Countrywoman*

Jane Solomon, *Hotel 167*

Irini Spanidou, *God's Snake*

Natsume Soseki, *Light and Darkness*

Oliver Statler, *Japanese Inn* • *Japanese Pilgrimage*

CK Stead, *All Vistors Ashore*

Darcey Steinke, *Suicide Blonde*

James Stephens, *The Crock of Gold*

IF Stone, *The Trial of Socrates*

Robert Stone, *Bear and His Daughter* • *Dog Soldiers* • *A Flag for Sunrise* • *A Hall of Mirrors* • *Outerbridge Reach*

Randolph Stow, *To the Islands* • *Visitants*

William Styron, *The Confessions of Nat Turner* • *Darkness Visible* • *Lie Down in Darkness* • *The Long March* • *Set This House on Fire* • *Sophie's Choice* • *A Tidewater Morning*

Andrew Sullivan, *Virtually Normal*

Eamonn Sweeney, *Waiting For the Healer*

Graham Swift, *Ever After* • *Last Orders* • *Learning to Swim and Other Stories* • *Out of This World* • *Shuttlecock* • *Waterland*

Junichiro Tanizaki, *The Makioka Sisters*

John Taylor, *Superminds* • *When the Clock Struck Zero*

Emma Tennant, *Alice Fell* • *The Bad Sister* • *Hotel de Dream* • *Queen of Stones* • *Wild Nights* • *Woman Beware Woman*

Shashi Tharoor, *The Great Indian Novel*

DM Thomas, *The Flute-Player*

Hunter S Thompson, *Generation of Swine* • *The Great Shark Hunt* • *Songs of the Doomed*

Jim Thompson, *Omnibus* • *Omnibus 2*

David Thomson, *Silver Light*

Richard Thornley, *Zig-Zag*
Christopher Tilghman, *In a Father's Place*
Jacobo Timerman, Chile • *The Longest War*
Uwe Timm, *The Snake Tree*
Colm Tóibín, *The Heather Blazing* • *The South* • *The Story of the Night*
Viktoria Tokareva, *Talisman and Other Tales*
Kevin Toolis, *Rebel Hearts*
Sam Toperoff, *Queen of Desire*
Lee Tulloch, *Fabulous Nobodies*
Colin Turnbull, *The Forest People* • *The Mountain People*
Jill Tweedie, *Letters From a Fainthearted Feminist* • *More From Martha: Further Letters From a Fainthearted Feminist*
JEA Tyler, *The Tolkien Companion*

Sigrid Undset, *Kristin Lavransdatter*

Raymond Van Over, *A Chinese Anthology*
Mario Vargas Llosa, *Aunt Julia and the Scriptwriter* • *The Green House* • *The Time of the Hero*
MG Vassanji, *The Book of Secrets*
William T Vollmann, *The Rainbow Stories* • *Whores For Gloria* • *You Bright and Risen Angels*
Gregor von Rezzori, *The Death of My Brother Abel* • *Memoirs of an Anti-Semite*

Peter Wahloo, *The Lorry*
Andy Warhol, *From A to B and Back Again*
Marina Warner, *Alone of All Her Sex: The Myth and the Cult of the Virgin Mary* • *Monuments and Maidens: The Allegory of the Female Form*

Fay Weldon, *Female Friends*

Nathanael West, *The Complete Works of Nathanael West*

Edmund White, *The Beautiful Room is Empty* • *A Boy's Own Story* • *The Burning Library* • *Caracole* • *Forgetting Elena &* *Nocturnes For the King of Naples* • *Genet* • *Skinned Alive* • *States of Desire: Travels in Gay America*

Tyler Whittle, *The Plant Hunters*

Peter C Whybrow, *A Mood Apart*

John Edgar Wideman, *All Stories are True* • *Father Along* • *Philadelphia Fire*

Leon Wieseltier, *Kaddish*

Richard Wiley, *Fools' Gold* • *Soldiers in Hiding*

Binjamin Wilkomirski, *Fragments*

Hugo Williams, *No Particular Place to Go*

Niall Williams, *Four Letters of Love*

Colin Wilson, *The Outsider*

Deirdre Wilson, *Slave of the Passions*

Leslie Wilson, *Malefice*

Dick Wimmer, *Irish Wine*

Tim Winton, *Blood and Water* • *Cloudstreet* • *The Riders* • *Shallows*

Monique Wittig, *The Guérillères*

Tom Wolfe, *The Bonfire of the Vanities* • *From Bauhaus to Our House* • *The Kandy-Colored Tangerine-Flake Streamline Baby* • *Mauve Gloves & Madmen, Clutter & Vine* • *The Purple Decades* • *The Right Stuff*

Tom Wolfe & EW Johnson (eds), *The New Journalism*

Tobias Wolff, *Hunters in the Snow* • *In Pharaoh's Army* • *The Stories of Tobias Wolff*

Tobias Wolff (ed), *The Picador Book of Contemporary American Stories*

B Wongar, *The Track to Bralgu*
Richard Wright, *Black Boy* • *Native Son*
Rudolph Wurlitzer, *Quake* • *Slow Fade*

WB Yeats, *Collected Poems*
WB Yeats (ed), *Fairy and Folk Tales of Ireland*

Andrzej Zaniewski, *Rat*
Frank Zappa with Peter Occhiogrosso, *The Real Frank Zappa Book*
William Zaranka (ed), *Brand-X Fiction: A Parody Anthology* • *Brand-X Poetry: A Parody Anthology*
Fritz Zorn, *Mars*

Anomalies

This is a list of the B-format Picador paperback 'anomalies' published between 1972 and 1999/2000 that I have collected between 1982 and 2021. The designation, 'anomalies', is mine, not Picador's.

Dee Brown, *Bury My Heart at Wounded Knee*
William Faulkner, *The Sound and the Fury*
John Gardner, *Grendel*
Albert Goldman, *Ladies and Gentlemen, Lenny Bruce!!*
Brothers Grimm, *Household Tales*
Russell Hoban, *The Lion of Boaz-Jachin and Jachin-Boaz*
Denis Johnson, *Already Dead*
Maxine Hong Kingston, *Tripmaster Monkey*
Anita Loos, *Gentlemen Prefer Blondes & But Gentlemen Marry Brunettes*
Barry Lopez, *Arctic Dreams*
Ian McEwan, *A Move Abroad*
Daniel L Magida, *The Rules of Seduction*
Noel Redding & Carol Appleby, *Are You Experienced?*
Jonathan Schell, *The Fate of the Earth*
Graham Swift, *Waterland & Last Orders*
David Thomson, *Suspects*
Marina Warner, *The Lost Father*
Niall Williams, *As it is in Heaven*

Picador Classics

This is a list of Picador Classics published in the late 1980s and early 1990s that I have collected between 1982 and 2021, not a list of all the books published as Picador Classics during those years.

Nelson Algren, *The Man With the Golden Arm* • *A Walk on the Wild Side*
Louis Aragon, *Paris Peasant*
Ambrose Bierce, *The Collected Writings of Ambrose Bierce*
Truman Capote, *Other Voices, Other Rooms*
Joseph Conrad, *Nostromo*
Simone de Beauvoir, *The Second Sex*
Henry de Montherlant, *The Girls*
James T Farrell, *Studs Lonigan*
William Faulkner, *Mosquitoes* • *Sanctuary* • *Soldiers' Pay*
Ronald Firbank, *The Complete Firbank*
Knut Hamsun, *Hunger* • *Mysteries* • *Victoria*
Hermann Hesse, *The Glass Bead Game* • *Siddharta*
Anna Kavan, *My Madness: The Selected Writings of Anna Kavan*
Franz Kafka, *The Trial*
Jules Laforgue, *Moral Tales*
Claude Lévi-Strauss, *Tristes Tropiques*
Malcolm Lowry, *Under the Volcano*
Curzio Malaparte, *The Skin*

Robert Musil, *The Man Without Qualities III*
Erich Maria Remarque, *All Quiet on the Western Front* • *Arch of Triumph*
Rimbaud, *Complete Works*
Fr Rolfe, *Hadrian the Seventh*
Antoine de Saint-Exupéry, *Wartime Writings 1939–1944*
André Schwarz-Bart, *A Woman Named Solitude*
Sigrid Undset, *Kristin Lavransdatter*
TH White, *The Goshawk*
Tennessee Williams, *The Collected Stories of Tennessee Williams*
Richard Wright, *Native Son*
WB Yeats, *Collected Poems*

This book has been typeset by
SALT PUBLISHING LIMITED
using Granjon, a font designed by George W. Jones
for the British branch of the Linotype company in the
United Kingdom. It is manufactured using Creamy 70gsm,
a Forest Stewardship Council™ certified paper from Stora
Enso's Anjala Mill in Finland. It was printed and bound
by Clays Limited in Bungay, Suffolk, Great Britain.

CROMER
GREAT BRITAIN
MMXXI